ALEXANDRE DUMAS'

Adventures in Spain

ALEXANDRE DUMAS'
Adventures in Spain

Translated by

ALMA ELIZABETH MURCH

Illustrations by

GUSTAVE DORÉ

CHILTON COMPANY—BOOK DIVISION
Publishers

Philadelphia   *New York*

Foreword

⚜   ⚜   ⚜

A hundred-odd years ago, when this book was written in 1846, Alexandre Dumas was approaching the very peak of his literary career. His fame and prestige as a dramatist were already so great that, with the influence of a royal patron, *le duc de Montpensier,* a new theater was being built for him in Paris. His novels (especially *The Three Musketeers* and the recently completed *Count of Monte Cristo*) had made him renowned far beyond the borders of France, publishers were pressing him to complete promised manuscripts, and he was writing serials at top speed, an installment at a time, for several important newspapers—in particular *Joseph Balsamo* for *La Presse* and *Le Bâtard de Mauléon* for *Commerce.* His time was further taken up by frequent visits to the fantastically elaborate *château,* later given the name *Monte Cristo,* which he was having built for himself at Port-Marly.

In the midst of this whirl of activity he received two invitations. In September, *M. le comte de Salvandy,* Minister of Public Instruction, anxious that Frenchmen should become better informed about Algeria since it had recently passed under French control, suggested that Dumas should visit that beautiful country and publish his impressions.* Learning of this plan, *le duc de Montpensier* invited Dumas to travel via Spain to attend his wedding to the Spanish Infanta in Madrid on October 10th.

---

* Dumas' first travel book, *En Suisse,* written in 1833 (and translated into English in 1958 by A. Craig Bell and R. W. Plummer, titled *Travels in Switzerland*), caused a marked increase in the number of French tourists visiting Switzerland. The Count of Salvandy hoped that Algeria might be popularized in the same way.

v

Instantly Dumas accepted both invitations. Though it was a most inopportune moment for him to leave Paris, with his theater nearing completion and his serials unfinished, in a few hours he was on his way. As companions for the journey he took with him an old friend, Louis Boulanger, the painter; Auguste Maquet, a former schoolmaster who turned to literature and became Dumas' most prolific collaborator; and his only son, Alexandre Dumas *fils*, then a youth of twenty-two, still dreaming of his love affair in the previous year with Marie Duplessis, whom he was later to immortalize in *La Dame aux Camélias*.

For two crowded months they explored Spain, and Dumas' account of their adventures fills four sparkling volumes, each of several hundred pages. To condense this profusion within the covers of a single volume has necessarily involved abbreviating many of Dumas' descriptions of scenery, his lengthy conversations, and his philosophical musings; but in this, the first English translation, every effort has been made to retain the essential characteristics of the original and to convey Dumas' own vivid picture of the places they visited—the people they met in towns or lonely mountains, palaces, or wayside inns— the humor, hardship, or actual danger awaiting them at every turn of the road—their delight in the dances, the bullfights, the fiestas, and all the excitement of Spain, where a hundred years ago is only yesterday.

Who was the mysterious "Madame" to whom these exciting letters were addressed? That is Dumas' secret! There were several ladies of Paris who must have missed him during his absence, and speculation as to the identity of "Madame" was rife as the letters appeared serially in *La Presse*, but even Dumas' biographer, Glinel, ventured no more than a tentative suggestion that she might have been a fair unknown named Suzanne Brohan. Possibly "Madame" was a figment of Dumas' imagination, a device to enhance the personal atmosphere of this work. If, on the other hand, she really existed, her identity is one of the enigmas left to posterity by the originator of the phrase: *"Cherchez la femme!"*

A. E. M.

ALEXANDRE DUMAS'

Adventures in Spain

1

✤   ✤   ✤

Bayonne, the evening of October 5th, 1846

Madame,

When I set out on my travels you made me promise to write you—not just a letter, but three or four volumes of letters. You were right, knowing me enthusiastic for big things, forgetful of small ones; loving to give lavishly, not in little. On arriving at Bayonne I am beginning, as you see, to fulfill my promise.

I make no pretense of modesty, Madame, and I am well aware that the letters I send you will appear in print. With that pert *naïveté* which turns those I meet into my good friends or inveterate enemies, according to their nature, I at once confess that I shall write with this expectation in mind. But have no fear. The prospect will in no way affect the tone of my letters. For the past fifteen years my readers have traveled with me along the various paths I have traced through that vast labyrinth of literature which is to some an arid desert, to others a virgin forest. This time too, I hope, they will accompany me with their customary kindness along whatever familiar or unexpected byways I chance to beckon them—roads where I shall be disporting myself for the first time.

Besides, my public will lose nothing thereby. A journey like the one I am starting, with no fixed plan, braving the risks of Spanish roads and the winds of Algeria—such a journey will fit in marvelously well with the free-and-easy style of personal letters, which can stoop to the most humdrum details or soar to the loftiest themes.

1

There is, too, for me, the lure of casting my thought into a different mold; refining my style in a fresh crucible; polishing some new facet of that stone, diamond or paste, which I hew from the mine of my spirit and which Time, that incorruptible jeweler, will one day assess at its true value.

It is to you I write, Madame, because your spirit is grave, yet gay; sincere and childlike; punctilious, yet whimsical. Your position in the world renders you familiar with accepted customs, with literature, politics, the arts, even the sciences. The most essential element for producing that *verve* which the public expects of me is conversation—that evocative muse which presides at our *salons* and is so rarely met with outside France. When writing, I shall simply be conversing with you. True, the public will make a third in our conversations, but I have always noticed that I am wittier than usual when I sense some eavesdropper standing outside with his ear to the door!

After this brief preface, let me tell you the conditions of my departure, my purpose in leaving you, and the plans with which I shall probably return.

In society there is a certain man of high intelligence, whose spirit has withstood ten years of the Academy.* Fifteen years of parliamentary debates have not ruffled his sophisticated charm, nor has the burden of five or six ministerial portfolios changed his natural kindness of heart. One morning he sent me an invitation to lunch. It was almost two years since I had seen him, for we are both busy men. But for this I should certainly have called on him more often, no matter what the varying political factions might have inferred from my action. As I rather suspected, the invitation was only a pretext, a means of bringing us face to face across a table which was not exactly a desk. His real purpose was to make the twofold suggestion that I should attend the wedding of Monseigneur the Duke of Montpensier in Spain, and also visit Algeria. Either of these proposals I would have accepted gratefully. What joy to be offered both!

Your banker would tell you it was a most unreasonable prop-

* M. de Salvandy.

osition for me to go at that moment, with *Balsamo* less than half published and my newly built theater* on the point of completion. But there it is, Madame! I am impulsive, I know, and your banker would have the greatest difficulty in reforming me. So I decided to leave *Balsamo* as it stood and to desert my theater, for the time being, at least.

Do you recall the first performance of my play, *The King's Musketeers*, at the Variety? His Highness the Duke of Montpensier was there, sitting so near to me that I could study his every expression, the more attentively since I had known and devotedly served his brother. When the Duke seemed upset by the scaffold scene in the play I forgot all else, rushed around to his box, and begged my friend Dr. Pasquier, who was with the Duke, to present me and to assure His Highness that on the morrow this particular scene would have vanished. I was graciously received, and a week later I was at Vincennes chatting with the Duke of Montpensier, almost forgetting for a few moments that his brother, my patron and hero, the Duke of Orleans, was dead. But to return to Saint-Germain and my luncheon party.

When I went to call upon my friend the Minister, I had no idea of leaving that ancient, charitable town. When I returned, my departure was already arranged for the following day. There was no time to lose. Twenty-four hours under any circumstances, more especially those in which I found myself at that moment, make a very brief period of preparation for a journey of three or four months. Besides, I was counting on setting out in good company. To travel alone, on foot, staff in hand, may suit a carefree student or a poet-dreamer, but I, alas, have passed the age at which university scholars tramp the highroads, their cheery choruses vying with the rough oaths of carters; and, if I am a poet, I am first of all a man of action.

---

* Begun in 1845 on a site at the corner of the Faubourg du Temple, and opened early in 1847, with the name *Théâtre Historique*. As author-director, Dumas was to produce his own plays there, and, in addition, the works of Shakespeare, Calderon, Goethe, and Schiller.

3

Six months or so ago, on one of those companionable evenings that Giraud, Boulanger, Maquet, my son, and I so often spent in my garden, the idea of a visit to Spain first dawned upon us like an inspired dream, and we swore we would all go there together. Indeed, one fine day three months later, Giraud and Desbarolles, dressed for the journey, knocked at my door and asked if I was ready. Chained to my desk, slaving away at *Joseph Balsamo* and the designs for my theater, what could I do but listen wistfully to their plans and speed them on their way, following them with longing eyes as far as the first bend in the road? And now, you see, a totally unexpected turn of fate has snatched me away from my novel, out of my theater, and set me speeding on the road to Spain, my longed-for country of romance.

As you know, Madame, I am a man of quick decisions. Walking up the hill from Saint-Germain I met my son and persuaded him to come with me. The moment I reached home I sent my servant Paul with brief, identical notes to Maquet and to Boulanger, telling them I should be leaving for Spain the next day and inviting them to accompany me. They could each bring one trunk, the smaller the better. I would be responsible for everything else.

My man found Maquet enjoying a day's fishing on the Isle of Chatou, and at the same time writing one of those lovely passages of limpid prose you know so well. Lying on the grass in the throes of composition he was, for the moment, completely oblivious of his fishing lines, which, instead of serving to land the fish, were actually being dragged by them into the water. Paul was just in time to save a superb rod from shooting downstream like an arrow, towed by a carp with urgent business in Le Havre. Maquet read my letter once or twice, packed up his fishing tackle, and rushed off to Chatou to look for a suitable trunk.

Paul went on by train to No. 16, rue de l'Ouest, where he discovered Boulanger, loaded palette in one hand, brush in the other, gazing dreamily at a great, white canvas, on the point of starting his masterpiece for next year's Exhibition. Slipping

4

his brush between his lips and tossing his palette on a chair, he took my note from Paul's hands, read it, pinched himself to make sure he was awake, asked whether the whole thing was a joke, and on being assured that I was quite serious, sank down to collect his thoughts—into the chair where he had thrown his palette! Five minutes later, his mind made up, he was furiously searching around his studio in the hope of finding a little trunk hidden away behind some canvas or other.

At 6 o'clock the next evening we all met in the courtyard where passengers embark in the Lafitte and Caillard coaches. You can imagine the confusion, with each of us bidding our dear ones *adieu;* disconnected phrases assailing the ears from every direction; arms waving from carriage windows; the guard urging passengers to take their places; friends calling them back for yet another last word, exchanging final instructions, promises, reassurances.

In the midst of this uproar the clock struck six, and the most tightly clinging arms perforce must slacken their hold. I set an example by jumping quickly to my seat, Boulanger followed me, Alexandre came next, and, lastly, Maquet, still giving directions for letters to be forwarded to him at Burgos, Madrid, Granada, Cordova, Seville, and Cadiz, after which he would send further details. As for Paul, with no leave-taking to occupy him, he had long ago settled himself in the seat next to the driver.

A quarter of an hour later, an extremely ingenious mechanism lifted us from our coach and gently set us down in a railway carriage. At once the engine drew a loud, harsh breath, the immense machine quivered to life, we heard the grating shudder of iron, lamps began to move quickly past us on left and right like torches carried by evil spirits at a witches' revel, and, leaving a long fiery trail behind us, we rolled on toward Orleans.

2

❧ ❧ ❧

I talked so much about myself in my last letter that I scarcely mentioned my companions, and I must tell you a little about them. Giraud will show you what they look like. I will describe to you their personalities.

Louis Boulanger is that painter and visionary whom you know, always susceptible to beauty in all its aspects, with Raphael's appreciation of form, Rubens' love of color, Goya's flights of fancy. For him, every great thing is indeed great. A man of learning, brought up in his studio, his whole life devoted to art, he has none of those energetic habits so essential to a traveler. He has never ridden a horse or touched a firearm. Yet I am certain that, should the occasion arise in the course of this journey, you will see him bestriding a saddle like a *picador* or shooting away like an *escopetero*.

Maquet, my friend and collaborator, you know less well. Next to myself, he works harder, perhaps, than any man in the world, is rarely seen in society, and speaks seldom. His mind is critical, yet richly imaginative, and his study of ancient languages has given him an analytical bent without affecting his originality. With him, will power rules all, and his supreme self-control has brought about a kind of physical and ethical stiffness, his only fault apart from his exaggerated sense of loyalty. For the rest, he is skilled in all sports, adept at everything that calls for perseverance, courage, and presence of mind.

You already know my son, whom you spoil outrageously, Madame. Born between daylight and dark, he is an extraordinary mixture of opposites: indolent, yet active; self-indulgent, yet sober; lavish, yet thrifty; distrustful, yet credulous. His words are cold, but his hands are quick to help. He flouts me,

6

yet loves me with all his heart; would filch my purse like Valère, and champion me like *le Cid*. He is a fearless horseman, expert with firearms, dances beautifully, and displays the most sparkling vivacity I have ever known in a young man of twenty-one. Now and again we have differences, and, like the prodigal son, he stands on his rights and leaves home. Then I buy a calf and start to fatten it, certain that in less than a month he will be back to partake of it. True, gossips say he comes back for the calf, not for me, but I know what to believe about that.

Now for Paul, whom you must have clearly in mind if you are to visualize us as we travel along. He is a being apart, calling for special mention. To begin with, his name is not Paul, but Pierre. No! I'm wrong! He is Eau-de-Benjoin, black-skinned, a native of Abyssinia and by habit cosmopolitan. As a lad he was bought in Gondar for a bottle of rum by an English globetrotter traveling home from India. A week later, Eau-de-Benjoin had dried his tears and begun to enjoy his new life. For six years he served this Englishman, journeying through Italy, France, and Spain, and picking up those languages as well as English. Indeed, he never deserted his master. When that indefatigable traveler had seen every country in this world, he decided to visit the next. One morning, when he had not rung for his servant at the usual time, Eau-de-Benjoin went into his room and found him hanging from the bell rope. That was why he had not rung.

While serving this Englishman, a generous master, Eau-de-Benjoin could have saved a good deal, but thrift was not in his nature. A true son of the equator, loving everything that glittered, he squandered all he had on trash—or on rum. Not till his last *sou* was spent did he look for a new situation, and with his candid eyes, ingenuous smile, and flashing teeth he was not long in finding one.

His new master, a French colonel, took him to Algeria, where his native language made him completely at home among the Arabs. During his five happy years there Eau-de-Benjoin, moved by the grace of God, was baptized and chose the name

7

of Peter, doubtless reserving for himself the indulgence of denying the Lord three times, as his patron had done. Unhappily for Eau-de-Benjoin, his colonel returned to France to protest against certain regulations and was put on the retired list at half pay, so that he was forced to dismiss his servant, and Pierre was once again unemployed.

Chevet recommended him to me as an invaluable valet, speaking four languages besides his own, his one fault being that he lost everything he was asked to look after. Chevet said nothing to me about Pierre's fondness for rum, doubtless guessing that I should soon find that out for myself. In this, Chevet was mistaken. I attributed Pierre's occasional aberrations to sickness, and the only thing I entrusted to him was the cellar key, which, contrary to his usual habit, he never mislaid. However, one morning I set out on a week's hunting trip but came back unexpectedly the next day. Entering my home I called for Paul, as I always did.

(Ah! I must tell you how Pierre, formerly Eau-de-Benjoin, came to change his name yet again. My old gardener, also called Pierre, took it very hard that my new man, and a Negro at that, should bear the same name. His seniority in my service, and his white skin, made him flatly refuse to change his own. Eau-de-Benjoin, on the other hand, having changed his once already, was quite content to change it again, merely asking me to choose for him as noble a name as the one he found for himself. I suggested Paul, and he was satisfied.)

Coming in from hunting, then, I called for Paul. No reply. I opened the door of his room, fearing that he might have followed his former master's example and hanged himself. But no! Paul was horizontal, not perpendicular. I called him, shook him, stood him upright. His legs wavered unsteadily so I propped him up against the wall, where he remained stiffly motionless. I summoned Pierre, who gruffly pronounced Paul to be dead drunk, and went off without another word. I knew that Pierre cherished a grudge against Paul because of that unfortunate business of their names, and I had never paid much attention to the tales he told me about his fellow servant. But this time his accusation was clearly true.

I ordered the coachman to put Paul to bed and inform me the moment he woke up. Twenty-four hours later I was brought word that Paul had just opened his eyes. I went down, composing my face to its utmost severity, and informed Paul he was no longer in my service.

Ten minutes later the house resounded with frightful yells. Paul was in hysterics, shouting at the top of his voice that he had lost his first master because he had hanged himself, and his second because of his retirement. In his view, these were the only two possible causes why employment should terminate, and as long as I was neither hanged nor put on the retired list he was not going to leave me.

No one responds to a sound argument more quickly than I do. Paul's seemed to me excellent, so I made him promise to stop drinking, took charge of the key of the cellar, and all went on as before. Naturally Paul broke his promise now and then, but knowing the reason for his indispositions I was not worried, and since I detest scenes I did not risk dismissing him again. Now that I'm going to Africa, my leniency is rewarded. The Arab, Eau-de-Benjoin, will be of the greatest service as my interpreter.

To return to our journey, we all slept peacefully as the train rolled smoothly onward through the night. Suddenly the cessation of movement roused us, and we peered anxiously through the windows. No sign of a station. An accident, then? We could make out a crowd of people tramping up and down beside the track. Realizing after a moment or two that they were merely passengers taking advantage of the stop to get out and stretch their legs, we joined them and learned the cause of the trouble. Something had gone wrong with the boiler, the water had put the fire out, and the engine had died of dropsy. We were just beyond Beaugency, and should have to wait for the relief that would be sent out to search for us when we failed to arrive at Blois on time.

Two hours later we glimpsed a red point of light growing larger and brighter until we could hear the rasping breath of the monster. It rushed past us roaring like the lion in Holy Writ, halted, grew tame, and allowed itself to be coupled to the train. We resumed our seats, the dead engine was tied on behind, off we went, and at 6 in the morning we reached Tours.

Toward 3 o'clock in the afternoon we arrived at Châtellerault. Heaven preserve you from Châtellerault, Madame, unless you are passionately fond of little knives. In five minutes you could acquire the most comprehensive collection of them in the world. Unfortunately, we stayed there a quarter of an hour. The doors of our coach were at once blocked by a crowd of women of all ages from seven to eighty with voices of every conceivable pitch, soliciting us to buy their wares. We had intended exploring the town a little, all together, and called the guard to clear a passage for us to alight.

It was no use. The instant we set foot on the ground we were scattered, followed, surrounded, vanquished. Instead of picking us up in a body at the far end of the town, as planned, the coach had to collect us one at a time, here and there, like a lifeboat rescuing shipwrecked sailors, each of us shamefacedly carrying a set of razors, a pruning knife, a lancet, or a pair of scissors. To cap everything, Alexandre had bought a huge dagger with a mother-of-pearl sheath and a hilt of copper disguised as silver. He had been offered it for a louis. Thinking to cut the transaction short he contemptuously suggested five francs, and it was his! Bear this instructive detail in mind, Madame, if ever you visit Châtellerault.

I cannot tell you what time we reached Bordeaux, but I well remember that, because we were four hours behind schedule, the last coach for Bayonne left that town as we entered it. That made us twenty-four hours late, since there was no other coach until the next day. It was already the fifth of the month, the royal wedding would take place on the tenth, and we were still a hundred twenty-five miles from the frontier. Not a moment to lose if we were to arrive in time!

For thirteen hundred francs I bought a traveling carriage

10

that was well worth five. The vendor assured me I was making a wonderful speculation, for French carriages are so highly esteemed in Spain that I could be certain of selling it in Madrid for three times what it cost me. I had my doubts—not that I would question the statement of a carriage maker, Heaven forbid!—but because of my natural inaptitude for speculation. However, it was no time for hesitation. This post chaise was the only means of transport that would get me to Bayonne in time to catch the stagecoach for Madrid the next day, so the horses were harnessed and we set off.

Spain, I had been told, begins as you leave Bordeaux, and we saw the sun set over vast plains such as Cervantes describes in *Don Quixote*. When we awoke, nearing Roquefort, we found ourselves in very different country. If the Landes were thousands of miles away, instead of in France, we should appreciate them more. At sunrise they looked wonderful as to left and right of us stretched rolling prairies, marked like a tiger skin with dark streaks of fog. The east was aflame with light; to the west, night was in retreat, trailing its mantle still studded with stars. Southward, ahead of us, the clear-cut edge of the Pyrenees stood out like silver lace against the azure of the Spanish sky.

After changing horses at Roquefort, we noticed that our stubborn Percherons had been replaced by thin little horses with flying manes and tails, not built for pulling a carriage, but bringing to this task all the zest inherited from their remote Arab ancestry and shortening our time four minutes for every mile. Never have I seen anything finer than the road beyond Mont-de-Marsan. The last great trees in France grow there, and you will find no more like them in Spain. Bid farewell, also, to the Dordogne, here more than a mile wide. From now on you will see many rivers with their beds full of stones, sand, even shrubs—but seldom running water.

We arrived at Bayonne about noon. The pleasure of our journey from Bordeaux, not to mention the coachmaker's golden prophecies, had decided us to continue traveling by post chaise, so the moment we reached Bayonne I rushed to the consul, M. Leroy, to beg him to attend to our visas and help us to leave quickly. He was a most kindly, courteous man, anxious to give us every assistance, but I learned from him two things that brought our plans to naught. A carriage entering Spain from France must pay a tariff of eighteen hundred francs, and, owing to the assembly of princes for the royal wedding, we should find it impossible to change horses along our route.

I dashed to the office of the mail coach and booked the only four seats available, then ran to tell my companions of our change of plan. To crowd ourselves and all our luggage on to a vehicle not really intended to carry anything but letters was quite a problem. Fortunately, Spanish coachmen are more accommodating than their French counterparts, and after ten minutes' conversation, with animated gestures of explanation, everything was satisfactorily arranged. Now, three things compel me to say good-by: the length of my letter, the postal collection, and the coachman who is calling his missing passenger. I will write to you again at our next stop, probably at Madrid.

3

❦ ❦ ❦

Madrid, the evening of October 5th

Ouf! Here we are at last installed in the capital of Spain, but, as you will see, Madame, not without difficulties.

As we journeyed on from Bayonne (still, to some extent, under the protection of France, since for a couple more relays the postillions were Frenchmen), we could hear on our right, from time to time, the low roar of the sea, and now and then in the moonlight caught a glimpse of the bays of Fontarabia or of San Sebastian, the coast line fringed with silver by the breaking waves.

The Bidassoa, as you know, forms the ancient frontier of Spain, and half of the bridge spanning that river is French territory, the other half Spanish. A man may stand on it with a foot in each country, and would have beneath him the famous Isle of Pheasants, where Mazarin held conferences with Don Louis de Haro, and where the marriage of Louis XIV to the Infanta Maria Theresa was decided. At the far side of the bridge, with France behind you, your way is blocked by the Irún customhouse. Are you expecting me to tell you how severely we were treated by these lace-encrusted officials? Not at all! At Irún began that series of triumphant entries which I enjoyed for the remainder of my trip.

Each of us brought his baggage forward with some trepidation, for we had been warned that nothing could be taken into Spain except soiled linen and old clothes. As for firearms, they were completely out of the question. Merely to possess them would brand one as a revolutionary. Now I had three trunks bursting with new clothes and white linen, six cases of rifles, small arms, hunting knives, and a case of cartridges.

To my amazement the chief officer, having read my name upon my luggage, came over and complimented me in excellent French, and in Spanish even more gratifying to my ears ordered his men to show the utmost respect to everything I owned, opening nothing. He went on to advise me to keep the box of cartridges in a safer place, lest some passenger with a light should accidentally blow us all up. A very reasonable suggestion, I thought, so I gave the box to Paul to take care of, with the result that it now seems irretrievably lost. To counterbalance the lenient treatment I enjoyed, the other travelers were searched to the skin, and my friends spent two hours arguing with the custom officials while I smoked a cigarette with their chief.

Eventually, on we went through Hernani and Andouin, reaching Tolosa at daybreak, hungry as hunters and eager for

13

the breakfast we had been told would be waiting for us there. You know, Madame, how cordially French hotels welcome travelers at any hour, providing sumptuous profusion for two or three francs a head, and how aggravating it is to be snatched away, halfway through the meal, by the coachman's order, "Take your seats, gentlemen." Expecting the same at Tolosa, we rushed from the coach, inquiring where breakfast was served. But in Spain such haste is unheard-of. Our coachman took five minutes to reply that *if* we wanted some breakfast we had better go and look for it.

"You sound like the Evangelist," said Maquet. " 'Seek and ye shall find.' "

I fancied, to my horror, that the coachman murmured "Maybe," as he turned to hide a half-smile. Imagine the despair of four starving men, told that *perhaps* they might find breakfast somewhere, seeking vainly for a hotel, for we could see no signs such as hang above French hostelries, only endless rows of small private houses all exactly alike and not the slightest aroma of cooking from even one of them!

The outside passengers had by now alighted, and among them I recognized one as being French. He had lived in Spain for twenty years, he told me, traveling to France twice annually, on business.

"You can save our lives, sir," I exclaimed, "for if you pass through Tolosa four times a year you must know *somewhere* we can get a meal."

"A meal?" said he, and at last added, "Would a cup of chocolate content you? Well, then, follow me."

Turning a corner or two, he led us to a house which he entered as though on familiar ground, motioning us to remain out of sight in a corner near the door. There was nothing to distinguish the house from its neighbors, yet it was a sort of café. We could see a man sitting smoking and a woman warming herself over a brazier. Neither of them made the slightest movement. Our guide approached them like a neighbor paying a call, inquired conversationally about the proprietor's health and the woman's family, relighted his own cigar from that of his host, and having thus arrived at a sufficient degree of familiarity ventured to inquire tentatively whether it might be possible to have a little chocolate.

"That might be managed," replied the host, laconically.

This reply drew us forward, until a gesture from our guide reproved our premature advance.

"Ah!" said the master of the café, scowling horribly. "How many cups?"

"Five."

"—and the largest possible," ventured Alexandre.

The host grumbled darkly to himself in Spanish that cups were cups, and no one was going to make any special size for the likes of us. Our guide saved the situation by offering a fine cigar to the indignant proprietor, who only just managed to prevent a flicker of satisfaction from showing in his eyes.

"Five?" he said at length.

"Yes," returned our guide, "though I myself am not unduly in need and could . . ."

With a gesture of regal dignity the host interrupted him. "Not at all. *Muchacho*, five cups of chocolate for these gentlemen."

A deep sigh came from the inner room and was echoed by another of satisfaction from ourselves. The host glanced at us with scorn and devoted his attention to lighting his cigar with leisurely appreciation. Five minutes later a servant entered bearing a tray upon which were arranged five thimble-sized cups full of a thick black fluid, five glasses of clear water, and a little basket containing small sticks of bread, pink and white.

From our earliest days we had heard of the wonderful chocolate one gets in Spain, and we hardly dared raise the cups to our lips lest this impression should vanish like so many other illusions of childhood. But no! The chocolate was excellent. Unfortunately, there was only just enough to taste.

"Would it not be possible to have five more cups?" I hazarded.

"Ten," suggested Boulanger.

"Fifteen," said Maquet.

15

"Twenty," demanded Alexandre.

"*Chut!*" reproved our mentor. "Let us enjoy this refreshment, not abuse it. Dip your *azucarillo* in your glass and then we will go back to the coach."

Indeed, we found this refreshment as acceptable as the chocolate. The quality was superb; only the quantity fell short.

When we wished to pay, our guide stopped us with a gesture, took a *peseta* from his pocket, and placed it on the edge of a chest.

"*Vaya usted con Dios,*" he murmured, with a gracious bow of farewell. The proprietor, without even glancing to see whether he had been correctly paid, took his cigar from his lips for long enough to reply, "*Vaya usted con Dios.*"

"Go with God," repeated Alexandre as we rejoined our coach, waiting with fresh horses already harnessed. "Go with God. That's fine. I could ask nothing better. But it's a long way from here to Heaven, and if I'm to have nothing on the journey but chocolate, sugared water, and breadsticks, I'd as soon go elsewhere."

"Sirs," interrupted our guide, who seemed increasingly disturbed at our distress, "would you allow me to offer you a cooked chicken, a two-pound loaf, and a bottle of Bordeaux?"

When I could speak, "Give us your name, sir," I stammered, "so that when we reach home again we may have it engraved on marble in letters of gold!"

"I am Faure," he replied, "a merchant in Madrid."

We accepted his gifts as though he were Providence itself, without, I'm sorry to say, even pausing to wonder whether he had a similar store for his own use, and not until the last crumb had vanished did we lift our eyes to the countryside around us. We were racing along through Guipuscoa, one of the most fertile provinces of Spain. If the heights that surrounded us were mere foothills, compared with the Pyrenees, they were nevertheless quite considerable mountains compared with Montmartre, their rusty-brown slopes brightened here and there with patches of yellow, red, or green, wherever the owners of this rocky land found a plot of earth large enough

16

to cultivate laboriously, by hand, a little crop of corn, pimiento, or clover. The road itself was delightful, with sparkling brooks and pretty villages, red and white, basking in the sunshine; crowds of children laughing, shouting, swarming everywhere; while now and then as we flashed past the open doors of cottages we caught a glimpse of a dusky interior and the serene, clear-cut profile of a woman spinning.

Our vehicle was drawn by eight mules, sometimes by ten. Their coats, thickening for winter, had been clipped along their backs only, and as one looked down on them they seemed just like huge rats harnessed to a fairy coach. They were handled by a team of three men: the *mayoral*, corresponding to our coachman, the *sotacochero*, or postillion, and the *zagal*, for whom there is no equivalent in any language. The *zagal* seems scarcely human. He jumps on and off the coach like a monkey; bounds along like a tiger; like a demon he hounds his team onward with sticks, a whip, even stones. His official station is a little platform on the front of the coach, near the driver, but he is never there. He canters, gallops with the mules, yelling encouragement or a stream of profanities. When they run flat out, so does he. If they bolt, he heads them off and catches them. A coach without its *zagal* is just a coach. With him it is an eagle pursuing a cloud, the wind that follows a whirlwind. Never shall I understand why the coach does not shake to pieces or overturn.

His colleague, the *sotacochero*, is a mere lad of fifteen or sixteen, mounted on the left-hand leader of the team. His Spanish nickname means "one condemned to death," and indeed the poor devil may well be riding continuously for three days and two nights, from Bayonne to Madrid, and on arriving he often enough leaves one saddle only to mount another. Quite apart from the greater speed of the Spanish coaches, I found this triple team of *mayoral*, *sotacochero*, and *zagal*, with their picturesque uniforms of pointed hats, velvet-trimmed jackets, red belts, wide-cut breeches, and top-boots or sandals, infinitely more entertaining than our dual partnership of coachman and postillion.

17

The highroad, too, offered us endless variety. In France, all the wayfarers one meets in any particular district are dressed very much alike. In Spain, what a contrast! Quite apart from the priests with their fantastically enormous hats, there is the copper-skinned Valencian with his voluminous white breeches, his feet shod with *alpargatas;* a man from the plains of La Mancha, with his brown jerkin, red belt, short trousers, and brightly colored stockings, his scarf knotted crosswise over his chest and his blunderbuss at his saddlebow; an Andalusian, whose hat, with its two silk pompons, has a widely curving, turned-up brim, and whose customary dress is a vividly checkered coat, brilliant waistcoat, crimson tie, trousers cut off at mid-thigh, and high, embroidered top-boots, slashed at the side; the Catalonian, the length and thickness of his staff regulated by order of the police, a silk square knotted around his head with the ends hanging down his back —all these one can recognize at sight, as well as others from the dozen or so different regions of Spain which have grudgingly consented to form one kingdom but will never bind themselves into a united people.

Now and again we met an amazingly primitive vehicle drawn by a couple of oxen, its approach heralded by a most extraordinary screeching that puzzled me a great deal, the first time I heard it. It is caused, no doubt, by the dryness of the axle which turns (or, for all I know, is turned by) the great solid mushroom-shaped wooden wheels, and can easily be heard a mile away when not drowned out by other sounds. I was surprised that the driver of the cart, who was generally placidly smoking a cigarette, seemed quite undisturbed by the din from his musical box, incessantly grinding out the same tune.

Another noise I must warn you about, Madame, lest you should take it for someone being murdered, or a soul in purgatory, is that made by a *noria.* Your dictionary, with the discretion of all such volumes, will inform you that a *noria* is a machine, but that is to tell you absolutely nothing. A *noria* is the wheel of a water mill, so gigantic that it would make the great wheel of the Marley mill seem like a wheel from a watch, and it makes four times as much noise as the cart I spoke of just now.

In time we reached Vittoria where, thanks to the breakfast supplied by our good friend M. Faure, we awaited dinner without anxiety, though with some impatience. We were offered saffron soup, a *puchero*, and a dish of *garbanzos*, and the saffron was one of the best soups I have ever tasted, though I suspect it was made from mutton, not beef. Still, it was excellent. (Note that I mention the good things as well as the bad.)

Then came the *puchero*, essentially a Spanish dish, the staple diet of the country. It would go hard with you, Madame, if you were to visit Spain and could not eat this fare, so I suggest you accustom yourself to it by degrees. It consists of a large joint of cow meat (in Spain the bull seems completely unknown as a source of food), a little mutton, a chicken, slices of a sausage called *chorizo*, all cooked with dripping, ham, tomatoes, saffron, and cabbage. These would be acceptable enough if served separately, but I could never get used to eating them all together, and in my opinion they form a most unfortunate mixture. Try to do better than I did, Madame, for if you cannot enjoy *puchero* you will be obliged to make do with *garbanzos*. These are hard, bullet-sized peas, quite beyond my powers of digestion, but if you were to begin by eating one on the first day, two on the second, and on the third day three, it is just possible that you might survive. I hasten to add that the meal was beautifully served with exquisite cleanliness, and we were waited on by servants like maids of honor, or by the daughters of the house who bore themselves like princesses. Nevertheless, we decided that in future we would prepare our own meals as far as possible.

A notice fixed to the wall bore the tariff for breakfast, and I asked our hostess for the first item, "a couple of boiled eggs." She understood my Spanish at once, but puzzled me by asking whether I would like a monk's couple or a layman's. "Surely 'a couple of eggs' means simply 'a couple of eggs'?" I learned that "a monk's couple" consists of three eggs, but "a couple of eggs for a layman" means two only. It seems that the monks enjoyed wide privileges before the revolution drove them from Spain, privileges now remembered only in such catch phrases as this.

We set out once more between 7 and 8 at night, reaching Burgos toward 5 or 6 the following morning, entering the land of the Cid by the self-same gate that this national hero passed through eight hundred years ago, on his way to the King's palace. You will certainly know the story of the day when the Cid's father, Diègue Layne, rode in with his three hundred Gentlemen-at-Arms, his son among them, to swear fealty to the good king Ferdinand, ordering his men to follow his example. Curbing his fierce Castilian pride, Don Roderigo was dismounting to obey his father's behest when his dagger slipped by accident to the King's feet, alarming His Majesty so much that he harshly commanded the Cid to leave his presence.

"Sire," retorted Roderigo, "I count it no honor to kiss the King's hand; rather I consider myself humiliated because my father has done so," and remounting his horse he whirled away, followed by his three hundred noblemen.

Burgos, that once boasted thirty-five thousand inhabitants, is now a poor city of scarcely eight or nine thousand, but it still remains famous as the shrine of its most illustrious son, the Cid. The colossal shadow of this hero of eight centuries ago still looms over the life of the place. Any child in the street, unable to name the present Queen of Spain, can tell you every detail of the exploits of Don Roderigo. Yet, Madame, there are learned scholars who contend that the Cid never existed; that this world-renowned figure was a creation of the imagination of twelfth- and thirteenth-century poets. What luster a scholar can add to a nation's glory when he is clever enough to find out such things as that!

If ever you go to Burgos, Madame, you must visit the immense cathedral with its bas-reliefs showing our Lord's entry into Jerusalem; its wonderful iron-work choir screen; its dome like a Florentine jewel; its priceless art treasures—Murillo's *Ecce Homo*, El Greco's *Christ on the Cross*, Leonardo da

Vinci's *Magdalene*. Then, ask to see the coffer that belonged to the Cid, and the sacristan, who, fortunately, is not a scholar, will lead you to the room of Jean Cuchiller and show you this venerable relic secured to the wall with hooks of steel.

I am allowed three hours at Burgos—two for sightseeing and one for sleeping. If I slept I might not dream of you, so I am using that last hour to write to you. The Cid himself could have done no more for his love, Ximena.

4

🙢 🙢 🙢

If ever you leave Burgos to travel southward, Madame, you will cross a bridge. (I did not see the river it spans and cannot tell you its name.) When you reach the middle of the bridge, turn and cast one last look at the Queen of Old Castile. Before you is its finest gateway, built in honor of Charles V and bearing statues of Nuno-Rasura, Lain Calvo, Fernand Gonzales, Charles I, the Cid, and Diego Percel. To the right, like arrows of stone, rise the twin steeples of the fine cathedral, while the whole town lies before you like an amphitheater. Look beyond the town to the plains and green valleys you have passed through, and say good-by to the rushing streams, the cool shade, and the lovely mountains of Guipuscoa, for henceforth you must journey over the red sands and gray heather of Old Castile, where the horizon stretches without a break and the mere sight of a spindly oak or a stunted elm will call forth a joyous exclamation of surprise.

The first noteworthy sight on our road was the castle of Lerma, where the famous duke of that name died in exile and disgrace. It was seized after his death, with all his other property, for a sum of fourteen hundred thousand crowns, and has

21

now fallen into ruin. M. Faure, our fellow traveler and guide, who gave us these details, added that five years ago he was held up by a gang of robbers who had made this old castle their headquarters.

As we drove onward, the blue summits of the Somo-Sierra seemed by an optical illusion to be moving toward us. This is one of the mountains to the left of the road from Aranda to Madrid, and its sides are as steep as the roof of a house. It was about 5 o'clock in the afternoon when we began to climb its lower slopes, and to negotiate this pass, formerly as much feared by travelers as the road past the castle of Lerma, our team of mules was increased to twelve.

In the morning, as we awoke, we could see, across the desert, points of light standing out against a purple haze. It was Madrid, and in an hour or so we entered this capital of Spain through its finest gateway, that of Alcala, and dismounted at the stagecoach terminus. To arrive, however, was not everything, for we still had to find somewhere to stay—not at all an easy thing to do under the special circumstances that prevailed. Our hurried departure had left us no time to arrange accommodation in advance. Moreover, the papers had announced that all Spain was in a state of revolution, guerilla warfare was causing havoc on the highways, and a pitched battle was being waged in the streets of Madrid. This seemed encouraging news to us, for if people were out fighting in the streets they were obviously not at home, and their houses would presumably have that much more room to receive us. But we found Spain enjoying profound calm. We had just come from Bayonne to Madrid, a hundred and fifty leagues, without encountering a single guerilla or even a highwayman, and we found the streets of the capital empty in the peace of early morning, covered with the stands of traveling theaters, erected in preparation for the festivities we had come to join.

Leaving our luggage at the coach office, we began our search, knocking at every hotel, every boardinghouse, every possible lodging in Madrid. Not one single room could we find, not a garret, not even a cupboard large enough to shelter a dwarf, and as we found ourselves back in the street after each fresh disappointment our spirits sank lower and lower. We had tried everywhere and had lost almost our last shred of hope when by chance I raised my head and read over a doorway the words *"Monnier: French bookseller."* I uttered a cry of joy. Our fellow countryman would surely offer us hospitality, or would at least do everything in his power to find us accommodation elsewhere.

The shop door was closed, and looking for another entrance to the house I found an alleyway with *Casa de banos* written above it. This was miraculous good fortune. Next to a furnished lodging, what we needed most was a bath. I pushed open a little glazed door that rang a bell, and went along a passageway that ended in a courtyard with a glass roof. All around this courtyard were the doors of the various bathrooms, and above them a suite of private rooms. In the courtyard were two women and five cats, and when I inquired for M. Monnier something in my manner or appearance seemed to displease them, for the women began to grumble and the cats to mew loudly. At the noise, a window of the *entresol* flew open and a man's head appeared, crowned with a nightcap, asking what was the matter. (I hasten to add, Madame, that this head, whose features and expression were so important to me at that moment, appeared prepossessing.)

"My dear M. Monnier," I replied, "the matter is that I and my companions have been searching for a lodging since early morning and if you cannot help us we shall be obliged to buy a tent from some retired soldier and camp out in the square of Alcala."

M. Monnier's eyes grew wider and wider as he listened and tried to recognize me.

"Pardon me," he said, "but you address me as your dear M. Monnier. Are we, then, acquainted?"

"Undoubtedly, since I address you by name."

"Oh, that's not surprising, since my name is on my door."

"So is mine."

"What! Your name is on my door?"

"Indeed, yes. I have just read it there."

"What is your name, then?"

"Alexandre Dumas."

M. Monnier gave a loud cry, knocked his head against the crossbar of the window, and disappeared. A moment later he joined us in the courtyard, clad simply in a pair of bathing trunks.

"What!" he exclaimed, "*the* Alexandre Dumas? Our own Dumas? This is a wonderful day for me. What can I do for you?" and we shook each other warmly by the hand.

"Can you offer me hospitality?"

"My eminent friend, my house is yours."

"Dear M. Monnier, I am not alone. My son is with me."

"Well, I suppose that a room big enough for one could take two."

"We are, unfortunately, more than two. I have a friend . . ."

"*Diable!*" said M. Monnier, scratching his ear. "Well, we will do our best to find enough space for your friend. What's the matter now?"

"My friend . . . has another friend with him."

"Then there are four of you?"

"And a manservant."

M. Monnier sank back into a chair. "Then I simply don't know what we can do."

"Let's see. Haven't you some room or other that would take two beds?"

"Yes, but there are already two beds in it, occupied by two Frenchmen, Messieurs Blanchard and Girardet."

"Why, these are friends of ours! They'll certainly be willing to share with us."

"Impossible. Their room is so small that they can hardly get into it themselves."

"Have you any other room?"

"One very large one that would, indeed, take you all, but it is their studio."

"Then it shall be our studio, too. After all, I can claim to be a painter!"

24

"I also have a few tiny attics, mere garrets."

"Then we shall be as snug as mice in a Dutch cheese."

My companions were still waiting anxiously at the door and broke into cheers when I told them what sumptuous accommodation I had managed to find. Alexandre came in first, bowing low; then Boulanger and Maquet. Paul brought up the rear, his fingers held stiffly against the seams of his trousers, a gesture that always means we have taken our eyes off him long enough for him to slip away and get a drink. I frowned at him sternly and he smiled amiably back at me.

M. Monnier led us upstairs, where we found Blanchard and Girardet already at work in their studio. They and a third artist, M. Gisnain, had been sent to Madrid with an official commission to paint the most important scenes of the forthcoming celebrations. As we entered they greeted us with cries of delight, agreeing enthusiastically to the proposition I had put to M. Monnier. They quickly painted a white line marking off roughly one third of the studio for their own use, leaving for us the remainder of the room which M. Monnier arranged to furnish for our needs. Paul was sent to collect our luggage while our host, beaming ecstatically, led us to the two little whitewashed attics where we were to sleep, Maquet and I sharing one, Boulanger and my son the other. The good French bookseller was almost overcome with joy at finding himself the center of a whole colony of Frenchmen, among them the official artists and a guest invited to the royal wedding.

Our affairs thus pleasantly settled, we hastened to enjoy the amenity of the *casa de banos*, for after traveling sixty leagues by train, four hundred by post chaise and two hundred by stagecoach, nothing could be more welcome than a bath, and soon, from four separate bathrooms, our voices were jointly raised in thanks to the Lord for the repose and refreshment He had sent us.

We had a thousand questions to ask M. Monnier, but he had disappeared to ransack all the furniture shops of Madrid, so we discussed among ourselves with animation our first impressions of this city where everything was so new to us; these still, silent people who stood like shadows to watch us pass; women lovely beneath their rags; proud men, dignified in tattered clothing; children hung about with shapeless fragments fallen from their father's cloak;—all of them seemed to us not just a different race, but beings living in another century. Boulanger was in a state of delight at finding such models awaiting his skill as an artist—and gratis, too!

As we left the baths M. Monnier rejoined us, rubbing his hands with satisfaction and assuring us that everything was now ready for us. "Yes, you can settle in at once. The tables are steady on three legs at least, your beds are almost made up, and the chairs won't let you down, provided that two of you don't try to use them at the same time."

"You are a truly great man," we assured him thankfully, and our host bowed to us with modest grace.

On our way upstairs we glanced in the studio, where I was more than surprised to see Paul working away really hard, unpacking our luggage, even our firearms. He had already taken our trunks to our rooms and laid out our clothes ready for us. Such an outburst of energy on his part always means that he hopes to be pardoned for some lapse, and I strongly suspected that some item of baggage was probably missing.

"Paul," I said, taking the list from my pocket, "we will check over the inventory of our belongings."

Paul's color is by nature roughly the shade of India ink. When he blushes he turns the color of a Florentine bronze, and when he is afraid he grows as gray as a mouse, as at this moment. He did his best to distract me, but I insisted on a detailed examination and found that our case of cartridges was missing. This was a serious matter. We had seven guns in all, one double-barreled, and four of them needed a special type of cartridge. Now, except for about sixty that had been packed in odd spaces in the gun cases, we had no ammunition at all.

Paul was ordered to search with the utmost diligence, and, indeed, gave every impression of doing so, but after two or three days, when he felt the barometer had risen again from "Stormy" to "Set Fair," he confessed with a smile showing all his thirty-two dazzling teeth that the box of cartridges had been left in the customhouse at Irún or Bayonne, as he distinctly remembered.

While Paul was still busily hunting for this missing box, my companions and I made ourselves at home in our new quarters, and, as soon as we had achieved that comfortable untidiness so indispensable to writers and painters, we began to think about a meal. Do not be surprised, Madame, that I so often mention the subject of food. You, in Paris, have only to glance through your windows to see both sides of the street filled by luxurious restaurants competing to tempt your appetite with every imaginable delicacy, or you could send out for whatever you fancy for a dinner prepared at home—a game bird stuffed with truffles, some pâté de foie gras, or perhaps a fresh lobster. But here in Madrid we are too far away from Strasbourg and its pâté de foie gras, the lobster pots of Brest, and the poultry farms of Périgord. Such essentially French fare could not survive the long journey to Madrid, and one is forced to fall back on such food as the country provides. After two or three hours of investigation we learned that the only chefs or cooks still extant in Madrid are employed in noble houses. Ordinary people who wish to eat (foreigners, of course), must buy what they fancy in the market and cook it themselves.

Fortunately, from my early childhood I have been a hunter —I might add quite a good hunter. At the age of ten or twelve I would sometimes run away from home—(I almost said from my father's house, but, alas, my father died when I was three. From my mother's house, then)—to live like a poacher in those great woods surrounding my birthplace. For a day or two, perhaps even a week, I would wander from village to village relying solely upon my gun, bartering a hare, a rabbit, or a young partridge for some bread and a bottle of wine. These, with a further part of my catch, made me many a fine meal. The remaining third of my spoils I always carried home to my mother, like Hippolytus laying his trophies at the feet of Theseus to appease his wrath.

This habit of mine may have prejudiced my intellectual

27

education, but it certainly taught me how to cook. Many of my readers have adversely criticized my books, but no gourmand who has tasted my sauces has ever found the slightest fault with them. I was therefore unanimously elected *maître d'hôtel* of our little French colony, Paul to do the actual fetching and carrying. We all clubbed together to buy a large basket for his use, hoping that he would thus manage not to lose more than an irreducible minimum of our eggs, carrots, ham, or cutlets.

So, Madame, our luncheon arrangements are settled. As for dinner, M. Monnier recommends us to try a restaurant owned by an Italian, Lardi by name, where we should be able to obtain a reasonably good meal. In Italy, where one has poor meals, the good innkeepers are French; in Spain, where one finds no meals at all, the best innkeepers are Italian. Farewell, Madame. I must leave you and go to the market as well as the French Embassy.

5

Madrid, 10th October, 1846

Guess whom I brought back with me from my errands to the market and the Embassy! Giraud and Desbarolles!

In the middle of *la strada Mayor* my carriage suddenly jolted to a standstill and a swarthy, bearded head appeared at each window. Shaken thus rudely from my reverie by the sight of these two formidable heads and their attendant bodies in Spanish dress, I thought at first I was being attacked by bandits in some dense forest or rocky defile, and reached instinctively for my pistols. Not having deemed it necessary to take them with me when shopping, I failed to find them, and was preparing to repel aggression with my fists when I realized the intruders were laughing at me, one of them showing thirty-two white teeth, the other two yellow ones. Looking at them more closely, I recognized Giraud and Desbarolles—chiefly, I must confess, by those two yellow teeth, for, quite apart from the deep tan burned into their faces by the sun of Catalonia and Andalusia, their whole appearance had changed enormously. Giraud, almost hairless when he left France, now had a mane like a lion, while Desbarolles, who had a magnificent growth of hair before setting out for Spain, was now almost bald. Why their journey should have had such opposite effects on these two travelers I must leave to medical science and to the researches of those who make hair restorers.

With a joyful cry I opened the carriage door and they settled in beside me. They had just completed a marvelous expedition, on foot all the way, traveling like true artists with a drawing case thrust through their belts, pencil in hand, and a musket slung over the shoulder; sleeping and eating as and when they could, laughing, singing, dashing off a sketch or two all along the road. At Seville, twelve days ago, they had heard of the forthcoming wedding festivities and had at once set out for Madrid. In those twelve days they had walked two hundred fifty miles and had just arrived.

Before leaving Seville they had bought a greyhound, which trotted along in front of them for the first three days. On the fourth and fifth it walked beside them, and on the sixth lagged behind, quite exhausted. The next day it was too stiff to walk at all, so Giraud took it in his arms and carried it until, six and a half hours later, the poor creature lay on his breast and died. They hollowed out a grave for it on the far side of a ditch, and that day Giraud and Desbarolles walked no more than thirty miles, but they made up for it next day by walking forty-five. On reaching Madrid they learned that I, also, had just arrived, so they set out to look for me, and, by great good luck, came up against my carriage straight away.

As soon as we had warmly exchanged greetings, my first word was, "You'll come to Algeria with me, won't you?"

They exchanged a look, for they should both have been back in France a month ago. Desbarolles sighed deeply, while Giraud raised his hands to Heaven and murmured, "My poor family." However, both of them at once accepted my suggestion.

Thus our whole party was complete, just as we had visualized on that long-ago evening in my garden which I told you of earlier. We were now all together in Spain, with half of the country still to be explored, and I ought to tell you something of Giraud and Desbarolles, as I have already done for Boulanger, Maquet, and my son. You must have seen Giraud's *Permission de Dix Heures* reproduced as an engraving, in print, on snuffboxes, even at the theater, and he has done a thousand other charming things besides—historical paintings, scenes of country life, portraits, pastels. When he draws, he is not dependent on any conventional tool. If his pencil is missing, his charcoal mislaid, when his brush is not at hand or his pen does not come at his call, then Giraud will draw with a piece of coal, a match, a walking stick, or a toothpick and what always strikes his subtle, humorous spirit is the funny side of his subjects. His eye is like one of those distorting mirrors that caricature everything they reflect. He is one of the wittiest men I know, and I have seldom met in a studio, a drawing room, or even a palace, an artist who can appreciate more sensitively than he does the conventions due to his surroundings, whatever they may be.

It is more difficult to portray Desbarolles, though he is in some ways more true to type than Giraud. He is a blend of artist and traveler, and in both roles essentially Parisian. He handles a sword like Grisier, a baton like Fanfan, and he can box as well as Lacour. This multiplicity of accomplishments, quite apart from that skill with a pencil or pen to which he devotes his moments of leisure, has given to his hands a multiplicity of habitual gestures, some of them devastating. Furthermore, Desbarolles is a most absent-minded man, as I have already mentioned. As long as he is standing, the only result of his distraction is that he hears nothing one says to him, or forgets it the moment he hears it. That's all. But when Desbarolles is seated, the matter becomes more serious, for, where-ever he may be, he passes quite simply and naturally from reverie to sleep—a sleep so peaceful and dignified that his most wide-awake companions respect his slumbers, all except Giraud. It seems as though something awakes in Giraud the moment Desbarolles drops off to sleep, and impels him to press his thumb againt his friend's nose until that feature almost entirely disappears in his mustache. Desbarolles wakes up all ready to pick a quarrel with the insolent tormentor taking such liberties with an organ whose shape he values, even to the extent of denying it snuff, for fear of spoiling its native elegance. Then, recognizing Giraud, he gives him that sweet and friendly smile, the like of which I have never seen save on Desbarolles' lips. They have known each other for twenty years. Giraud must have flattened Desbarolles' nose a million times, and a million times Desbarolles has smiled at Giraud for this reason alone.

When I met them on my way home from the market they were both in Spanish dress—pie-shaped hat with a turned-up brim and two silk pompons, brightly decorated jacket, dazzling waistcoat, red belt, knee-length trousers, embroidered gaiters, and an Andalusian cloak, but this attire had been forced upon them by circumstances rather than adopted out of enthusiasm for the national costume. On leaving France they took with them, in addition to what they were wearing, a trunk containing two suits, two frock coats, two pairs of trousers, and two opera hats. The suits retained their shape and their Parisian style until they were worn to shreds, but the opera hats, those still uncertain products of our modern civilization, failed to withstand the tropical sunshine of Barcelona and Murcia and took to bending forward instead of remaining upright. In France such a curvature would have been corrected in a matter of seconds, but it defied the best efforts of Spanish hatters who, indeed, have not yet progressed beyond the Andalusian sombrero and the felt hats worn in the days of Louis XIII. Consequently, Giraud and Desbarolles appeared to be wearing wind-battered chimney pots on their heads. As long as they took care to wear their hats at the same angle, whether pointing forward or backward, all was reasonably well, but if, through an oversight very understandable in travelers delighting in the air, the sunshine, the people, all the unfamiliar things around them, they forgot this precaution and put on their hats tilting in opposite directions, they presented the fantastic appearance of an enormous pair of scissors walking wide open on four feet.

One day Desbarolles had the idea of taking his hat to a watchmaker, who managed to put it right with the mainspring from a clock, and Desbarolles, to Giraud's great astonishment, returned to the hotel with his opera hat proudly erect. This very satisfactory state of affairs continued for three days, and then, while Desbarolles was enjoying a nap, the spring uncoiled itself with a loud cuckoo. The result of all these clothing problems was that Giraud and Desbarolles adopted the national dress in which they appeared before me, and subsequently before our little French colony, who greeted them with delight.

In response to their inquiries about my visits to the market and the French Embassy, Paul, dealing with the first of these subjects, opened his basket and displayed, all neatly set out on beds of cabbage leaves, a dozen eggs, six partridges, two hares, and a Granada ham.

I must tell you, Madame, that if people eat but poorly in Spain it is, quite frankly, because they will not take the trouble to eat well. The soil there is amazingly fertile and the finest vegetables, the most luscious fruits, grow almost of themselves. At any time of the year one can stoop and gather strawberries, almost hidden among the flowering violets, and for six months one has only to stand on tiptoe to pick the fragrant, golden oranges swinging overhead, or ripe pomegranates ready to burst in a shower of rubies. Then, too, Spain is a sportsman's paradise. The endless, heather-covered moors shelter countless partridges and hares, while the sierras provide a safe refuge for larger game: stags, fallow deer, wild boars. There is in Spain an unaccountable age-old superstition that hares, which, jugged or roasted, are so highly esteemed by us, must not be served at table because they are supposed to prowl around like scavengers in graveyards, so in that country hares die of old age, watching Spaniards eating rabbits.

Furthermore, I fancy that the race of partridges must have bribed Spanish cooks never to serve them at table in the ways we enjoy so much—roasted, or in a *salmi*, or cold with tartare sauce—but always prepared with a horrid vinegar sauce, so that anyone unversed in culinary arts is given the impression that the partridge, *vice-reine* of our banquets, second only to the royal pheasant, is scarcely more eatable than a jackdaw or a crow. I had a vision of making it my task to correct these fatal errors and restore the hare and partridge to popular favor, a work of justice and humanity with which our French colony, delighted at my purchases, was in full agreement.

My friends were anxious to know how I had fared at the Embassy, and I quickly reassured them. M. Bresson had been advised of my arrival by the Count of Salvandy, and though extremely occupied by the political complexities and the social obligations of his ambassadorial position, he left orders that I was to be admitted to his presence as soon as I called. I had not met M. Bresson before—a tall man with a frigid, serious expression, his head held high, a thing one likes to see in people who have achieved distinction by their own efforts. M. Bresson has shown most commendable firmness throughout the important business of this marriage, and has not allowed himself to be moved by Lord Palmerston's threats or by the antagonism of the newspapers.

M. Bresson received me cordially, repeating to me what the Prince had said concerning his pleasure at the prospect of seeing me again, and in order to bring about our meeting as soon as possible he invited me to dine with His Highness this very evening. My friends were *all* invited to the *soirée* that was to follow. I emphasize the word *all* to show that the number to which the invitation should extend was left to my choice.

I left M. Bresson, delighted with his warm welcome, for I knew he was not prodigal with such favors, and went in search of Glucksberg, Talleyrand, and Guitaut. I had left Paris at such short notice that I had no time to ask M. le duc Decazes (one of my first literary patrons, whom I shall never forget), whether he would like me to take any message to his son, Glucksberg, whom I have known since Boulanger painted his portrait as a child, and whom I was looking forward to seeing again. You well know, Madame, how rarely I have leisure to visit those I love, and what difficulty they have in getting rid of me once I am there. I stayed a whole hour with Glucksberg.

I was equally anxious to see Talleyrand again. I have known him ever since he was attached to our Embassy in Florence, and introduced him to you during one of his visits to Paris. Can anyone surpass his delightful vivacity or the quick intelligence that shines in his face? He is the perfect attaché at an embassy, especially at our Embassy in Spain. I will whisper that Talleyrand has enjoyed all sorts of success in Madrid, representing France in his own particular way, and in consequence has acquired a pallor that goes very well with his blue eyes and fair hair. Glucksberg represents the more serious side of diplomacy, Talleyrand the more interesting.

Guitaut is Mme Bresson's brother-in-law, a descendant of that brave and noble Guitaut who was so devoted to the service of Queen Anne of Austria. His was the iron hand chosen to expel the Prince of Condé who was terrorizing the little court of the Palais-Royal, and it was this same Guitaut who, in the Queen's name, sought and found Louis XIII in the very presence of Mlle de la Fayette in her convent of Les Dames de la Visitation and brought him back to the Louvre to his own bed, precisely nine months before the birth of Louis XIV. Young Guitaut is a proud and handsome lad of twenty-two, well aware of the worthy name he bears and fully prepared to devote himself to any queen in need of his services.

Thus I returned home delighted with my excursion. I had found a well-stocked market, an embassy such as exists nowhere else, and on the way I had gathered in two friends I thought to be at the other end of the peninsula. I forgot to add that, besides my own invitation to dinner and the general invitation for the evening, I brought back tickets for all the royal functions, including a balcony for the great bullfight due to take place in three or four days' time at the *plaza Mayor*. We had been assured that this would be a marvelous spectacle, devised with the utmost splendor and originality. Not for sixteen years has such a display been seen in Madrid. Yet bullfight enthusiasts shake their heads and make those little "tut-tut" sounds indicating doubt, so I am curious enough to inquire why. I learn that they consider the *plaza Mayor* too large. When the scene of combat between the bull and his enemies is too extensive, there is extra space for avoiding danger and the fight is correspondingly less fierce. We are therefore told not to expect to see, during the four days this festivity will last, more than two or three hundred horses killed, ten or twelve men injured. In an ordinary bullfight one could count on twice as many casualties. Hence the disapproval evinced by the real devotees of tauromachy. However, we shall know what we are in for tomorrow, when there is an ordinary bullfight at the Alcala gate. All Madrid is in a fever of anticipation, and we are as excited as the rest. The fever is catching.

Now, Madame, I must leave you and go to dine at the Embassy. My companions are dining at Lardi's restaurant, escorted by Théophile Gautier, whom they found wandering about the streets. He claims to know Spain better than Spaniards do, and on the strength of that has predicted that they will have an extremely poor dinner.

6

✤   ✤   ✤

Madrid, the morning of October 11th

Now, Madame, we know what it is, that terrible emotion they told us we should feel at our first bullfight. One of us grew pale, another was thoroughly upset, and the remaining four remained as apparently unmoved as those ancient Romans whom the conquering Gauls took to be the gods of the Capitol.

First, however, our young prince received us in audience, charming as always, with a friendly word for each. My friends were astonished that so young a prince already possessed such a delightful flexibility of conversation, but nothing is so inspiring as happiness, and last night the Duke of Montpensier seemed to me the happiest prince in the world.

I would describe the occasion, but certain newspapers have erroneously announced that I came here to act as His Highness' official chronicler,* a piece of foolishness that will deprive you of the glowing account I would otherwise have sent you. You will be able to read the details in a letter palpitating with excitement that Achard is sending to the *Époque*.

Our French colony increases daily and will soon amount to an Occupation. In the streets one meets as many Parisians as Spaniards, and could believe oneself still in France, but for the blazing sunshine; the mantillas everywhere; dark, flashing eyes, blacker than I have ever seen; and the tiny whistling note of fans ceaselessly fluttering.

After visiting the Embassy I called upon two good friends of mine whom you know by name, the politician Rocca de

---

* This report, which Dumas resented since he was invited as a private guest by the Duke personally, was spread by Victor Hugo, who added details of the Treasury and other sources which had placed funds at Dumas' service for the journey. Cf. Victor Hugo, *Choses Vues*, Vol. 1, p. 199. Ed. Imprimerie Nationale.

Togores who will be Minister one day,* and the Duke of Ossuna, who would probably already possess that title if he had so wished. Rocca de Togores is one of the finest poets in Spain today, and one of her wittiest men. Spain has the good taste to appreciate that her poets have a power beyond their skill in writing poetry, and that her brilliant men can do more than coin a fine phrase. Responding to this confidence, Rocca de Togores has become one of the most popular figures in Spain today.

Nowadays there are very few noblemen left of the quality of the Duke of Ossuna. Thirteen or fourteen times a Spanish Grandee, decorated with more orders than he can wear, he is the last of his race, the sole representative of a family which combined the three great houses of Lerna, Benevente, and Infantado. For five hundred years his ancestors have stood on the steps of the throne or have occupied the throne itself. His revenue is so immense that he is said not to know how much it is, and his estates are spread over Spain and Flanders. In the Low Countries he owns castles finer than those of the late king; in Spain his great fortresses, manned solely by his servants, could withstand for a year all the armies of the Spanish king, were he not a loyal subject; he owns whole plains, chains of mountains, forests, and in those forests (listen to this, Madame), he has his own bandits, a gang of seven. He is not their chief, but their proprietor, and he acquired this singular property under the following circumstances.

Three or four years ago, determined action was taken to wipe out brigandage in Spain, but some sixty robbers escaped. Thirty or forty took refuge in the impenetrable gorges of the Sierra, eight or ten in the wild country between Castro de Rio and Alcandete, and the remainder in the forests of Alamina, which belongs to Ossuna. For some time Ossuna's guards hunted the brigands and there were losses on both sides, until a truce was agreed on the following terms: the guards would cease trying to round up the bandits provided that they would undertake

* Alexandre Dumas' prophecy was soon fulfilled. M. Rocca de Togores became a Minister by the time this work first appeared in print.

never to molest any traveler known to be a relative, a friend, or a messenger of the Duke's. In addition, the priest of one of Ossuna's villages was instructed to attend to the religious needs of the robbers, hearing their confessions, administering sacraments, and burying them when, from natural or accidental causes, they passed from this life to the next. The priest duly carried out these services to the best of his ability, and, as time passed, the bandits, originally ten or so, were reduced to seven.

One evening they were lying in wait for passing travelers when they saw approaching them the carriage of the Marquise of Santa-C . . . , one of the loveliest women in Madrid—indeed, in the whole world. She was idly dreaming as her coach went galloping along, when suddenly seven muskets were leveled at the coachman with a command to halt. The Marquise looked out, realized her danger, and swooned. Gently the bandits helped themselves to all her luggage, leaving not a single jewel, not the smallest coin, then signaled to the coachman to drive on. The movement of the carriage restored the Marquise to consciousness, and on arriving at Madrid she drove straight to the Duke of Ossuna to inform him of her loss.

"Did you not inform them that I have the honor to be your cousin?" asked Ossuna.

"I could not tell them anything. I had fainted," replied the Marquise.

"Ah," returned the Duke, "then I quite understand the position, odd though that may seem. Go home and await a message from me."

Nine days later, her cousin invited her to his house, where she found him in conversation with a man she did not know. "My dear Marquise," he said, leading her to a table on which lay a bag of money and a pile of jewels, "please tell me whether all that you lost is here restored to you. This gentleman is the leader of the robbers who molested you. I complained to him, pointing out that we are closely related, and he is greatly distressed that he was not told this at the time. He offers you his most sincere apologies. Come, will you forgive him?"

"With all my heart," replied the Marquise, "but now that I understand I should like him to keep these things."

"My good fellow," commented the Duke, "my cousin is very headstrong, and must be humored."

Without a word the bandit gathered up the money and the jewels, bowed respectfully, and departed. When the Marquise reached home she found awaiting her a package containing everything stolen from her, which she had perforce to accept, being unable to pursue the robber-chief into the forests of Alamina. Since that day the Duke of Ossuna has never had the least occasion to reproach his gang of brigands. See what it is to be a great Spanish overlord, so different from the lordlings of France! The Duke has invited me to lunch with him tomorrow, and promises me a surprise.

Madrid awoke today in holiday mood. All the theaters and the great squares, empty yesterday, were by 6 o'clock this morning thronged with actors and spectators. Taking their turn on every stage were the national dances of each of the fourteen great provinces of Spain, performed by men and women really belonging to the regions they represented, ceaselessly clacking their inevitable castanets and displaying the costumes of their own country. In Spain, as elsewhere, alas, national dress is becoming rarer every day, but for this occasion the characteristic garb reappeared in all its original freshness.

What a special feeling for color, what an eye for harmonious effect, Nature has given to these children of the sun! Have you noticed, Madame, that the farther north one travels, the more drab is the clothing people wear? Rubens, that painter with a name and heart of flame, must have been overjoyed when he was sent as an ambassador to Spain and saw, blazing before his eyes, that magnificent rainbow formed by the men and women of Madrid, where dresses are like a palette of bold colors that mingle but never clash. If only it were possible to fly like a bird and look down on the streets of Madrid from above, I am certain one would take them for an immense flower bed, starry with blossoms.

When a group of dancers finish their performance in one

place they move along the road, making music all the way, seeking a fresh audience. Wherever they pass, windows grow bright with lovely women, bare of head and shoulder, their smooth, blue-black hair shining like a raven's wing and bedecked with a crimson rose, a camellia, or a glowing carnation, a mantilla covering all but hiding nothing, while all around is the fascinating little sound of fans opening, closing, fluttering between slender fingers in gestures of incredible dexterity and adorable coquetry.

The theater the dancers have left does not remain empty long. Moors wearing turbans and armed with scimitars clash in mock combat with crusaders in plumed helmets and chain mail, mounted on chargers caparisoned in bright blue, giving a spirited representation of the capture of Granada and the valiant deeds of its captain. To stimulate the players a band of drums and trumpets keeps up such an exciting, barbaric rhythm that a spectator could well imagine he was watching the fall of Jericho rather than the siege of Granada.

On another stage we saw a troupe of Chinese actors in pagoda-shaped hats, with their slanting eyes, long drooping mustaches, and silk robes all glistening with little silver bells. But unquestionably the honors of the day fell to the dancers and the Moors. The Chinese, though not quite neglected, struck me as a little old-fashioned, even for Spain.

Every moment great coaches, apparently from the stables of King Louis XIV and drawn by plumed horses, cut a furrow through this feverishly excited crowd, and only with great difficulty did we succeed in reaching the Church of Atocha where the marriages of Spanish princes and Infantas customarily are solemnized.

No one, I should think, has ever seen more people crowded into a smaller space, or so much gold displayed on ceremonial robes. Against this setting of fabulous luxury the military neatness of our two young princes was all the more striking. Each of them was wearing the uniform of a brigadier general: white breeches, high-cut riding boots, a broad red sash across his breast, and at his neck the Order of the Golden Fleece, the emblem worn by His Highness the Duke of Montpensier being of diamonds. The Queen was graciously charming and the Infanta a shining vision of loveliness. I did warn you, Madame, that I should not be the one to give you details of all these marvels, so I will simply add that the Patriarch pronounced the nuptial benediction at 2 o'clock.

On leaving the church we found the crowd as dense as ever, and we were further delayed by bystanders thronging around us to admire Eau-de-Benjoin in his Egyptian robes. This was most unfortunate. We were anxious to hurry home and change out of our wedding finery, for the bullfight was due to commence at half-past two and it never waits for its public, not even for the Queen. I ordered our driver to leave the Prado, which was obstructed by preparations for illuminations and fireworks, and to drive through the deserted back streets. We reached M. Monnier's house at a quarter-past two and by half-past were ready to leave again, but the cabman refused to allow five of us to crowd into his vehicle and left us standing on the pavement, so that we had to walk, or rather run, to the gate of Alcala, a good half mile away.

It really is an amazing sight to see the populace of Madrid making its way to a bullfight. Like a river bursting its banks, or the souls Dante saw in Hell being blown along like a whirlwind of leaves, people were rushing wildly onward, fearful of being late for their favorite spectacle. The whole of the Alcala road, as broad as our Champs-Elysées and ending in a gateway almost as gigantic as the *Arc de Triomphe*, was as full of men and women as a field is full of wheat, all of them bending forward at the same angle under the wind of their burning curiosity. Through the crowd ancient carriages forced their way, and horsemen from outlying districts, a carbine at their saddlebow, their aspect as fierce as though they expected to fight for, not pay for, their seats at the ringside, while the mule-drawn omnibus, tightly packed with passengers, battled on at an unwonted speed like leviathan through the waves. We managed to stop a passing cab carrying no more than its legal complement, a generous tip persuaded the driver to squeeze

41

us in upon the knees of his original customers, and so we arrived at the Alcala gate.

Before going in I should have liked to look at the chapel where the last mass is said over the bodies of men killed in the arena; the dispensary where two doctors wait to attend the wounded; the sacristy with its priest who hears the confessions of the dying. But there was no time. Already we heard the fanfare announcing that the President had just thrown the key of the bull pen to the attendant waiting in the ring. We bought our tickets, the great gateway engulfed us, and with that beating of the heart one always feels when about to look upon the unknown and the terrible we climbed the stairs leading to our seats.

I have just been warned, Madame, that it is already 7 o'clock and I must dress for this evening's ceremonies at the palace. I will tell you of the bullfight later tonight, or tomorrow.

7

❧ ❧ ❧

Madrid, midnight

We are living in such a whirl, Madame, that it is already forty-eight hours since I last chatted with you—hours of endless fêtes, illuminations, bullfights, ballets that passed before my eyes like a mirage.

You left us rushing, pushing, struggling along through dark passageways leading upward inside that modern equivalent of the Tower of Babel, the amphitheater of a bull ring. At last we came out into the blazing Spanish sunshine and the noise of the waiting crowd, like no other noise on earth. Imagine twenty thousand people packed close together on tiers in the full glare of the sun or in the shade, depending on what they can afford to pay, all shouting and waving handkerchiefs, fans, parasols, umbrellas! Our seats, in the shade of course, were facing the gate of the *toril*, that gate which the attendant was just on the point of opening with a key decked with gay ribbons.

To the left of the bull entering the ring were the three *picadors*, motionless in their Arab saddles, lance in rest. The remainder of the bull-fighting squadron, the *chulos*, the *banderilleros*, and the *torero*, took up their positions on the right, spread out over the arena like pawns on a chessboard.

It is the *picador*, in my opinion, who faces the greatest danger, mounted on horseback, lance in hand, waiting for the bull to charge. His lance is no weapon, merely a spur, a pole tipped with an iron point just long enough to pierce the animal's hide, and the purpose of the wound it inflicts is to rouse or redouble the bull's ferocity. The sharper the pain, the fiercer the attack on horse and rider, so that the *picador*, protected only by iron leg-guards under his leather trousers, runs the twofold risk of being gored by the bull or crushed by his own mount. When a bull is about to vent his rage upon a prostrate horse or a dismounted *picador*, the *chulos* are the men who rush forward to divert his attention by waving a cloak of green, blue, or yellow before his eyes.

The work of the *banderilleros* is to keep the bull's rage at fever pitch. At the moment when the great beast, weary and bewildered, loses heart, they close in and plant through his withers the *banderillas*, wooden rods barbed like a fishhook and trimmed with little frills of colored paper such as children use on the tail of a kite.

The *torero* is the king of the drama, dominating the arena where every living thing obeys his gestures—even the bull, for he lures it here and there as he chooses, he determines in advance the exact spot where the bull shall die at his feet. Should the *torero's* lady-love be present, that spot will be as near as possible to the place where she sits watching. On this occasion there were three *toreros*, Cuchares, Lucas Blanco, and Salamanchino, each of them superbly elegant in a short jacket

43

of green, blue, or scarlet, heavily embroidered in gold and silver, a waistcoat to correspond and a brilliant sash, soft black cap with its artificial pigtail, skintight stockinet breeches, silk stockings, and heelless satin slippers. Around the great arena runs a partition of oak planks six feet high, painted red in its upper part, black below, and called an *olivo*. Against it, a short distance from the ground, is fixed a white springboard, enabling a man closely pursued by the bull to vault over the barrier to safety, a maneuver called "taking the olive." Only very rarely does a *torero* resort to this expedient: he eludes the bull, but would think it shameful to run away from him.

Beyond this partition is a second barrier, and in the corridor between them stand any fighters not actually engaged in the arena, the *alguazil*, the *picadors*, *chulos*, and *banderilleros* with their reserves, and the *cachetero*, who plays an ignominious part. If the bull, felled at last by the *torero's* sword, still has the strength to raise his bellowing, blood-stained head, the *cachetero* bestrides the barrier, glides sinuously like a cat or a jackal across the sand to the prostrate beast, and treacherously, from behind, administers the *coup de grâce* with a little heart-shaped dagger between the second and third cervical vertebrae, killing him instantly.

This barrier is by no means a safe refuge, for bulls have been known to jump it like a race horse clearing a fence. One of Goya's engravings shows the Alcayde of Terrasson being gored and trampled by a bull that had leaped from the arena, and at the royal fêtes I myself saw a bull clear the barrier three times. When this happens, the corridor empties like magic, a *peon* opens one of the doors in the partition, and the bull, raging furiously in the narrow space, rushes through into the arena where his enemies await him. Sometimes a large arena is divided so that two bullfights can take place simultaneously, as in the *plaza Mayor*. One day both bulls jumped the barrier and met in the corridor, where they fought and killed each other.

During the night before the fight the bulls are brought down from their lonely pastures to the *toril* in Madrid, where each one is penned in a separate cell and remains there, unfed, for ten or twelve hours. Then, at the moment when he is released into the ring, a barb bearing ribbons in his breeder's colors is thrust into his left shoulder. Every *picador*, every *chulo*, aspires to win this tuft of ribbons, a charming token to present to his mistress.

Thus, Madame, the stage is set. On our right is the Queen's box, on our left the *ayuntamiento*, reserved for the municipal dignitaries. Facing us across the arena is the *toril* and above it the band. Rocca de Togores sits at my left, and at my right Alexandre, Maquet, and Boulanger, all of us white-faced and wild-eyed in an agony of anticipation. Giraud and Desbarolles, who have already seen ten bullfights, are standing by the second barrier, glancing at us now and then like old veterans of the Empire pitying new conscripts.

The *garçon du cirque* opens the *toril* door and hides behind it. The bull appears, advances ten steps and stops short, dazzled by the light, bewildered by the roar of the crowd—a black bull bearing the colors of Ossuna and Veragua, his muzzle white with foam, his eyes two shafts of fire. My heart thumps as though I were at a duel.

"Look! Look!" cries Rocca. "This bull is good."

Like lightning the bull charged the first *picador*, who thrust in his *pic* to no avail. The bull did not flinch from the iron but pressed against it and plunged his horn deep between the horse's ribs to its very heart, tossing it so that its four feet beat the air. The *picador* grabbed the crest of the barrier and dropped to earth inside as his horse crashed down outside and tried to rise, blood pouring from the holes in his chest as from two taps. He staggered and fell. The bull turned on him and in a second inflicted ten more wounds.

"Good!" exclaimed Rocca, that charming poet. "This bull is a thruster. It will be a grand fight!"

I turned to my companions. Boulanger did not seem unduly troubled, but Alexandre was extremely pale and Maquet was mopping the sweat from his brow.

The second *picador* rode forward and his horse shied, well aware, in spite of his bandaged eyes, that death lay before him.

The bull hurled himself at this new antagonist and quicker than thought the horse was overthrown, falling backward with all its weight on its rider's chest, so that we heard the breaking of his bones. A great cheer went up and twenty thousand voices yelled in unison, "*Bravo toro! Bravo toro!*"—Rocca, even I myself, with the rest. The animal was beyond question superb, all his body black as jet, with the blood of his two victims streaming over his head and across his shoulders like a crimson coif, as he attacked the fallen horse and with implacable fury sought underneath him for his rider.

Cuchares, the chief *torero* of this fight, made a signal and the whole troupe of *chulos* and *banderilleros* surrounded the bull, among them Lucas Blanco, the second *torero*, a handsome young man of twenty-four or five who has been killing bulls for only two seasons. To mix with the *chulos* was really below his dignity, but his enthusiasm carried him away.

By dint of waving their capes before the eyes of the bull, the *chulos* managed to distract him. He raised his head, looked for a moment at this crowd of new enemies, and charged the nearest one, Lucas Blanco. Lucas calmly swung on his heel in a gesture of infinite grace and the bull rushed past him to pursue the *chulos* so closely that the hindmost man could feel the animal's breath burning his shoulders. They flew over the barrier, their brightly colored capes spreading out like wings, the last man dropping his on the bull's head, where its vermilion deepened to purple as the blood soaked through. For a moment it encumbered the great beast as he trod on the edge of the cloak, his horns piercing the middle folds. Then it flew in pieces under his maddened onslaught, one long fragment of it remaining fixed to his right horn like a pennant. When he could see again he encircled the whole arena with a swift and somber scrutiny.

Above the barrier, the fugitive *chulos* and *banderilleros* were raising their heads, ready to leap into the ring again as soon as the bull moved off. At their chosen points Lucas Blanco and Cuchares stood waiting, both calm, each watching the other. Three men had dragged the fallen *picador* from beneath his

46

horse and were trying to set him on his feet. He staggered wildly, his legs clumsy in their iron guards. He was pale as death and a bloody foam stained his lips. Of the two horses one was quite dead. The other was still trying to kick Death away from him. The third *picador*, the only one remaining, sat his horse as though he were a statue of bronze.

For an instant the bull stood motionless. Then his questing eye lighted on the little group helping the injured *picador*. The sand spurted high as his forefeet scraped a furrow, down went his head, and with a terrifying bellow he rushed to attack. The three men ran for the barrier, deserting their wounded comrade who staggered a step or two and collapsed, barely conscious, while the bull bore down on him. The third *picador* moved in to shield his colleague and oppose the raging beast with his *pic*, but the bull bent the stout pole like a reed and in passing gored the horse, which, grievously wounded, pivoted on its hind legs and bolted with its rider to the far side of the arena.

Hesitating a second between the horse, still alive, and the man who lay apparently dead, the bull chose to pursue the horse, riddling it with his horns and leaving in one of the wounds the relic from the *chulo's* cape. Then he turned again on the man, now being helped by Lucas Blanco, while the circus re-echoed with applause for the *bravo toro*. Lucas stepped aside, extending his cape of blue silk to lure the bull away from his intended victim.

I looked at my companions; Boulanger was pale, Alexandre green, and Maquet's face was streaming wet. If I had had a mirror, Madame, I could tell you how I looked myself. All I know is that I was so strongly moved that I felt none of the revulsion I had been promised. I, who cannot bear to see the cook kill a chicken, could not tear my eyes away from this bull that had already slain three horses and sorely wounded a human being.

He had stopped in his tracks, all unaware of how flimsy was the obstacle that opposed him, while Lucas Blanco, the fluttering cape his only protection, his only weapon, challenged him

47

to renew the combat. As the bull charged, Lucas made another pass like the first, and the bull pulled up, ten paces beyond him. By now the injured man had been assisted to the barrier, the *chulos* and *banderilleros* had re-entered the arena, surrounding the bull and waving their capes. But the bull had eyes only for Lucas. The battle lay between him and this one man, and no other attack should divert him. When a bull looks thus at a man, almost always that man is doomed.

"You'll see!" said Rocca, his hand on my arm. "You'll see!"

"Back, Lucas! Get back!" shouted all the *banderilleros* and the *chulos* with one voice. "Get back!" called Cuchares, but Lucas gazed contemptuously at the bull. Head down, it rushed at him. Lucas placed his toe between the murderous horns and vaulted neatly over the animal's back. The crowd roared with delight. "Bravo, Lucas! Viva! Viva!" Men threw down their hats, women their fans and bouquets, while Lucas waved and smiled as though he had been playing with a little goat. But no shouts, no wild applause, could turn the bull from his vengeful purpose. Among all his enemies it was Lucas whom he followed with his eyes, and the many capes fluttering around him could not make him forget the one sky-blue cloak at which he had twice hurled himself in vain. He charged Lucas once more, this time measuring his rush so as not to pass him. Lucas eluded him by a clever turn, but the animal was no more than four steps away and came at him again without a pause. Lucas threw his cape over the bull's head and began to run backward toward the barrier, gaining a dozen paces before the bull tore the cloak in shreds and rushed to renew his attack. Lucas stepped upon a bouquet, slid, and fell. A great cry broke from twenty thousand throats, dying away to a profound stillness. A mist swam before my eyes, and through it I watched a man tossed fifteen feet in the air, particularly noticing, strangely enough, every detail of poor Lucas' brilliantly decorated costume, even the carved buttons of his pink waistcoat. He fell to earth again, where the bull was waiting for him.

But now another adversary was waiting for the bull. The first *picador*, mounted on a fresh horse, had re-entered the arena and galloped up to attack the bull at the moment when it lowered its head upon Lucas. Feeling the wound of the *pic*, and confident he could come back to deal with Lucas where he lay, the bull turned on the *picador*. The instant he moved away Lucas was on his feet again, smiling and waving at the crowd. By a miracle the horns had passed one each side of his body. Only the animal's forehead had thrown him into space, and his fall had done no harm. A great murmur of relief and joy ran through the amphitheater and twenty thousand people breathed again. Then we heard a new uproar and the bugles sounded.

Forgive me, Madame, but there are two inexorable moments in one's life: the time when the post leaves, and the hour of Death. The first is all but come. I am yours until the other.

8

Madrid, 15th October

As I remember, Madame, we left Lucas Blanco, miraculously still alive, saluting the public amid universal applause; the bull was at close quarters with the *picador* whose timely intervention had saved Lucas; and a fanfare from the bugles was announcing some new and unexpected event.

This was the arrival of the Queen Mother, that gracious, lovely lady whom you saw in Paris, who is as fond of bullfights as though she were merely a marquise. She had managed to get away from the festivities of the day and had come to spend an hour watching this feverish pageant. No sooner had the trumpets announced her presence than all the drama taking place in the ring ceased as if by magic. The *picador*, his horse, and the bull were left to their own devices, and all the other members of the troupe took their places in front of the *toril* for the ceremonial march. Cuchares, Salamanchino, and Lucas Blanco led the procession, then came the three *picadors*. The one whom we had thought dead had managed to mount a fresh horse, and but for his extreme pallor showed no outward sign of his ordeal. The third, who had been at grips with the bull as the bugles sounded, had left it and taken his place in line. Following the *picadors* came the four *chulos*, then the *banderilleros*, and after them the grooms. Only the *cachetero* was missing.

The bull, driven into a corner near the *ayuntamiento*, gazed at this procession in bewilderment. The cortège, marching in time with the music, ignored his very existence as they reached the space before the royal box and dropped to one knee. The Queen allowed them to remain so for several seconds to show that she accepted their homage, then she signaled them to rise. At a second sign they broke their ranks and returned each to his own station; the *picadors* lowered their lances, the *chulos* waved their cloaks, and the *banderilleros* ran to prepare their banderillas.

Meanwhile, the bull had busied himself by returning to savage one of the horses in which he detected signs of life, though we had thought it dead. Driving in his horns, he lifted it bodily and walked off, carrying it across his neck as it raised its head to utter one last feeble scream. Seeing his enemies returning to the attack, the great bull shook off the horse as though it were a mere feather. It fell, staggered to its feet with a final agonized effort, and tottered off to collapse near the *toril*, while the bull watched it go.

"Remember this," said Rocca to me, "and tell me afterward whether or not I know tauromachy. No matter where this bull is brought down, if he is not killed stone dead at once, he will get to that horse and die there. I told you. He's a real sticker!"

The *picadors* had done their work and suffered their casualties. They withdrew to the *olivo* while the *chulos* with their fluttering capes enticed the bull backward and forward across the arena, and three or four times we enjoyed the graceful spectacle of these men vaulting over the barrier, capes out-spread. Then the *banderilleros* entered the ring, each carrying one banderilla poised in his left hand, another in his right. It is by no means an easy thing to drive these barbed wooden rods through the bull's withers to lie parallel with each other, as they should. The first pair was successfully planted and the bull began perceptibly to lose his fixity of purpose, attacking one *chulo* after another, striking random blows with his horn as a wild boar does with his snout, but always allowing a fresh foe to distract him from the last.

A second *banderillero* came up, and on seeing him the bull at once grew quiet, with a calm that promised vengeance. Doubt-less he recognized in the newcomer's hands the same instruments of torture as those already in his shoulders, for he suddenly charged at him with a fury that nothing could halt or turn aside. Arrows in hand, the *banderillero* awaited him, but a mo-ment later only one of them protruded from the bull's neck, while the pink sleeve of the man's coat turned purple and his hand ran with blood that dripped from every finger. The horn had transfixed his upper arm. Refusing all assistance, he man-aged to get to the barrier, but in the very act of crossing it he swooned, falling headlong and unconscious into the safety of the corridor.

This sum of disasters wrought by one bull was enough. The bugles decreed his death, and instantly the center of the ring was deserted by the men of the bull-fighting squadron, leaving the final drama to the *torero*. From now on the combat lay between the bull and Cuchares, a man about thirty-six or forty years of age, of average height, lean and sunburned. He is per-haps not the cleverest bullfighter of the day—the Spaniards prefer Montès and Chiclanero—but he is at least one of the most daring, and performs amazingly audacious feats before the very nose of the bull. One day, when he and Montès were both in the arena and all the applause was for Montès, Cuchares won back his share of the *bravos* by actually kneeling in front of a charging bull.

Cuchares stepped forward, in his hand his sword, concealed

by the *muleta*, a piece of red cloth on a short stick. He crossed
the ring and dropped to one knee before the royal box, seeking
the Queen's permission to kill the bull. He received a sign and
a smile, whereupon he tossed his hat far from him with a gesture
of such arrogance as a man may feel when he goes forth to
battle with death single-handed, and advanced toward the bull.
From now on, nothing would be done save at his direction. He
had already decided the spot where the bull should be killed, in
the space below the Queen's box, and the *chulos* maneuvered
the animal into this position, first tiring him by a long detour
around the arena and past the *toril*, where he turned aside to the
horse he had slaughtered and plunged his horns again and again
into the lifeless body.

"Look at that! What did I tell you?" shouted Rocca.

At last Cuchares and the bull stood face to face, the man with
his thin little needle-sharp sword and the beast with its horns
and its immeasurable strength, its incredible speed of movement.
Yet all the advantage lay with the man, for the light of intelligence sparkled in his eyes, while those of the bull gleamed only
with ferocity, and in this duel the strong would be vanquished
by the weak.

Cuchares passed his *muleta* across the bull's eyes, and, as it
charged, pivoted on his heel, the horns grazing his chest. A
magnificent pass, loudly applauded. The cheers seemed to irri-
tate the bull, and he turned again on Cuchares who awaited him
calmly, sword in hand. A terrific clash, and the sword bent
like a bow, then flew whistling high in the air, having struck
bone.

The fickle public was about to boo Cuchares, and the *chulos*
were coming forward to distract the bull, when Cuchares
signaled them to stay where they were. Then we witnessed a
wonderful sight, showing how profound was this man's understanding of the bull's mentality. For five whole minutes, armed
with nothing more than a piece of red cloth, Cuchares drew the
bull wherever he chose, provoking it till it lost all reason. Ten
times it attacked him, brushing past him to right or left, but
never touching him. At length, having had his fill of applause,

Cuchares picked up his sword, wiped it calmly, and stood once more on guard. This time the delicate blade plunged its full length between the bull's shoulders and he halted shuddering on his four feet. The chill of the steel, if not the steel itself, had entered his heart, and as Cuchares walked away to make his bow to the Queen the mortally wounded beast looked around the arena for the last time. Then at a trot already slowed down by the pangs of death, he made his way to the body of the horse, fell to his knees, uttered one defiant bellow, lowered his hindquarters and lay prostrate, only his head still raised. The *cachetero* emerged from the corridor, crept stealthily up to the bull, drew his dagger, took his time, and struck. The beast fell dead without a sound.

The band began to play, a door in the barrier opened, and four mules, their harness resplendent with silk tassels and silver bells, dragged in a kind of sled. One at a time the bodies of the three dead horses were attached to it and quickly removed, then, finally, the bull. Four grooms, two with rakes and two carrying baskets of sand, leveled out the furrows these carcasses had made in the arena, covered the bloodstained patches, and in ten seconds every trace of the first bullfight had vanished completely.

Once more the *picadors* took their places to the left of the *toril*, the *chulos* and the *banderilleros* to the right, with Lucas Blanco, who succeeded Cuchares, a little to the rear. The bugles announced the overture, the gate opened, and the second bull appeared. One of the advantages of these marvelous spectacles, Madame, is that there are no intervals. Even the death of a man is a normal accident that causes no interruption, and, as in our own highly organized theaters, two or even three people can take the same role.

With bulls as with men, some are brave, others cowardly; some straightforward, others cunning; some tenacious of purpose, others irresolute. The bull now before us was black, like the first, both were seven years old, both came from the forests of Alamina. They were apparently exactly alike, but Rocca was not deceived.

"If you want to go out at all," he said to me, "go now. This bull is no good."

One day, Madame, I will get Rocca to tell my fortune. Take care if he prophesies that one day you will love me, for that day would surely come. He is infallible, and the bull was a bad one. Like the first he ran upon the horses, but at each prick of the lance he halted and drew away, bellowing with pain, while the spectators booed and whistled.

An audience at a bullfight is the most impartial one I know. Without bias they applaud or condemn men or bulls according to their deserts, and they never miss one single blow, whether given by the horn, the lance, or the sword. On one occasion twelve thousand spectators with one voice demanded mercy for a bull that had disemboweled nine horses and killed a *picador*, and that bull left the arena alive—an almost unheard-of event. The one before us now was not destined to be saved in such a glorious fashion. In vain the *picadors* spurred him and the *banderilleros* drove in their banderillas; nothing would induce him to fight, and the crowd began to shout for the *perros*, that is, the dogs.

The *alguazil* directed an inquiring glance at the Queen's box, received permission, and gave his orders. Immediately everyone in the arena drew away from the bull as though the poor animal had the plague, and he stood alone in the midst of the arena, perhaps thinking that now he was left in peace he would be led back to the quiet mountains where he was reared. If so, his dream was vain. The gate opened. One after another there entered six men, each carrying a hound that furiously gave tongue at sight of the bull. On seeing them the bull guessed what was to happen and backed up against the barrier. In a second the baying pack had crossed the arena and the battle began. Against these new antagonists, his natural enemies, the bull recovered his spirit and showed more courage. As for the dogs, they were well-bred mastiffs and bulldogs, the smallest and fiercest of all being a bulldog from London. This was no new experience for me, for in our lovely forests of Compiègne, Villers-Cotterets, or Orléans I have often seen a wild boar at bay against a rock or the trunk of a tree, facing a pack of hounds. Every now and again one of them, more venturesome than the rest, would be struck by that terrible, tusked snout and tossed ten or twelve feet in the air to fall back dying, dragging its entrails. It was the same in this new combat. One dog was thrown into the midst of the crowd. Another, tossed straight up into the air, fell on the barrier and broke its back. The others, trampled underfoot, managed to get up again, and two of them seized the bull's ears; another, the smallest one, gripped his muzzle; and the fourth made him turn. Overcome with pain, the bull gave a fearful bellow and tried to flee from this ever-growing agony, but the dogs held firm. Twice he encircled the arena, dashed to right and left, shook himself, rolled in the sand, and bucked like a horse. All was useless. The jaws that held him stayed firmly locked and at last he stood defeated, his head down, while the dogs dragged him to his knees. A bull that has to be baited by hounds is considered unworthy of the matador's sword and of the stroke from the front, between the shoulders, so one of the *chulos* came forward and thrust his sword into the great beast's flank. His third blow reached the heart and the bull fell prone.

The dogs still kept their hold upon their prey, dead though he was, and their masters had to come and make them unlock their jaws. Do you know, Madame, the only way to force a bulldog to release its hold? Nothing simpler! One must bite its tail!

One day I was almost carried in triumph. In my carriage I was passing down the Rue Sainte-Anne when my way was blocked by a huge crowd. An elderly marquise was taking a walk, followed by her Pekinese and a servant, when suddenly a little iron-jawed bulldog rushed at the Pekinese and bit it in the fleshy part of its rear. The Pekinese howled, the marquise wept, the servant swore, and, to their shame, the inhabitants of the Rue Sainte-Anne stood laughing. Some more kindly souls were trying to separate the animals without avail, and the marquise was in despair. I decided to play the role of a *deus ex machina*, or *ex-cabriolet*, and, leaning over the apron of my carriage, I called, "Bring those two animals to me!"

"Oh! Sir! Save my dog!" cried the marquise, clasping her hands.

"Madame, I will do what I can," I replied modestly.

The cluster of dogs was carried across to me. Since I was not acquainted with the bulldog, and therefore could not presume to be overfamiliar toward him, I wrapped my handkerchief carefully round his tail before giving it a hard bite. The Pekinese dropped like a ripe fruit and ran to his mistress, while the bulldog, his eyes bloodshot and his jaws gaping, tried his best to attach himself to some part of my person. But I know my job as a detacher of bulldogs, and I threw him ten feet away as I called to my coachman to drive on.

Three days later, the old marquise, having traced my address, offered me her heart and hand. If I had married her, I should today be a widower with an income of a hundred fifty thousand francs!

With this thought I must leave you, Madame. It never grows tedious to watch bullfights, and every day for a week I have seen all the bullfights in Madrid. But to see is not the same thing as to hear, and I fear my letter may already be overlong, especially since I shall have to return to that subject, for royal bullfights, as I have the honor to inform you, are conducted under conditions very different from those of an ordinary bullfight.

9

Madrid, the evening of October 12th

Madrid is truly a city of miracles, Madame. I do not know whether there are always such illuminations here, such ballets, such lovely women, but I do know that I feel a tremendous urge to make Spain my country and Madrid my home. No one who did not see the Prado lit up, last night, has any idea how wonderful such an illumination can be; no one has really seen dancing if he missed Mme Guy Stephen at the Circus Theater; and unless one has watched Romero fighting a bull one has no conception of what courage means.

On leaving the Palace last evening I was escorted to the Prado, where the whole length of the Avenue blazed with lights that shot up in every imaginable color, forming every conceivable shape,—cathedrals, flowers, Gothic castles and Moorish palaces, stars, garlands, the whole planetary system! Never have I seen anything like it, except the Fête of the Luminara, at Pisa, and if it is true, as I was told, that this illumination costs a hundred thousand francs a day, it would not surprise me in the least.

There were so many beautiful women passing up and down in the lights of the Prado that it became simply impossible to take notice of each one. The task became too exhausting, and one had to give up trying. Only a plain woman is remarkable in Madrid!

After a couple of hours we made our way to the Circus Theater, arriving at the moment of the *baile nacional* when the *première danseuse* was on the stage, a Frenchwoman, Mme Guy Stephen. I must tell you, Madame, that there exists a sort of Freemasonry among artists of the theater, whereby we entertain one another even when we do not actually meet. If I go into a Parisian theater where Frédérick Lemaître is playing, or Déjazet, or Bouffé, I have only to let them know that I am in the audience and they respond by giving the performance of their lives! I wondered if this might still apply in Spain, so I sent word to my *compatriot* that I had come to watch her, begging her to dance especially for me.

Do you know these Spanish dances, Madame? The audience at the Circus that night thought they did, too, but as this well-loved artist took her opening steps, an astonished silence fell. Never before had Mme Stephen entered with such inspired *verve* into the *jaleo* of Xérès, or portrayed so sensitively its

57

theme of fierce pride and languorous surrender, bitter scorn and voluptuous desire. The silence broke in a trembling sigh of ecstasy, then came a tumult of cheers that would not be stilled until the dance had been encored again and again. Afterward I went backstage to see Mme Guy Stephen. We had never met before, never exchanged a single word, but she held out her hand to me and said, "Well? Are you satisfied?" What a wonderful thing is this fellowship between artists, which so simply, so naturally, achieves complete mutual understanding! I feel that by a single stroke I have amply repaid Madrid for all the hospitality that city has so lavishly extended to me.

On reaching M. Monnier's house, I found a letter awaiting me from Ossuna, inviting me to lunch next day with his *caballero rejoneador*, a term I must explain to you. Royal bullfights are arranged to celebrate the births or marriages of kings and queens, and, as I have mentioned, are marked by special ceremonials that apply to them alone. The bullfighters are not professionals, but impoverished noblemen of exalted birth whose chances of survival are slender, since they face the bull handicapped by complete inexperience. If, however, they manage to escape death in the arena, their reward is a position as equerry at the palace and an income of fifteen hundred francs a year, a fortune in Madrid.

There are no *picadors* at a royal bullfight, no *torero* to confront the bull on foot, sword in hand. Instead, the cavaliers attack him with javelins, mounted not on wretched nags that the knacker will slaughter tomorrow if the bull does not kill them today, but upon superb, gallant horses from the Queen's own stables. This was originally intended as a helpful concession, but proves in fact a great disadvantage, because the rider has to wage a twofold battle, grappling with the ferocity of the bull and the terror of his own mount. The stronger the horse, the more terrible is this struggle, and the casualties among the cavaliers are caused more often by their horses than by the bull.

Each cavalier, or *caballero rejoneador*, chooses a patron from one of the foremost families of the town, and the patron responds by paying his *protégé's* expenses, equipping him with the approved costume—court dress of the time of Philip IV— in the patron's own colors. The patron also appoints a first-class professional *torero* who will act as a sort of guardian to the cavalier in the arena, using his expert knowledge to entice the bull within reach of the cavalier's lance, or to distract the animal if it attacks him.

The Duke of Ossuna, then, invited me to lunch with him, to meet his *protégé*, Don Federigo Varela y Ulloa, and the guardian angel appointed to aid him, Francisco Montès. Montès, I need hardly tell you, is the King of Bullfighters, so important that he responds only to invitations from royalty, or from a city. He is a millionaire—every time he fights a bull he is paid a thousand francs—a general who has won five thousand battles. Only outstanding merit can win a man fame as a bullfighter. No influence, no intrigue can lend him any aid. He must win his reputation at his sword's point, standing alone in full view of his public and under the eye of God. You may be sure I was most anxious to meet Montès, and at 10 o'clock I was at Ossuna's home.

But Montès had decided to reserve all his energies for the afternoon's ordeal, and did not attend the luncheon party. We were six or eight at table, and never in my life have I seen anything more sad. Don Federigo was about twenty-two years old, still suffering from a horn thrust in the thigh, received three months earlier. Desperate at seeing his mother and sister living in abject poverty in spite of all his efforts, he had resolved to risk his life to ensure them an income. In his Philip IV costume, which he wore very awkwardly, he was extremely pale and preoccupied, scarcely swallowing a crumb, as though the poor devil knew this would be his last meal. The matter was the more serious since he had no experience of those maneuvers that could lessen his danger. He would be mounting a horse for the first time, and had never borne arms. Clearly he had no chance at all against the bulls he was to face, and though we made what encouraging remarks we could he sat in silence, as if Death itself were his fellow guest. When he left us and retired to the next room, Ossuna followed him. As I learned later, the Duke urged him to withdraw, and offered him a sum equal to the pension he hoped to win, but the *caballero* declined, asking only that Ossuna should take care of his mother and sister if he were killed.

At eleven-thirty we set out for the *Plaza Mayor*, and ten minutes later were installed in the Duke's magnificent balcony, overlooking this immense square. For a month past, workmen had been busy pulling up the paving stones, laying sand everywhere, erecting barriers, and raising tiers of seats up to the level of the first-floor windows of the houses. Above that, the windows, roofs, even the church steeples, served as a grandstand where a hundred thousand people crowded to see and be seen.

On our left was the royal box, and in the space below it a company of halberdiers stood to attention, not moving a muscle. (Should the bull charge them, they are permitted to lower their halberds, and if the animal impales himself on these weapons he becomes their perquisite.) Facing them were six *alguazils* in their traditional black costume, mounted on black horses and unarmed except for a short sword and, of all things, a whip, as though to provide a touch of comedy in the tragic drama. (Indeed, the bull himself, puzzled by these men with whips, and perhaps having a private grudge to work off, often seems to take malicious delight in attacking them, whereupon the good people of Madrid collapse in fits of laughter.)

Imagine three rows of balconies, lavishly decked with red and gold, or yellow and silver; imagine the riot of color in the dress of a hundred thousand Spaniards; imagine their ceaseless movement and the sound of their voices; and your imagination will still fall short of the actual reality. More than half the people were talking only of one man, Romero, the *caballero* sponsored by the Duke of Alba. The rumor ran that this young fellow's political opinions had cost him his rank as an officer of the Queen's guard, though he claimed to be falsely accused. So he had volunteered as a *cavalier en place* at this royal bull-

60

fight, declaring he would either be killed or would win for himself a better place than the one he had lost.

Meanwhile, a great cheer heralded the arrival of the Queen, who entered with the King, the Duke and Duchess of Montpensier (the bride receiving a special welcome from the crowd at this, her first, public appearance), also the Duke of Aumale and the Queen Mother. As soon as the royal party was seated, the bugles sounded a fanfare and four magnificently decorated carriages entered the arena, each drawn by four horses and bearing a cavalier with his sponsor around the ring to pass in single file before the royal box. Then the *chulos*, *banderilleros*, and *toreros* began their ceremonial parade, finally kneeling before the Queen's balcony. As they rose to their feet again, two richly caparisoned horses were led in, followed by two cavaliers, Don Federigo, my fellow guest at lunch, and Don Romano, sponsored by the Count of Altamira. The bugles blared again as they mounted, and Don Federigo's horse reared. Instead of giving him his head, the inexpert cavalier reined him in so tightly that both horse and rider fell backward and rolled in the sand. It was a bad start, but fortunately neither was hurt and Federigo soon settled himself again in the saddle. The other cavalier seemed to me a man of forty or forty-five, a rather more skilled horseman than poor Federigo, for at least he knew how to trot.

Each rider was now handed a further embarrassment, his javelin—a wooden pole about six feet long, ending in a sharp steel blade. The pole itself was of very brittle white wood which would break off as the cavalier struck, leaving the blade and the broken shaft in the bull's body. Another fanfare, the gate of the *toril* opened, and a red bull with pointed curving horns rushed in and circled a third of the arena before halting to glare fiercely around at the great crowd. His eye fell on the unhappy *alguazils*, who paled visibly, and with a great bellow he charged, scattering them like cockroaches. One lost his stirrups and clutched his saddle with both hands. His broad hat blew off and was trampled by the bull while the crowd hooted their derision. Montès took Federigo's horse by the bridle and led it toward the bull, which was still too blinded by rage to notice this move. Federigo did not lack courage, only confidence, and he urged his horse up to the bull, raised his arm and buried his lance in its side, while those who appreciated his triumph of will power gave him a cheer. For a second the bull stood stunned, then turned on his adversary and we all thought poor Federigo was done for, as, indeed, he would have been but for Montès, who dodged under the horse's neck and took his stand between his *protégé* and the bull, his red cloak flickering in his hand. Dazzled, the bull charged Montès, and we were privileged to watch an amazing sight—a man, armed only with a silk cape, playing with an enraged animal, making it pass now to his right, now to his left, without stirring a step himself, though at every pass the horns grazed the silver of his waistcoat. It was incredible, as though Montès was protected by a charm, a talisman.

Meanwhile Federigo was rearmed, and the second cavalier was led forward by his *torero*-protector to break his lance in the bull's neck. As before, the bull turned on his enemy, but this time the *torero*, less skilled or less daring than Montès, failed to divert him and he buried his horns in the horse's chest. It reared, pounding the bull with its iron-shod forefeet, then fell backward upon its rider, whose scream was suddenly cut short as the saddlebow crushed his chest. The horse struggled to its feet, blood gushing from its wounds, one leg paralyzed, but the man lay prone and unconscious as the bull returned to attack. Don Federigo buried another lance in the bull's shoulder, and once again we watched Montès play the bull while the injured man was rescued and the third *caballero* entered to a welcoming roar from the crowd.

It was Romero, a handsome young man of twenty-five or so, his skin clear and pale, his short hair black, like the small mustache that outlined his sensitive mouth. He wore green velvet, and the costume of Philip IV, which on the others seemed a mere fancy dress, on him looked elegant and well-fitting. He vaulted lightly to the saddle, rode across to pay his respects to the Queen, then maneuvered his horse up and down in the arena, completely ignoring the bull. After exchanging a word or two with his *torero, le Chiclanero,* he spurred his horse toward the bull, not as yet to attack it, but riding around it once or twice, like a falcon around its prey, to accustom his mount to the sight and the scent of the animal. Then he halted as it charged, drove his lance deep between the bull's shoulders, and cantered off to collect another weapon. For ten steps the doomed animal pursued him, then fell on one knee, struggled up again, bent both knees, stretched its full length in the sand, and at last dropped its lifeless head as Romero rode up to renew the attack.

There was a moment of stunned, incredulous silence. No professional *torero* could have shown more grace and skill, and the great crowd broke into a frenzy of cheering which Romero received with an air of quizzical pride, as if to say, "Gentlemen, you are too kind! Wait a little. There's more to come!"

A second bull entered the ring and Romero grasped the sword in his right hand, while his left hand waved the *muleta* before the animal's eyes as it charged. We saw a bright flash of light, and the sword was buried to its very hilt between the bull's shoulders, bringing it instantly to its knees before its conqueror, while the spectators applauded hysterically.

Five minutes later the third bull was released, a black one which at once charged the *alguazils,* as though it knew the routine. Romero galloped up, broke a lance in its left flank, seized a fresh weapon, doubled back, and drove the second lance into the bull's right flank. You should have seen that immense amphitheater, filled with waving hands, fluttering handkerchiefs; you should have heard the *vivas* for Romero, the invincible, the invulnerable! He was acknowledging the applause as the bull pawed the sand and bellowed defiance; calmly he replaced his hat and waited for the charge. It came, so violently that the horns lifted both horse and rider high in the air.

Now, listen to this, Madame, and add your applause for a feat that was witnessed by a hundred thousand spectators.

While Romero was thus being tossed, he leaned forward and drove his lance into the bull, pushing it in deeper with his foot until the huge beast, horse, and rider all fell together in one confused heap of struggling bodies. The bull was the first to free himself, and with no more fight left in him he backed away to take refuge against the barrier, as the horse, strangely enough almost unharmed, regained its footing with Romero still in the saddle.

"Another lance!" he cried, but his adversary, stabbed to the heart, had already collapsed on the sand. "Another bull!" shouted Romero. He was at the highest pitch of exaltation, his lips and nostrils quivering, his eyes blazing with excitement.

But the Queen made a sign and whispered an order. Romero left the arena and presented himself in the royal box, where the Queen gave him her hand to kiss and the Duke of Montpensier presented him with his own sword. Henceforth Romero's bravery would be well rewarded, and if ever a man was completely happy for a whole day, that man was Romero.

The celebrations continued; my friends and I have seen the death of forty-six bulls, a mere half of the total, but nothing is worth the telling after Romero's spectacular achievement. I will write you one more letter from Madrid. What it will tell you, events must decide.

10

Madrid, 21st October, 1846

The festivities are over, Madame, and flocks of thankless foreigners are taking flight from Madrid like birds darting back to their nests. The Duke of Aumale left this evening, the Duke of Montpensier goes tomorrow, and in a week's time the city will be deserted, but I shall not be here to see it, for we leave for Toledo tomorrow.

Two hours ago I returned from a visit to the Escorial, that shrine, palace, and mausoleum of Spanish kings, but before telling you about it I should mention that in preparation for continuing our travels we have organized our party and agreed upon the duties each shall undertake. I retain the title bestowed on me by all our Spanish servants, *l'amo*, "the boss" and general provider. Desbarolles is sworn in as our interpreter, officially in charge of arrangements with coachmen and innkeepers. Maquet will continue as our steward, and in his leisure moments he will keep us informed of the time, since his repeater is the only watch still in working order. Giraud, our treasurer, carries our funds in a leather belt around his waist, and will be responsible for buying provisions *en route*, as well as for keeping them safe. Boulanger is to be in charge of our personal baggage.

Three days ago, when we decided to visit the Escorial, Desbarolles was accordingly sent to find a suitable vehicle to convey us to this favorite palace of Philip II. We were still busy with our preparations when Desbarolles returned, the expanse of his waistcoat eloquent of triumph as he announced that our carriage was waiting, so we went down. There stood four mules, harnessed to a light *berline* with a green hood and yellow bodywork, a startling color scheme that we were willing to overlook. It was, however, too small for eight passengers. Giraud offered to ride on a shaft, and Desbarolles to balance on the step, but I decided we must have a second carriage and asked Desbarolles to find one quickly, for it was already an hour past midday and the Escorial was seven hours' drive. (So the coachman said, Madame, but in Spain the miles, and the hours, are a third longer than in France.)

We waited for almost an hour, and then Achard, at the window, called to us with lively interest: "Gentlemen, you probably imagine you know every sort of carriage in the world, but come and look! You've never seen anything like the one coming this way across the *Plaza Mayor*. Quickly, or you'll miss it!"

We crowded to the windows, and saw, drawn by one thin horse whose protruding bones were almost hidden by the pompons of its elaborate Spanish harness, a fantastic coach that would have fetched an enormous price in Paris as an antique. Its two great wheels were bright vermilion; its pale blue coachwork was decorated with a latticework of fruit, flowers, and bright green leaves, among which sported myriads of bright-hued birds, dominated by a magnificent purple parrot with outspread wings, eating an orange. The upholstery *à la pompadour*, now a mass of patches, still retained its original tasseled fringes and gold lace.

To our amazement it drew up before our door and Desbarolles stepped proudly down. We fell on his neck, helpless with laughter, and christened it "the Desbarolles" in his honor, while everyone begged to ride in it. I signed to Don Riego to follow me, we took our seats, gave the driver his orders and started off, ignoring the protests that broke out behind us as our companions piled hastily into the *berline* and set out in pursuit. Keep that green and yellow carriage in mind, Madame, for it is destined to play an important role in our lives.

Once outside the town we made only slow progress, for in places the road had been washed away by recent storms. Climbing the foothills we enjoyed a fine view of Madrid, its gigantic palace towering above the little white houses like a whale in the midst of a shoal of fishes, while beyond it the great plain stretched in austere grandeur to the peaks fringing the horizon. On we went for four hours, plunging into a valley, crossing a bridge, then scaling the flanks of the Guadarrama, a mountain range like a herd of enormous buffaloes, where, on one of the highest crests, stands the Escorial. Since the gradient rose sharply, we dismounted and spread out on foot over the mountainside. Rarely have I seen a prospect so wild and awe-inspiring. A thousand feet below us, beyond precipitous crags, beyond chasms with their far side in deep shadow, the infinite plain lay like a leopard skin, marked with tawny patches and great streaks of black. To our left, the view was limited by the mountains we were climbing, their summits crowned with snow, while in the distance the white pinpoints of Madrid pricked through the dusk that was rolling on toward us like a darkening flood.

Giraud and Boulanger were in ecstasies, especially Boulanger, who was less familiar with Spain. Never had he set eyes upon such contrasts of light and shadow, and every other moment he clasped his hands, crying: "How beautiful it is! God! How beautiful!" Among men like us, traveling as we are, there are moments of infinite sweetness. Man, as an individual, is far from complete, and can experience fulfillment only when his own personality merges with the minds of others with whom he is linked by chance or choice. With us, poets and painters complement each other, and the sublime verses of Hugo that Alexandre declaimed to the winds were in perfect harmony with the grandeur around us. So we stood, delighting in this communion of spirit, till dusk gave place to night, and, from the heavens a million stars blinked their golden eyelids to peep curiously down at the earth.

The country we were passing through was formerly infested with bandits. Our *mayoral* assured us that to travel this road after sunset would once have cost us our luggage at least, and the wooden crosses we saw stretching their sorrowful arms beside the road or at the foot of a rock confirmed his story. A further confirmation was a light that suddenly appeared, two hundred yards ahead. Learning that it shone from a police post, I rather suspected its existence implied that there were still robbers in the vicinity, so we looked to the loading of our guns—unnecessarily, as it proved, for we crossed the danger area without incident. We were still some distance from our journey's end, and the *mayoral* persuaded us to resume our seats in the carriage, promising to make his mules trot, which hitherto they had refused to do. Now, for a few moments at least, they did so, since the road sloped downhill and the weight of the carriage forced them forward. We drove on through the darkness for two hours, then seemed to pass

67

through a gateway into a park where the sound of our wheels was deadened by sand. Still we pressed on, uphill toward a few scattered lights on the mountainside, and an hour later we were on a metaled road, passing a few ramshackle houses, crossing an open square, and pulling up at the *Posada*, where a large sign over the door bore the name of the landlord, Calisto Burguillos.

To our great surprise, the inn was bustling with activity in spite of the lateness of the hour, and we surmised that something unusual was afoot, as indeed it was. A party of English travelers had arrived in two carriages, three hours before us, and were about to have supper. Never arrive at a Spanish inn, Madame, at a moment when they are serving supper to English visitors! The aforesaid Calisto Burguillos received us churlishly, declaring that he was far too busy to attend to any supper or rooms for us. But if a man puts up an inn sign to attract wayfarers, I maintain he has no right to turn them away, so I told Giraud to bring our loaded guns from the coach to the kitchen. Obeying my glance, Alexandre, Maquet, Achard, and Desbarolles followed to assist him.

"Now, Boulanger," I continued, "you are a tactful man. Take Don Riego with you to look for four small bedrooms or two large ones." Burguillos followed this byplay with his eyes.

"Good!" he said to his wife, "they've gone, those *pugnateros* of Frenchmen."

This epithet of *pugnateros*, "dirty fighters," is one we have frequently encountered since we entered Spain. I do not know if it is well-deserved, but it is certainly used everywhere. Don Calisto had not noticed me, hidden as I was by the chimney breast, but his wife warned him with a gesture and he left his ovens to come and ask me what I wanted.

"A grill," I said, "to cook some cutlets."

"You have some?"

"No. But you have," and I pointed to a quarter of mutton hanging in the chimney corner.

"Those are for the English, not for you."

"You're wrong. You have just served them twelve cutlets, and that is plenty. The rest is for us."

The landlord was still protesting when Giraud returned, followed by Desbarolles, Maquet, Achard, and Alexandre, all carrying guns which I instructed them to bring to the fireplace.

"Giraud," I said, "Master Burguillos will have the goodness to spare us this quarter of mutton. Ask him the price. Pay for it generously; unhook it deftly, and cut it up neatly."

"Those three adverbs accord very harmoniously," observed Desbarolles, as he brought his carbine to the fire.

"Not too close, my friend, not too close," cried Achard. "You know these guns are all loaded."

"How much is the quarter of mutton?" inquired Giraud, passing me his gun and taking up the carving knife from the kitchen table.

"Two *duros*," replied the landlord, with one eye on our weapons and the other on his quarter of mutton.

"Give him three *duros*, Giraud." In doing so, Giraud allowed five or six gold coins to fall to the floor, while the *Señora* opened her eyes wide. Giraud took the meat, carved it with a facility that did credit to his anatomical studies, dusted the cutlets with salt and pepper and placed them daintily on the grill, which he then laid on a bed of red-hot coals that Achard had leveled in readiness.

"Now, Desbarolles," I continued, "offer our hostess your arm, beg her to lead you to her potato store, and if you come across any eggs on the way, slip a dozen into your game bag. Inquire after the health of her family, flatter her, gain her confidence."

Madame Burguillos, already somewhat softened toward us by the sight of our gold, deigned to accept Desbarolles' arm and conduct him through a door that apparently led to the bowels of the earth. At the same moment, Boulanger and Don Riego returned from their expedition of exploration. They had set their course toward the South Pole, and been blown by favorable winds into a corridor where, at the far end, they discovered a long room that could take eight beds. Boulanger, sensible man, had locked the door of this room and brought me the key.

The cutlets were still cooking, and at a word from me Achard seized a frying pan and Giraud a saucepan, while Master Calisto watched our proceedings in stupefaction. But he was one against eight, with no weapon but a cooking spoon against five rifles. For a moment he seemed on the point of calling his English guests to his aid, but as a well-informed man he was doubtless aware that in the Peninsular War the Spanish suffered more from their English allies than from their French enemies, so he made no move.

Desbarolles returned with a game bag full of eggs and his pockets crammed with potatoes. Achard started to beat the eggs, Giraud prepared the potatoes, and Desbarolles cajoled Madame Burguillos to such good effect that a table laid for eight was set in a corner of the room. Ten minutes later our meal was almost ready, and Don Calisto's kitchen presented an entertaining spectacle. Your devoted servant, M. Alexandre Dumas, with a fan in each hand, was maintaining an even draught on the glowing coals that were grilling the cutlets and frying the potatoes. Giraud was busily peeling more potatoes for a second cooking; Don Riego, while pretending to read his breviary, was savoring the grill and keeping the corner of his eye on the frying pan that Maquet was handling; Achard was grinding pepper; Desbarolles was resting after his labors; Boulanger, chilled by his expedition into high latitudes, was warming himself by the blaze; Alexandre, as usual, had gone to sleep; while Master Calisto Burguillos contemplated this French invasion in utter amazement. In another ten minutes we were all sitting at table to enjoy twelve smoking cutlets, two pyramids of potatoes, and an immense omelette, laughing so uproariously that Mme Burguillos peeped through the doorway with two or three servants behind her, while in the shadows beyond appeared the astonished faces of the English travelers.

I took advantage of Mme Burguillos' presence to slip the key of the bedroom into Desbarolles' hand. "One last sacrifice," I begged. "Get them to make up our beds. We will keep your share of the supper hot, and on your return will vote you a crown of laurel, as the Romans did to Caesar." An hour later, seven of us were lying on mats arranged symmetrically on the floor. One Spanish bed—that is to say, two trestles with four planks and a mattress—dominated the room, and this we all gratefully assigned to Desbarolles, without prejudice to his laurel crown.

11

❦ ❦ ❦

Toledo, the evening of the 23rd of October

The day dawned gray, overcast with cloud, and I was glad, for that seemed to me the right light in which to see the Escorial. At a turn of the road we caught sight of its sepulchral immensity, truly worthy of the man who chose the desert for his capital and a tomb for his palace. You know how the Escorial came to be built, Madame? One day early in the year 1559,* while Philip was besieging Saint Quentin, his artillery destroyed the church of Saint Lawrence, and fearing that this saint might grieve for the loss of his shrine he vowed to build him another, far larger and richer. The victory won, Philip, unlike most monarchs, fulfilled his vow a hundredfold, giving his architect, Juan-Bautista, the strange instruction to build his monument in the shape of a gridiron lying on a dish.

No one can imagine how austere, how mournful, the Escorial looks, a granite monument on a granite mountain, like some

* Dumas is not quite accurate in this particular, for the date of Philip II's victory at St. Quentin was the 10th of August, 1557, St. Lawrence's Day. It was possibly from this circumstance, rather than because the old church of St. Lawrence in the town was demolished during the siege, that the new building was dedicated to that saint and given the title of *El Real monasterio de San Lorenzo del Escorial.*

natural phenomenon. Approaching it, one realizes the insignificance of man in the face of its gigantic bulk. A great door yawns, then shuts behind you, and though you are merely a casual visitor, if you are aware of what freedom means to you, you shudder as though you were fated never to leave this place.

Nothing can give you any idea of the Escorial, not Windsor in England, nor Peterhoff in Russia, nor Versailles in France. It is like nothing but itself, created by a man who bent his epoch to his will, a reverie fashioned in stone, conceived during the sleepless hours of a king on whose realms the sun never set. No one could call it beautiful. It evokes not admiration, but terror. Even Philip himself must have shuddered when his architect handed him the thousand keys of this monument conjured up by his inflexible spirit.

Have you ever descended a mine and felt that a whole mountain was pressing down on you? That is how one feels on entering the Escorial. In other monuments, one climbs; in this, one descends. Philip wished to leave himself no illusion, and while still living he went down to his tomb in the tradition of his family. There is everything in the Escorial; palace, chapel, convent, sepulcher. The chapel is admirable—perhaps the only place in the whole edifice where one can breathe freely. It is supported by four square pillars, each a hundred and twelve feet around the base. Nineteen marble steps lead up to the altar, which is decorated with fine paintings of scenes from the life of Christ. Between them stand doric columns, the most severe style in all architecture, and these columns are the only touch of decoration in the whole structure. The altar itself is lighted by a great lamp hanging from the vaulted roof, which makes the bright flecks in the granite shine like mother-of-pearl.

To right and left of the altar, at a height of about fifteen feet, are two great square-cut niches. The one on the left is the tomb of Charles V; on the right is the tomb of Philip, who doubtless considered that he and his father were the only ones worthy of burial outside the *real podridero*. Below is this inscription in letters of gold: "Philip II, King of all the realms of Spain, Sicily and Jerusalem, lies here in the tomb which, in his lifetime, he built for himself. With him rest his first wife, Elisabeth, his second wife, Marie, and his first-born son, Don Carlos." Thus this unyielding father, good Christian king, ordained that his son should be reconciled with him in death. Above the tomb are sculptures of Philip, his son, and his two successive queens, all kneeling at prayer. Above the tomb to the left kneels Charles V, surrounded by other kneeling figures whose identity one learns from the inscription: "To the memory of Charles V, Roman Emperor; King of Spain and of Jerusalem; Archduke of Austria. Erected by his son Philip. With him repose his wife, Elisabeth; his daughter, the Empress Marie; and his sisters, Eleanor, Queen of France, and Marie, Queen of Hungary." All these statues are of bronze-gilt, finely executed and striking in their effect, especially those of the two monarchs, sternly magnificent in cloaks emblazoned with their arms.

Turning from the altar one faces the chapter house, where you would find, Madame, none of the fascinating ornamentation of the Renaissance or the attractively simple sculpture of the fifteenth century. Here the stalls, instead of blossoming, like those at Burgos, into delightfully carved flowers or marvelously wrought borders, have no decoration beyond a simple molding of frigid straight lines. This inflexible and taciturn determination, this rigid squaring up of wood and granite, weighs upon your spirit the moment you enter this church. All other temples of the world give you back hope in exchange for prayer: the chapel of the Escorial is consecrated to the God of Vengeance, to the Christ at the Last Judgment of Michelangelo. Pray, if you like, but the chapel will give no response, returning no more echo than would a dungeon of the Holy Inquisition. Only two things break the funereal harmony of this church: the two thrones, like great lanterns, introduced by Ferdinand VII, and the paintings of the vaulted roof, executed by order of Charles II.

It is a strange thing, Madame, that whenever a powerful

personality expresses itself in creating a masterpiece, strong as granite, that work is not left inviolate as a sacred memorial. Once in the course of centuries there comes a man, typical of his own times, the mirror of a whole epoch, who leaves behind him a monument to make his spirit known to all future generations. Then comes another man, weak and paltry, who cannot endure the sublime melancholy from which his predecessor drew strength, so he brings in some bungling dauber or tinsmith, saying to the first: "All this is too sad, too funereal for me, poor frivolous creature that I am. Paint me something pretty on these walls," and to the other: "Make me a nice bit of decoration to smarten up this staircase." So the dauber and the tinker set happily to work, and profane for all time the masterpiece they think to embellish. God have mercy on M. Andrieux who renovated *Nicomède;** and on King Charles II, who touched up the Escorial.

So, Madame, if ever you visit the Escorial, limit your sightseeing to three things, the chapel, the *Podridero*, and the room where Philip died. All the rest would only weaken your first impressions. So rarely in life do we experience a profound sensation which, even while we tremble, opens new and strange horizons before our eyes, that I would never shrink from a deeply moving experience, even though it should drown me in sadness and terror as the Escorial has done.

The *Podridero* is the St. Denis of Madrid, the vault that holds the dust of kings. It is a kind of temple, lined with jasper and porphyry, but it lacks the solemn majesty of the crypts at St. Denis, where, on the final step, the king who died last stands waiting for his successor to join him.

Philip died in the room where he spent his last three years of life, crippled with gout. A narrow window in a recess allowed him to look upon the High Altar in the chapel, so that without

---

* Dumas evidently disapproved of certain fairly extensive alterations which M. Andrieux (lawyer, dramatist, and professor of literature at the Collège de Nance) had suggested should be made, for reasons of stagecraft, in Corneille's tragedy, *Nicomède*. Cf. *Oeuvres de François Guillaume Jean Stanislaus Andrieux, Paris, Chez-Nepveu, 1818, Tome III, p. 340 et seq.*

rising from his chair, or even his bed, he attended Holy Mass. His ministers came to this little room to work with him, and one can still see the wooden board that used to rest on the knees of the king, and of any man admitted to his presence, serving them as a table for their labors or for signing documents. Against the wall stands the great armchair to which Philip II used to be lifted when he left his bed, and near it are the footstools, one for use in summer, the other in winter, on which the king would stretch out his afflicted leg. They are both folding stools, one with a top made of rushes, the other in goatskin, and on both the powerful heel that oppressed half the world for forty years has left a mark that remains clearly visible and almost threatening.

Now, Madame, wander for a moment through these endless corridors, where a blind man, full of gaiety, will guide you to the middle of the maze if you wish. Then you will feel this stone tunnel pressing in upon you. Your breathing becomes labored between these granite walls, this granite floor and ceiling. You will urgently need daylight, air, and sunshine, and you will find them all by climbing the Cupola, whence you will see the monument at your feet and Madrid on the horizon.

But, Madame, on leaving the Escorial, there is one thing you will regret. There are now none of the fine monks of Zurbaran and Murillo, with their long trailing robes and shaven heads. The Escorial without monks is a paradox, with nothing to explain its meaning. The revolution abolished the monks, you are told. Do revolutions reach as high as the Escorial, then? Is the Escorial a part of earth, of this world? Drive the monks from the rest of Spain if you must, you philosophers, you social reformers, and planners of constitutions, but, in the name of Heaven, make an exception for the Escorial, as we have done in France for the monasteries of *La Trappe* and *la grande Chartreuse*.

As long as we remained in the Escorial we had no thought of a meal, so heavily did the sinister monument weigh upon our spirits, but once outside, hunger and life returned to us together. We therefore made our way back to the inn, where our host, Calisto Burguillos, was waiting on the doorstep to welcome us. The menu in Spain offers little variation, and at our disposal were cutlets, potatoes, and a salad, the same meal as the evening before, plus some greenstuff. But a salad in Spain knows nothing of oil or vinegar, and I defy any Frenchman, no matter how much he likes lettuce, endive, and rampion root, to swallow a single mouthful of them served alone, appetizing though they are when sprinkled with either of the liquids mentioned above.

It was then, Madame, that there came to me, for the first time, the sublime idea of how to make a salad without oil or vinegar. Certainly, if I were a speculator, I should have patented it and made a fortune by exploiting it in Spain—even exporting it to Italy. But, alas, as you know, the spirit of commercial enterprise was forgotten when I was christened, and, like a jealous fairy, not only gives me no help but actually persecutes me. I therefore will frankly and simply pass on my idea to those who, like myself, enjoy traveling. The secret is to use lemon juice and fresh eggs when mixing your salad.

As Master Calisto Burguillos displayed such intense interest during this operation of seasoning, I eventually snatched the salad bowl away as Giraud was about to take a third helping and sent the few remaining leaves to our host, adding a fragment of omelette cooked in my own special way. I had forgotten this parting gift until, as we were leaving, I found Master Calisto waiting for me on his doorstep, a glass in each hand and another under his arm, to accord me the ceremonial leave-taking reserved for members of the catering fraternity. He had, in fact, done me the honor of taking me for some celebrated French *maitre-chef*, visiting Madrid in connection with the Spanish festivities. I left him with this impression, which placed me far higher in his esteem than if I had told him I was the author of *The Three Musketeers* or of *Monte Cristo*.

Time was pressing, for it was already midday, and at 7 o'clock we were expected at a banquet the French Colony at Madrid was giving in my honor. Our compatriots are like that,

Madame. Out of France they welcome us with open arms, fete us, embrace us; while at home they criticize and tear us to pieces. Crossing the frontier one dies, and is received in a foreign country as in posterity. It is no longer you, yourself; it is your spirit, your shade, which inherits these proofs of appreciation that surge around you at every step, and I must say my glorious shade is received here in a fashion that fills my poor body with envy. One thing is beyond doubt. I am better known and perhaps more popular in Madrid than in France. The Spaniards recognize in me, that is to say in my works, some touch of Castille that warms their hearts. So true is this, that before France made me a *chevalier* of the *Légion d'honneur*, Spain bestowed on me the title of *commandeur d'Isabelle la Catholique*. I have no doubt, Madame, that when I go home I shall have to pay dearly for all the gracious courtesies that have been extended to me here. But at least, from the good opinion they have of me in Spain, I know more or less accurately what will be thought of me when I am dead.

Ever since my arrival, Spanish artists have shown us the most openhearted cordiality. Breton, the Scribe of Spain, and that great painter, Ribera, spend every evening with us; the two finest dramatic actors in the whole country, Romeo and Don Carlos de la Torre, gave us the freedom of the *foyer* at the Prince's Theater, the haunt of all the distinguished artists in Madrid. Every day one of these men has served us as a guide, conducting us to picture galleries, museums, parks—even royal palaces. The French Embassy has striven to satisfy our every wish, and M. Bresson, who has just been made Duke of Sainte-Isabelle and a Grandee, was kind enough to arrange a truly sumptuous reception for us in his royal residence.

To resume after this digression, the French colony at Madrid was expecting us at a dinner for a hundred guests, presided over by Colonel Camond's brother, one of the noblest merchants of Madrid. This, too, was a magnificent function. Strauss, himself one of the guests, arranged a surprise for us, and as dessert was served his whole orchestra entered, that wonderful orchestra which, a week ago, made kings and

77

queens dance like simple shepherds and shepherdesses. Until midnight it entertained us with waltzes, quadrilles, and military music, played as only German musicians can.

I do not know what my return to France has in store for me;* what unforeseen battles await me; what new seven-headed hydra will rear itself in my path; but one thing I do know— I shall come back with a heart so full of gratitude for my reception here that it will soar above any insults still to come.

It is 3 o'clock in the morning, Madame, and in two hours I shall leave Madrid, perhaps never to return. Pity me, Madame, for here I shall leave behind twelve of the happiest days of my life, and you, who know me so well, know that my happy days are few. So, farewell to Madrid, the home of hospitality; to those open-hearted friendships, born only yesterday, that will endure forever. Adieu to those velvet eyes that lured Byron from English beauties; those dainty hands that flutter the quick, shrill fan; those tiny feet that could wear Cinderella's slipper, or an even tinier one that only you and I know of, Madame.

The day before yesterday, when I took my leave of the Duke of Montpensier, he was so kind as to tell me that, at his suggestion, Her Majesty the Queen of Spain had just appointed me a Knight-Commander of Charles III; and when I came home two hours ago I found the cross and badge of the Duke of Ossuna, which he begged me to accept as a souvenir of himself.

You can see, Madame, how right I am to regret leaving Madrid.

* Dumas had good reason to anticipate trouble on his return to France. Lawsuits for broken contracts were already pending.

12

❦ ❦ ❦

Two hours after I sealed my last letter to you, Madame, we left for Toledo, Giraud, Maquet, Boulanger, Desbarolles, Achard, and Alexandre traveling in the famous green and yellow *berline* (having exchanged their tired mules for fresh ones), Don Riego and I by stagecoach. I have grown fond of this good priest, and shall postpone our parting as long as possible.

Our road out of Madrid followed the banks of the Tagus, which is fringed with green all along its course as it meanders through immense plains of sand or heath. I do not know whether we took the main road, or whether our coachman thought up some route of his own in the hope of saving a few kilometers. What I do know is that we made half the journey on foot out of pity for the wretched animals pulling the coach, and on two or three occasions, when they were stuck fast in sand or deep ruts, we even put our shoulders to the wheel, a form of co-operation they very much appreciated.

One tiresome detail I must warn you of, Madame, is the difference you will always find in Spain between the estimated and the actual time a journey will take. For instance, you are told it is about forty-eight miles from Madrid to Toledo, and you set out in the belief that this will mean six hours' traveling at a normal pace. Along the road you look out for the milestones that, in France, solace our impatience as pieces of chocolate solace an empty stomach, but here there are no milestones, no signposts, nothing. You say to yourself: "Bah! Even if we do not get on quite as quickly as we hope, it cannot take more than eight hours." So you travel on for six, eight, ten, twelve hours, asking every moment whether you are nearly there and receiving a vaguely reassuring reply. At last, after fifteen or sixteen hours, you see the outline of a town silhouetted against the setting sun and inquire, "Is that Toledo?" They tell you: "No, but when we reach it we shall be nearly at the end of our journey," and having set out at five in the morning you will arrive, as we did, at eight o'clock in the evening.

As we entered the town, Toledo won our hearts by its very atmosphere, perhaps more impressive by night than by day. As some consolation for the fatigues of the day, God vouchsafed us a warm clear night such as He gives only to the countries He loves. In the calm limpid clarity we could see a great gateway, a road running along the flank of a mountain, and at the summit an irregular outline of rooftops and steeples pointing their arrows to the skies, while in the darkness that girdled the mountain we could hear, leaping and roaring over its rocky bed, that same Tagus we had seen flowing so peacefully through the plain.

The stagecoach halted for the night at the *posada del Lino*. Our friends in the other carriage had arranged to leave Madrid an hour before we did, and, being misled by our impression that we should reach Toledo at 2 or 3 o'clock in the afternoon, a daylight hour in every country in the world except Lapland, we felt certain of finding each other easily and so had not arranged a rendezvous. Now, at 8 o'clock at night, our reunion was a matter of some urgency, and I therefore sent a servant of the *posada* to look for my companions, feeling sure that they, in their turn, would be sending the servant of their own hotel to look for me.

At eleven, news reached me that they were having supper at the *Fonda de los Caballeros,* and in my messenger's opinion they were not in the least concerned about me. I donned my cloak (one always does in Spain, Madame), and ordered the man to lead the way. After wandering for ten minutes over incredibly bad roads, and making our way along precipices edged with houses that I should have preferred to see by daylight, the servant halted at a modest dwelling and said: "This is the place." Once over the threshold I had no need of a guide.

You know my friends, Madame. They have extended the scale of laughter by an octave hitherto unheard-of, and were running up and down the whole range of this scale when I opened the door. The master and mistress of the house were waiting on them personally.

"Well, well! Here's papa!" cried Alexandre.

"The *amo*," murmured the whole group, as they rose and greeted me respectfully. I rarely swear, drink but little, and do not smoke. Consequently, if ever I indulge in one of these venial sins it is in no halfhearted fashion. For three hours I had been developing a furious temper, and I ripped out an oath that would have made the heart of a German leap with joy. Giraud murmured to the others: "I warned you our master would be annoyed," while the host and his wife whispered to each other: "It is the prince, the prince himself!"

I was completely at a loss to understand these titles of "prince," "master," and "*amo*," or the affected humility of my friends, so laughing off my annoyance I exclaimed: "Come, now! Let's get it over. What joke is this?"

"Achard," said Boulanger, "you are the orator. Explain to *l'amo*."

In the hope of discovering what it was all about, I decided to hear what the orator had to say. Besides, we had already agreed to indulge every caprice that might enliven our travels.

"Master," began Achard, bowing low. "Your Excellency," he continued, as I returned his bow, "in our haste to leave Madrid this morning we forgot the permit you obtained last night to ensure that the city gate would be especially opened for us."

"I gave it to Desbarolles," I interrupted.

"With all respect, that was a mistake. Desbarolles is so absent-minded that it was overlooked at the moment of departure. We went back to the *casa Monnier* and searched for half an hour before Desbarolles suddenly exclaimed: 'Ah! I remember now. I used it to load my gun!' Your Excellency can imagine how we cursed him! We got back to the gate at 5 o'clock, as it was opening for the day. Beyond the gate," he declaimed, swinging his cloak and striking an attitude, "there stood huge wagons with teams of mules; myriads of donkeys, patiently munching the vegetables with which they were loaded; great oxen quietly chewing the cud; shepherds with long staves, their flocks clustering around them."

"Bravo!" murmured several voices. "He speaks really well," said Giraud. "Neither Lepaule nor I could speak so eloquently. Continue, my learned friend!"

Achard resumed, his intonation as precisely right as though, like Caius Gracchus, he had a fluteplayer behind him to give him the note. "All the throng stood silent and still, the peasants resting their elbows on their wagon shafts like the harvesters in Leopold Robert's paintings; muleteers smoking cigarettes and dreaming beside their mules; tattered woodcutters wearing bright bandanas swathed around their heads. No one jostled his neighbor or tried to take his place. He who came last, remained the last. Such simple dignity made me think regretfully of the noisy tumult around the barriers of Paris."

"That's very well said," I commented.

"Can I send it to the *Epoque?*" inquired Achard, with a quick change of tone. Alexandre rose, took a piece of charcoal and scrawled on the whitewashed wall: "Read the *Epoque!*", while Achard went on: "When the iron gates swung open, we passed through in our turn. A cold white light lay over the land, and the dew-drenched furrows shone like silver bands in the rays of the new dawn. Like a wedding veil, strands of mist floated over the distant fields, while little pink clouds wandered across the sky like the cupids in Albani's pictures."

"That's enough," cried Boulanger, "or I shall take out my paint brushes!"

"Yes, yes," cried Alexandre, "that's enough, or we shall never finish! I will tell you the rest myself, papa. We traveled by an abominable road, taking fourteen hours instead of eight, and found absolutely nothing to eat on the way, so we had to use the basket of stores. Eventually we arrived, dying of hunger, and in order to get a good meal we said we were the retinue of a great lord who would soon join us. You are the great lord, of course, and now you have come. Are you hungry? Take Desbarolles' place, since he has gone to sleep again. Come to the table and eat." The landlord and his wife rushed forward to serve me, but I stopped them with a gesture, saying I had already supped.

"In that case, sit down and try this *mancenillo* and tell us about your own journey." When I had done so, they all escorted me ceremoniously back to my hotel, while their hostess prepared their beds. My own guide was given a *peseta* for his trouble, the first silver coin he had ever received in his life. He ejaculated "Long live your Lordship!", and in the morning all Toledo awoke to learn that within their walls was a prince, traveling *incognito*. Remember this detail, Madame. It is more important than you think, for this joke, whether good or bad, almost cost the lives of five of our party.

In view of my earlier comments on the churlishness of Spanish innkeepers, you may be surprised to know that in Toledo we received most attentive service. Toledo is a dying town, Madame, and, though too proud to admit it, dying of starvation. This once royal city, the fairest jewel in the crown for which Don Pedro *le Justicier* and Don Henri of Transtamare flew at each other's throats; Toledo, which formerly boasted 120,000 inhabitants, can now count scarcely 15,000 within its deserted walls. It is far from any main road, and except for its famous industry of swordmaking is cut off from all commerce. It lives—or, rather, it contrives to exist—upon the few travelers who are willing to cross the desert to reach it. You can appreciate that such travelers are cordially received, especially by innkeepers, who in Toledo will even come out of doors to welcome visitors and to buy special provisions for them, and it is in this, the hungriest town in Spain, that strangers are offered the finest fare.

Toledo does not deserve this neglect, for its position, its appearance, its sunlight, are all wonderful. It has twenty churches with finer stonework than you would find in any of our French churches. It has memories enough to keep a historian busy for ten years, and a chronicler for his whole lifetime.

Everyone has written a description of Toledo, from our excellent M. Delaborde down to our witty friend Achard, who, while I am writing to you, is writing to Solar and including in his account everything that has already been written on the subject. So, if you wish to know the town as well as though you had seen it yourself, take the advice that Alexandre scrawled in his abominable writing on the walls of the *Fonda de los Caballeros*: "Read the *Epoque!*"

From 6 o'clock in the morning until 4 in the afternoon we explored Toledo, circling its convents, entering its churches, climbing its towers and steeples, admiring everything we visited, until we had no strength left to admire any more. If ever you go to Spain, Madame, and visit Madrid, hire a carriage, find a coach, wait for a caravan if need be, but go to Toledo, Madame, go to Toledo! Only, take the precaution of arranging how to get back. I neglected this matter, and was almost compelled to stay in Toledo with Don Riego and found a French colony there.

You will recall, Madame, that I expected the stagecoach from Madrid to Toledo to take eight hours. Similarly, I had imagined the coach from Toledo to Aranjuez would take about three hours, but now I learned that I could consider myself especially favored by Heaven if it covered the distance in eight. This was a serious matter, for the morning coach leaving Toledo at six might not reach Aranjuez until two in the afternoon, an hour after the Peninsular coach had passed through, and it was in this coach that our seats were reserved for the next stage of our journey. We therefore needed to supplement the *berline* with some other means of transport, and Desbarolles was sent to find what he could. He came back with two saddle mules that we all longed to ride, except Boulanger, who knew nothing of equitation, and Don Riego, who thought it unsuitable for a man of his years and profession. The rest of us drew lots, and for the first part of the journey the mules fell to Giraud and Achard.

To make sure of reaching Aranjuez in good time, we decided to leave Toledo at 5 o'clock that evening, spend the night at the *Villa Mejor*, a little inn some eight miles from Toledo, set off early next morning, and arrive at Aranjuez for our midday meal. We had contracted to pay our *mayoral* a hundred and fifty francs for the three-day journey, and he, on his part, had agreed to set us down, safe and sound, at the *Parador de la Collurera* in Aranjuez on the due date. So it was arranged, but Man proposes and God disposes. Today I have told you what we proposed. Tomorrow you shall know what God disposed. While waiting, Madame, pray for us, for great danger threatens us.

13

✤   ✤   ✤

Aranjuez, 25th October

My last letter ended with us on the point of departure, Madame. Imagine your friends drawn up in echelon on a road as steep as a Russian mountain, outside the door of the *Fonda de los Caballeros*. Facing them on the other side of the street is the palace of the former kings of Toledo, now used as a barracks, I think, its stones the loveliest dead-leaf color from six centuries of baking sunshine, its walls standing out against an indigo sky on the mountaintop at our right. To our left we catch glimpses of the lower town with its red roofs and pointed steeples, while beyond it a russet plain stretches into the distance to merge into the violet horizon.

Standing before me, hat in hand, is our *mayoral*, asking for something on account of the one hundred fifty francs that I do not yet owe him, but shall owe him when he delivers us, *safe and sound*, at Aranjuez. He wants me to let him have as much as possible, in view of the large amounts he has had to pay out, so he says. I take out my purse, containing about sixteen hundred francs, and give him eighty.

Facing us is the carriage, loaded with all our trunks, the roof completely covered by our provision basket which Giraud is securing with a final cord. Maquet and Boulanger are tying up our rifles inside the *berline*, but Desbarolles prefers to keep his slung across his shoulder as he proudly takes his stand by the mules. Don Riego and Achard are smoking, while Alexandre is trying to find somewhere to put some magnificent pomegranates he has bought—a difficult matter since the carriage is too full to take anything else whatever, except its six passengers. The two saddle mules stand ready, held by the *zagal*.

An Englishman is waiting until I have finished with the *mayoral*, to say good-by to me. Who is he? A gentleman of fifty, with a fine head, elegant appearance, and the good manners of all cultured English people. He was touring Spain by post chaise, counting on hiring relays of horses, but had been compelled to leave his chaise in Madrid, so we met in the stagecoach. He had also counted upon finding palatable meals, and had already discovered his mistake. Like all men who order their lives well, he enjoys good food, and from the time he entered Spain he found nothing fit to eat until, at our first meal together, he tasted one of my salads mixed with fresh eggs and lemons. From that moment he began to live again, and attached himself to me like a shipwrecked sailor clinging to a floating spar. At Toledo he lunched with me, dined with me, and at this moment had but one regret: that he could not spend one more day with me. He took careful notes of our itinerary, hoping to rejoin me somewhere *en route*, and gave me his address in London and in the East Indies in case some mischance should prevent our meeting again.

At last all was ready. I took my seat in the carriage, five of my friends piled in with me, Giraud mounted *la Capitana* and Achard *la Carbonara* (these were the names of the mules), and we started off. Now we could see in broad daylight that steep road we had glimpsed in the dark the night before, which swoops down from the crest of the Muradora to the bank of the Tagus, crosses the bridge of Alcantara, and like a dusty ribbon follows the winding curves of the Tagus across the reddish brown plain. The whole scene was lovely; the ruins of an old mill stood beside the stream whose waters roared over their rocky bed; laundresses in picturesque garb were washing linen under the arch of the bridge; and two things very rare in Spain, foliage and a breeze, greeted us as we passed, bidding us good-by with a delightful murmuring of leaves.

For some time we followed an avenue of trees that drew moisture from the Tagus, but these at last gave place to stunted bushes and the bare plain. After an hour, a still, clear night spread its wings from one horizon to the other. The carriage rolled slowly along the sandy road, while Giraud and Achard tried to make their mules outdistance us, but the animals were more accustomed to traces than to the saddle and took their places in line with the team pulling our green and yellow carriage. Thus we traveled on for two hours under a dark blue sky studded with twinkling stars.

Suddenly, on the sky line, the stars were blotted out by the shape of a house with a kind of barn beside it. At a distance the barn augured well, suggesting to us, if not comfort, at least space and freedom, but as we drew nearer we could see that the barn had lost its roof—doubtless a careful search would have discovered it lying on the ground—and its windows were curtained only by the starry sky. There was the house itself, but it seemed far too small to accommodate eight travelers. True, it looked hospitable, for through the slits of the shutters shone lights that we hoped were coming from the kitchen, and as we drew nearer, cheerful, reassuring sounds reached our ears, the brisk click of castanets, the resounding boom of a Basque drum, the twang of a Spanish guitar. There was a party in progress at the *Villa Mejor*.

"Good!" said Alexandre. "We shall not only have supper and bed, but an evening of dancing, too. Desbarolles, my friend, jump down, present my compliments to the mistress of the house, and tell her in your best Spanish that I beg the honor of the first dance." The mules halted, the carriage followed suit, and we walked toward the house. At a closer view it lost its hospitable appearance; the doors were fast shut, and the absence of any living being at the threshold or anywhere around created a strange impression in our minds, the dwelling seemed so thronged, so merry and boisterous within, so deserted and silent without. We ordered the *mayoral* to knock, but no one answered. Alexandre picked up a large stone.

"Stop!" said Desbarolles. "I understand how things are done in Spain. You might, perhaps, force the door if you like, but no one will open it for you until the *fandango* is finished. A Spaniard never allows himself to be disturbed when he is dancing, smoking, or sleeping." Desbarolles had considerable authority among us, so Alexandre put his stone down and sat on it while we waited. The prophecy was as true as gospel. Scarcely had the sound of castanets died away and the drum throbbed into silence, when the door opened.

It gave on to a passage with two doors. The one on the left led to a kitchen, well lighted by three or four lamps and a great fireplace. This was the ballroom, and the door on the right showed us the refreshment room, a dark damp place lighted only by a night light. The man who had come to open the main entrance for us immediately returned to the ballroom, taking no further notice of us. The click of castanets broke out afresh, the drum rolled in fine style, the guitar thrummed away more merrily than ever, and the dance, interrupted for a moment, was again in full swing with true Spanish abandon. We went in, and our eight heads peered over the spectators already blocking the doorway. In France, everyone would have turned at our unexpected appearance, but at the *Villa Mejor* nobody stirred. There were forty or fifty people crowded into this kitchen, half of them dancing. One or two men stood out from the rest because of a certain elegance of dress and that resolute cast of features which is the great beauty of the peoples of the Midi. One or two others were leaning on their muskets, and, with no thought of striking a pose, were posed more perfectly than any model.

At first we were absorbed in the interest of the spectacle. For travelers in search of the picturesque it really was exhilarating to discover at night in the midst of a desert, in a *venta* isolated and almost in ruins, this gay company of dancers in national dress. Madrid, charming but civilized, has banned the picturesque as all civilized capitals must, and there we sought it vainly, finding little more than stereotyped, inadequate performances on stages erected in the squares, whereas this revelry, surging up so spontaneously and unexpectedly before our eyes, seemed a harmonious whole.

When one of the spectators needed something from the room behind us, he would sidle past his companions, then past ourselves, seeming to pay no more attention to us than to them. We, for our part, were more observant, and noticed that all those who went out were forming a group around our *mayoral* in the darkest corner of the refreshment room, where they were apparently debating a matter of the utmost importance. Possibly hunger was spurring us on, possibly our self-respect was piqued by the way we were being ignored, but when Achard suddenly exclaimed, "Gentlemen, it would be more to the point if we were to concern ourselves with supper and bed," we all instantly agreed.

As if in response, our *mayoral* left the group clustering closely around him and came toward us. "Come along, *señores*," he said. "Take your seats, and we will be off. The mules are getting cold."

"What do you mean? Aren't we at the *Villa Mejor*, where we are to sup and stay the night?"

"Yes. You were to do so, but the house has neither bed nor meal to offer you."

At first we could hardly believe he was serious, but when he assured us he was I cried: "Desbarolles, slip into that crowd and find the mistress of the house. Sit beside her, be as eloquent as you always are, and as persuasive as you were at the *posada* near the Escorial. Remember Madame Calisto Burguillos, and should you manage to escort this landlady to her cellar and her attic, as you did the other, bring us back some eggs and something to sleep on."

Desbarolles glided through the crowd, a sparkle in his eye and a smile on his lips. A moment later he was posing elegantly before the mistress of the house, his elbow resting against the wall and his legs crossed. Their conversation, begun on a note of ordinary courtesy, seemed to grow steadily more animated. Desbarolles had his back toward us and we could not see his expression; but we could see the face of the landlady, and it boded us no good. As Desbarolles turned around, we noted with alarm that his eye had lost its twinkle and his smile had disappeared. He rejoined us quite crestfallen, and said: "We must be on our way."

"What?" I asked. "No bed? No supper?"

"There is plenty of both, but we have unfortunately arrived while the mistress is giving a party, and she has no intention of putting herself out for us."

"A typical Spanish landlady!" said Giraud. "This is real Catalonian hospitality."

"Is there no way to persuade her to change her mind?" I asked.

"It's easy to see that you have spent only a week or ten days in Spain. If, like us, you had been here for four months, you would not ask such a question."

"Come along, gentlemen, come along. Take your seats!" cried the *mayoral*.

"What the devil d'you mean by 'Take your seats'? Our contract clearly states that we shall eat and sleep at *Villa Mejor*."

"Yes, I know, my good friend," replied Giraud, with his customary resignation, "but this is a case when we reckoned without our host, or rather, without our hostess."

"Suppose you offered to paint her portrait?"

Giraud shook his head. "When Spaniards are dancing, there is no proposition one can put to them. We must go."

"How far have we still to go to reach Aranjuez?" I asked the *mayoral*.

90

"Oh! It's very near, *señor*. Five miles."

I looked at him with a doubtful eye, and asked how long the journey would take. He hesitated an instant, and replied: "Three hours." "Well," I continued, "I will allow you four. But if in four hours we are not at Aranjuez" (here I placed my hand on his shoulder and let it weigh heavily), "you will have me to reckon with."

"Very good, sir," he murmured. "En route, gentlemen. Let us be off!"

"Devil take it! Let them at least give us a glass of wine. They cannot say they have none, for we saw three or four goatskins full."

"Oh! A glass of wine? That's a different thing!" said the *mayoral*, going back into the *venta* we had just left, and coming out again with a goatskin in one hand and a glass in the other.

I was the first to drink, and raised my glass to "Spanish hospitality," a toast that my companions all repeated in their turn. I even noticed that Don Riego spoke more bitterly than the others. Since he joined our company, the habits of the worthy priest have improved until he has become something of a Frenchman. Once more the *mayoral* urged us on. Boulanger threw a last glance at the house where he had hoped to sketch so much, and climbed into the carriage. Don Riego, who loves comfort, had already settled himself in his chosen seat; Giraud followed Boulanger, then came Desbarolles, and lastly, Maquet. With us, Maquet represents self-denial; Don Riego, egotism.

I bestrode a mule, Alexandre did likewise, and Achard took his place between us with a hand on the neck of each animal, looking forward to learning a good deal about dramatic art from listening to our plan for a tragedy. Some details concerning the safe disposal of Desbarolles' rifle delayed the carriage for a little while, while we went on ahead like scouts.

I am sorry to see, Madame, that my letter is already so long that I must postpone the next installment. Prepare yourself, therefore, to hear of terrible events tomorrow.

14

❧ ❧ ❧

Aranjuez, 25th October

Behind us, the coach began to move, lighted by a single lantern fixed in the middle of the roof like a pompon. A crescent moon was slowly rising, shedding a soft enchanting light over a countryside almost terrifying in its grandeur. To our right it was bounded by little hillocks where patches of prickly turf were interspersed with great lakes of shining sand. To our left stretched the limitless plain, farther than the eye could fathom, and a thousand paces from us a line of trees marked with their deeper shadow the course of the Tagus. Here and there an open stretch of the river reflected the moon's rays like a mirror, while before us the sandy, yellow road unrolled like a leather band. Now and again our mules turned from the path to avoid a precipice level with the road, or a gaping crevasse left by some forgotten earth tremor. From time to time we looked back and saw, three hundred, four hundred, then five hundred yards behind us, the light of the coach wavering like some will-o'-the-wisp. It was moving more slowly than we were, for its wheels were almost half buried in the sand. We crossed a little hill and lost sight of it while we went on our way. After half an hour, Alexandre's mule made a sudden swerve to the right where a deep cleft, stemming from a precipice, had cut away almost a third of the road, but we paid it no special attention and rode on for another three-quarters of an hour, laughing, talking, without the slightest thought of the tragedy we had intended to discuss.

I had, however, looked back five or six times, surprised not to see the celebrated lantern, set like the eye of a cyclops in the forefront of our carriage. At last I halted and said: "Gentlemen, something must have happened. We have not noticed any rise or fall in the terrain, except the little mound we crossed almost three-quarters of an hour ago, yet since then we have seen no light. I think we should be wise to stop." We did so, and turned our mules around.

The moon was wonderfully calm and bright; no sound could be heard in all these wide moors, except the far-off barking of a watchdog on some isolated farm. The mules twitched their ears anxiously, and seemed to be listening to something we could not hear. Suddenly the wind brought us an almost imperceptible quiver of sound, like the wandering echo of a human voice lost in space.

"What's that?" I asked. Alexandre and Achard had also caught the faint sound, without hearing anything distinctly, so we stayed silent and still, as one does when faced with some unforeseen emergency. A few seconds passed, then the same quavering note reached us, this time more intelligible, more clearly a cry of distress. We redoubled our attention, and at last we distinctly heard my name called by a voice that was drawing nearer.

"Oh!" said Achard. "It's for you. Someone has a grudge against you!"

"It must be our friends," replied Alexandre.

"You will see," said I in my turn, still trying to laugh. "Perhaps they have been held up by the bandits of the Duke of Ossuna."

A new cry was heard, more distinctly than before. "Certainly someone is calling me," I continued. "Let us make for the direction of the voice." Alexandre and I spurred on our mules while Achard ran behind, whipping them with a switch. Scarcely had we gone ten paces when the same cry reached us again, and this time the note of distress was unmistakable. "Come on! Come on!" I cried, doing my best to set my mule at a gallop. "Beyond question, something has happened. Let us shout in reply." We made trumpets of our hands and shouted three times, but we were facing the wind and the sound was carried away behind us. Once more we heard the cry, breathless, broken, uttered by a voice trembling on the brink of exhaustion, and a shudder struck us to the heart. Again we strove to answer, but we knew the wind was too strong for us, and besides it was evident that whoever was calling us so piteously, so wearily, was running toward us as fast as he could. We urged our mules to their utmost speed and the sound grew nearer.

"That is Giraud's voice!" said Achard. We were well aware that Giraud was not easily disturbed, and, forced to realize that it really was Giraud uttering these cries of distress, we grew more anxious than if it had been anyone else. For ten minutes more we rode forward, and then began to distinguish against the clear outline of the road a shadow coming toward us, running like a winged Mercury. Soon we could recognize Giraud's silhouette, as we had already recognized his voice.

"What is the matter?" we all three cried together.

"Ah!" panted Giraud with an effort. "It's you! You, at last!" He staggered up to us, breathless, ready to drop with fatigue, managing to stay upright by leaning one hand on Achard's shoulder and the other on the neck of my mule.

"What has happened?" we asked again. But our poor friend was so spent by his grueling race to overtake us that for a moment he was incapable of speaking. After a moment he gasped: "The carriage has overturned."

"Where was that?"

"Over the edge of a precipice."

"Good God! No one injured, I hope?"

"By a miracle, no!"

For a moment a personal consideration moved my heart, and I glanced around to reassure myself that Alexandre was indeed with me, and safe.

"Is that the whole trouble?" I asked, for another possibility suddenly occurred to me.

"That's just it," replied Giraud. "I am afraid that may not be all. That's why I ran after you."

"Then mount my mule, and I'll go on foot," said Alexandre, and so we started off, retracing our course with all the speed that Carbonara and Capitana could achieve. On the way

94

I tried to get Giraud to talk, but to all my questions he would reply only: "You'll see! You'll see!" This was far from reassuring, and obviously he was keeping something from us.

We pressed forward for half an hour—we scarcely realized that we had traveled so far—and at last, on reaching the crest of the little hill I mentioned earlier, we saw a light moving about, two hundred yards away, and shadowy forms hovering around it. One last burst of speed from our mules, and we had reached the scene of the accident.

"Ah! Here you are!" cried our friends. "We've certainly had a lucky escape!"

I glanced rapidly around. "Where are Desbarolles and Boulanger?" I asked. Both of them put their heads out of the carriage window and cried: "Here we are!" They were busy salvaging our luggage, passing it up to Maquet who then set it safely on the ground. The *zagal* and the *mayoral* were unharnessing the mules, still held by their traces. Don Riego was sitting on the edge of the ditch, complaining of an unspecified number of broken ribs.

"Now," said Giraud, "look at the lie of the land." He led me to the brink of the precipice. I fell back a step and a cold sweat broke out on my brow. "Truly, a miracle!" I murmured.

They had overturned into the very crevasse that had caused Alexandre's mule to swerve from the road. A rock, sticking out of the ground like the last remaining tooth in an immense jawbone, had checked their fall, and the roof of the carriage, completely upside down, was pressing against the rock. But for that, they would all have been thrown into an abyss a hundred feet deep. Achard and Alexandre in turn approached the brink of the precipice and were seized with the same vertigo that I had felt.

"But tell me," I asked, turning toward Maquet, "how did all this happen?"

"Ask Giraud," he replied. "As for me, I cannot speak four words together. I'm choking!"

"And when I think that it was I who caused it!" said Giraud. "My head was wedged against his chest."

"Not to mention that Don Riego had his foot on my neck," said Maquet.

"But how did that come about?"

"Oh! It happened very quickly. Desbarolles was dozing; Don Riego was snoring; I was leaning forward quietly to press my thumb against Desbarolles' nose when the carriage began to heel over. 'Heavens! I think we're going to overturn,' said Boulanger. 'We are overturning,' added Maquet. 'We have overturned,' said I. In fact, the carriage was lying quietly upon its side. Suddenly, as though finding this position uncomfortable, it capsized. The earth below it had given way. Now, things looked very much more serious. Our heads were downward, our feet in the air, and we were struggling in the midst of guns and hunting knives, Maquet underneath, I on top of him, and Don Riego on me, with Boulanger and Desbarolles flattened in between. 'Gentlemen, let's keep calm,' said Boulanger. 'I think we are in the precipice I was looking at when the carriage began to overturn. The less movement we make, the better our chances of coming out of this alive.' It was good advice, and we followed it. Only, with his characteristic composure, Maquet said: 'Do whatever is best, but just remember that I am suffocating, and if that goes on for five minutes I shall be dead.'

"You can appreciate the effect of this recommendation! Desbarolles, now completely awake and the only one on his feet—truly there is a God watching over those who sleep—hammered on the window and shouted to the *mayoral* to let us out. The *mayoral* was busy, unhitching his mules, and paid not the slightest attention to us. 'Open the door,' shouted Desbarolles, 'or I'll break it down!' This time the *mayoral* heeded, and came to open the carriage. Desbarolles stepped out first, gun in hand. This gave us a little more room, and Don Riego could lift his foot from Maquet's neck, so Maquet took the opportunity of renewing the air in his lungs. Once outside, Desbarolles began to drag Don Riego free, and after immense effort Don Riego found himself standing beside Desbarolles. Now we were much more comfortable, and Boulanger began his upward climb. Then it was a matter of my getting the right way up and turning Maquet over also, for he was almost unconscious, but with the aid of Desbarolles and Boulanger this was successfully accomplished. As for Don Riego, he went to sit where you now see him. Only Maquet still remained, of us all the one who suffered most. For that reason he was the most furious, and his first act, once he was standing safely erect, was to attack the *mayoral* with his fists."

"Bravo, Maquet!" I cried. "You're of my way of thinking. I take it you soon began to suspect that it might have been his fault?"

"Study the way the land lies," replied Maquet, "and judge for yourself."

In truth, a glance at the road made the accident, if attributed to mere chance, quite incomprehensible. The cleft lay across the road, and the *zagal*, who was leading the mules by their bridle rein, could not possibly have failed to see the precipice, since he was walking beside it, and since he necessarily must have turned the mules to avoid the crevasse, otherwise they would have fallen into it. There was a further significant fact. The moment he left his driving seat the *mayoral* had snatched down the lantern and extinguished it, an act that enlightened Maquet.

He stopped punching the *mayoral* and dragged him toward the abyss, stiffly resisting with his utmost strength and convinced that his last hour had come. But Maquet has a strong hand, and soon the *mayoral*, urged forward by the butt end of a gun, found himself at the edge of the precipice. He turned livid, closed his eyes, and said, "If you mean to kill me, kill me quickly." If he had still resisted he would probably have been lost, but his humility touched Maquet, who released him.

"Now," said Maquet, "someone must let Dumas know. We are only at the beginning of this business. Someone who has retained the use of his legs and has good lungs must run after Dumas."

"I'll go," said Giraud, and started off. You know the rest, Madame, or, rather, you know nothing yet, for at that very moment the sequel was coming down upon us from a little mountain sharply outlined against the sky, quite close to us and all silvered by the moon.

"Oh! Oh! A band of men," I cried, pointing, while Giraud counted seven of them. I saw the barrel of a gun flash for an instant in the moonlight. "Good! They are armed. This should be amusing! To your guns, gentlemen!" I said in a low voice but to good effect, for in a moment each of us stood armed. Achard, who had no gun, pounced on a hunting knife. Our weapons were not yet loaded, but the seven men were still a hundred yards away. "Gentlemen," I said, "we have three minutes, long enough to load three times, so take it calmly and load."

Everyone had gathered around me. Desbarolles, the only one whose gun was ready to fire, took his position four paces ahead. Alexandre was at my feet, looking for cartridges in his overnight case. His was the only breech-loading rifle: all the others had to be loaded with a ramrod. The men were twenty yards away when I finished loading and I cocked both barrels. At this sound, which carries so clearly under such circumstances and whose meaning is never in doubt, they halted. Alexandre was ready to fire: so was Maquet. We could fire ten shots, and three of us were hunters who certainly would not have missed our man at this distance.

"Now," said I to Desbarolles, "do me the pleasure of asking these people what they want, and hint that the first who comes a step nearer is a dead man." At this moment, either innocently or intentionally, the *mayoral*, whom we had forced to light his lantern, allowed it to drop, while Desbarolles translated our message to the newcomers and we noted its effect. I was giving him an order to translate to the *mayoral*, but it proved unnecessary, for that fellow understood my meaning and hastened to pick up his torch.

For a moment there was a solemn silence. We stood in two separate groups, linked by Desbarolles; the Spaniards in shadow, ourselves in the light of the trembling lantern that glinted on the gun barrels and the blades of our hunting knives.

98

"Now, Desbarolles," I continued, "ask these gentlemen what had procured us the honor of their visit."

"We came to bring you help," replied the one who seemed to be the leader of the band.

"Charming!" I retorted. "But since the *mayoral* and *zagal* have not left us, how did the gentlemen know that help was needed?"

"*Tiens*, that's very true!" said Desbarolles, going on to convey my question in Spanish. It was a difficult one to answer, and our nocturnal visitors made no attempt to do so.

"Papa!" cried Alexandre. "I've got an idea! Suppose we rob these gentlemen!"

"This young Dumas is full of imagination," said Giraud.

"Upon my word," said Achard, "since it's come to this, we might as well disembowel them right away." Our visitors made no reply but stood stunned while Desbarolles told them we proposed to slit them up if they did not immediately depart whence they came.

"But," cried their chief, seeing his comrades wavering, "we came with no evil intention. Quite the contrary."

"Well, there it is. Our spirit may be at fault, but we refuse to be helped unless we have asked for help."

They started to withdraw, when the *mayoral* cried, "Messieurs, allow these gentlemen to help me lift my carriage back to the road."

"By all means, but they must wait beyond the mountain until we have gone."

The *mayoral* said a few words to them in his own language and they at once took leave of us with the formal greeting "*Vaya usted con Dios*, Go with God."

"That scene," said Giraud, laying down his gun, "shall be the subject of my next painting."

15

✦ ✦ ✦

Aranjuez, 25th October

You left us dismissing our officious visitors, Madame, and following them with our eyes as they quickly vanished beyond the ridge. Desbarolles stood sentinel while the rest of us prepared to depart. Our luggage was lying in a great pile, topped with the basket of provisions so nobly rescued by Giraud. We looked in vain for Don Riego, but were not unduly anxious for he was unlikely to lose himself in his own country and we felt certain that he would turn up again at some well-chosen moment. The *mayoral* observed that the carriage could be dragged up to the road again by his four mules and his seven friends, so we left him his team and loaded one of the saddle mules with our luggage, placing the other at the disposal of the company. There ensued a contest of generosity and self-sacrifice that any spectators would have found very touching, but, alas, there were none, and the moving scene will remain for ever unrecorded.

"How unfortunate," I exclaimed, "that Don Riego is lost! He would have cut short this argument."

"Here I am!" said a voice. We turned, and there was Don Riego, looking much worse than when we had last seen him, holding his hand to his side, doubled up with pain and complaining to high heaven. One would have said the poor man had less than twenty-four hours to live. Obviously he had the greatest need for the mule, so we hoisted him upon Carbonara and set him at the head of our column, followed by Capitana and the luggage, while the rest of us shouldered our guns and brought up the rear on foot. We believed we were some six or seven miles from Aranjuez. Looking at our watches with a certain satisfaction that we still possessed them, and allowing

100

for the customary variations these little instruments show in the company of their own kind, we decided the time must be between ten o'clock and a quarter past. Walking at a reasonable pace, we ought to reach Aranjuez by one o'clock. One thing that cheered us was that Giraud and Desbarolles, on their walk from Seville to Madrid, had passed along the route we now had to follow, and so could act as guides.

Thus we set out lightheartedly, laughing at past dangers. Even Don Riego was cheerful. He had made a remarkable recovery, now that he was assured of not having to walk. For two hours we went gaily on, paying little attention to the time until Maquet glanced at his watch.

"Nearly midnight," he said. "We should be almost there."

"*Pardieu!*" returned Desbarolles. "I should think so! We've come at least seven French miles."

This reply, so free from evasion or subterfuge, quite satisfied us, and we stepped out blithely until, after another hour, Achard stopped and said: "That's all very well, Desbarolles, but . . ."

Each of us perfectly understood what Achard meant, and waited with some anxiety for our interpreter's reply.

"When you see a great avenue of trees," said Desbarolles, "you can feel certain you are near Aranjuez."

This response pleased us less: there seemed something indefinite and evasive about it. Besides, the moorland lay bare before us, as far as the eye could see. We strode on for another hour, then murmurs of complaint began to break out.

"Gentlemen," said I, "I propose that we cut enough heather and brushwood to make a great heap, set it alight, roll ourselves in our cloaks and sleep around the fire." The majority wavered an instant, then agreed with my suggestion.

"My friends," Desbarolles broke in, "I recognize this part of the country. We passed through it the day after our poor greyhound died, and we walked more than forty miles that day. We were therefore much more tired than you are now. Giraud even sat down on the very stone where young Dumas is sitting at this moment. Do you remember that, Giraud?"

"Perfectly. But don't wander from the point. What's the position now, Desbarolles?" retorted Giraud.

"We are still half an hour from the trees."

"And then?" I persisted.

"Ah!" said Giraud. "When we reach the trees we shall certainly be getting near Aranjuez." This reply was not quite all we could have wished, but at any rate it restored our courage somewhat, and we started off again—this time, however, with the steadiness of travelers preparing for a serious struggle against fatigue.

After half an hour we actually did see the trees etched against the sky line and came to a majestic avenue of elm trees and oaks, stretching away to right and left of us. Though the sight of it did not restore our good humor, it at least gave us a fresh heart, and we tramped on for another forty minutes.

"It's devilish long, this avenue of yours," said Boulanger.

"Yes," replied Desbarolles, blandly. "It's a very fine avenue!"

"That isn't what Boulanger means," I retorted. "He means that your avenue is endless!"

"Look, Desbarolles," said Achard. "Tell us the truth. Once, just once, my friend, say plainly whether we are still a long way from Aranjuez."

"When you hear the sound of a waterfall, you will be there."

We walked on for a quarter of an hour, and then could hear the lovely sound of falling water coming to us through the night. Ten minutes more, and we found ourselves on the bank of a little stream, shining in the moonlight like a ribbon of silver gauze. All around it cows were grazing, bells tinkling at their necks, and of all the mysterious sounds of the night the music of little bells is perhaps the most delightful. The herd and the waterfall made a beautiful rustic scene, but was not what we had been promised, and we still craved for the town.

"The first gate you come to will be that of Aranjuez," announced Desbarolles, "and from the gate to the town itself is barely half a mile." For a moment, Maquet, Achard, and Alexandre were ready to strangle Desbarolles, but realizing his danger he solemnly swore that this time he was really telling the truth. In a quarter of an hour we reached the gate, ten minutes later the town, and 5 o'clock was striking as we passed through its first arcades.

It was none too soon, for we were near exhaustion. We had been walking for seven hours, and nothing had passed our lips since 2 o'clock on the previous afternoon, except a few drops of water from Desbarolles' cascade. Fortunately, the inn *Parador de la Costurera* was nearby, and our only problem was how to present ourselves there in a way that would not alarm the landlord. Once inside, we should have to make ourselves particularly pleasant, if we were to obtain a meal. Traveling in Spain certainly teaches one ingratiating manners!

We knocked softly, then loudly, then more loudly still, and at last heard a sound inside.

"Is that you, Manuel?" asked Desbarolles. (He had stayed at this inn before, and had noticed that all the menservants were called Manuel, so he could make this inquiry without risk.)

"Yes, sir!" a voice replied, and the door was thrown open. For a moment the first Manuel was terror-stricken at the sight of seven men armed to the teeth, and our mules with Don Riego and the baggage.

"There's nothing to fear, my friend," explained Desbarolles. "We are peaceful travelers, but very hungry and very tired, so please be kind enough to wake up the other Manuels."

We carried in our luggage and closed the door, while the servant called the second Manuel, who, five minutes later, was up and waking a third. We found the dining room easily enough, an enormous place where a few dying embers still glowed in the stove. From them we lighted two lamps and set them on the table to illumine the vast solitude around us. The most surprising thing about dining rooms in Spain is that nothing about them suggests their function, either to one's eyes or one's sense of smell.

We summoned all the Manuels, of whom the first in command was *le mozo*, the second the butler, and the third the man in charge of the bedrooms. After a friendly interrogation, coupled with a certain firmness, there seemed some likelihood that we might be provided with a meal and beds, and we promised fabulous tips if these materialized. A quarter of an hour later, as dawn was breaking, the table was set with two cold chickens, the remainder of a *ragoût*, and an enormous cheese, with four bottles of wine, one at each corner. Nothing superfluous, but, at a pinch, adequate.

We woke up Alexandre who was sleeping on the table and began our meal, all of us dropping with weariness and looking like sleepwalkers. When we had finished we were given candles and shown to our rooms. Seeing Desbarolles take his rifle with him, I instinctively took my own. Alexandre and I were to sleep in a huge room with an alcove that was itself as big as an ordinary room. The Manuel attending to us closed the shutters and departed, while we mechanically and without conscious thought undressed and went to bed.

I was in bed when I was suddenly roused by an abrupt noise and a rough shake from a man who was holding me by the arm, while a second man was opening my shutters and calling out briskly. My mind was still full of the scene in the *Villa Mejor*, and I thought our bandits were returning to the attack, so I snatched up the gun I had put by the head of my bed, roaring a question and a curse at the intruders. The sound of my voice and the gesture accompanying it produced a remarkable effect. The man opening the shutter rushed toward the alcove, the one who had shaken my arm dashed toward the window, they collided with a crash, fell backward, scrambled up and fled as though the devil were at their heels. I heard the sound of their footsteps die away in the corridor and then cease altogether.

Cautiously I rose and went out of my alcove, my gun held ready to fire. On the field of battle were lying a hat and a tobacco pouch, which I collected as evidence. During all the infernal din Alexandre had not stirred, so I bolted the door and went back to bed. Five minutes later there came a scratching on the door, and I recognized the first Manuel's peculiar method of knocking. He came as a truce bearer. The men who had entered my room belonged to a caravan of *arrieros* who had arrived the night before, and as they were to leave all together in the morning they had promised to wake each other up. The two who woke first had mistaken the room and had awakened me instead of their comrades. They offered me their apologies and asked for the return of the hat and tobacco pouch. It was a reasonable explanation, so I accepted it and restored the desired objects to Manuel I.

I had suffered too many shocks, one after the other, to have any hope of getting to sleep again, so I dressed, and found Maquet and Boulanger already afoot. We roused our other companions, all except Alexandre, who would not open his eyes, so we left him in bed and sat down to breakfast. Halfway through the meal the stagecoach arrived from Toledo, bringing our English friend, who was just in time to take advantage of the scraps that remained on our table, giving us in exchange some tidings of our famous green and yellow *berline*.

The diligence had come to a halt where the carriage pole blocked the road, for our *mayoral* and his four mules had striven in vain to pull it up over the edge of the precipice where it hung, and had succeeded merely in damaging it still more. But at length, with the help of the eight mules from the stage-coach, the efforts of the postillion and the *mayoral* were crowned with success, and now the *berline* was coming along gently at an invalid's pace, expecting to arrive during the day.

News of our accident had spread through the town. Don Riego had given all the details, and had not minced his words on the subject of the dancers at the *Villa Mejor*. The consequence was that we received a visit from the *corrégidor*. (Perhaps you fancied, Madame, that *corrégidors*, like the monks, were abolished by the revolution?) Obliged to speak the truth in the presence of this representative of Justice, we more or less endorsed Don Riego's opinion of his fellow countrymen, and expressed our conviction that under the circumstances we were extremely fortunate in having our guns with us.

The *corrégidor* shook his head doubtfully, and told us that he knew of no robbers within forty miles, except the seven bandits of the Duke of Ossuna, and these could not have been the men we saw because last night they were holding up a post chaise in the woods of Alamina. However, he promised to make inquiries.

Two hours later we received a letter from *M. le corrégidor*, stating that he had information concerning *the men who had frightened us*. Far from being robbers, they were the militia, or so he said. I replied that it was fortunate for the men in question that they had *not* frightened us, for if they had, things could have turned out badly for them. I added that I begged any such gentlemen not to approach a French convoy in future as they had on this occasion, closing in without a word of warning at 10 o'clock at night, for, if they did, sooner or later they would come to grief.

I was finishing this letter when we heard a disturbance outside, and looking through the window we saw our *mayoral* dragging along the relics of his carriage, followed by all the population of Aranjuez. Scarcely had the *mayoral* made sure that we were at the *Parador* when he came up to our room to claim the money he said we owed him. He considered we should pay for the whole journey to Aranjuez; our view was that we owed him only up to the place where he had upset us. We argued; he threatened us with the *alcade;* I threatened to throw him out; he went.

A quarter of an hour later, as we were leaving the hotel to explore the town, a messenger came to announce that *le señor alcade* desired to make my acquaintance. I replied that, for my part, I should be no less happy to see a flesh and blood *alcade*, for the general impression in France is that an *alcade* is purely a convention. I called our interpreter, Desbarolles, who slung his rifle over his shoulder and came with me to *le señor alcade*, who proved to be a grocer, for in Spain an official may hold several offices. He thought we had come to order licorice or sugar, and was unpleasantly surprised to discover that our business was with the *alcade*, not the shopkeeper.

However, all honor to Spanish justice, the worthy man listened to both sides of the story, and, as Solomon would have done in his place, decided that we should pay the *mayoral* only up to the time of the accident, since we had hired his carriage with the object of riding, not walking. This made a difference of some sixty francs due to us, which were graciously received by our treasurer, Giraud, and our economist, Maquet. We saluted the *alcade* as a just man, and went to rejoin our companions in the market square.

Aranjuez claims to be the Versailles of Madrid, and in one respect, its solitude, it is far better. Nothing disturbed our contemplation of its beauties, and no one even glanced at us as we stayed to admire the twelve labors of Hercules carved in marble in the castle courtyard. We strolled on toward the park, crossing the Tagus by a stone bridge where a group of washerwomen were beating their linen with wooden pestles, and we wandered for an hour under beautiful trees, though if anyone had told us, twelve hours earlier, that we could ever again take pleasure in walking we should certainly not have believed him.

Time was growing short for Achard and Don Riego, who were now leaving us to return to Madrid, so we made our way back to the hotel, where Alexandre was still fast asleep. The coach was on the point of leaving; we embraced each other like friends uncertain whether they will ever meet again; and we followed them with our eyes until the coach was lost to sight.

16

❧ ❧ ❧

Oh, *Parador de la Costurera*, with your retinue of Manuels, your chilly rooms and your kindly welcome, your scrawny chickens that we thought so tender! Were I Cervantes, I would make you as immortal as Don Quixote's *Puerta Lapice! Parador*, with the relics of our green and yellow carriage in your courtyard shed, may you remain as long in my companions' memory as you will in my own! Have no fear, Madame. I will not burst into poetry. It is just that my heart must express its gratitude, for the *Parador de la Costurera* gave us a longed-for refuge, a breathing space after we had suffered much, and never did it open its doors to travelers more famished, more exhausted and desperate, than ourselves.

We left Aranjuez by the evening coach, borne swiftly along by eight mules, and settled down as comfortably as we could, hoping to make up for our lack of sleep the night before. We were, however, soon disturbed again. Because of the risk of bandits in this part of Spain, coaches do not travel, even on main roads, after 10 o'clock at night or before 3 in the morning, and we had hardly begun to doze when we were brusquely told that we should stop for the night at Ocana. The name struck a chord, and I remembered that, as a child, I had seen a picture of the battle of Ocana being won or lost (I forget which), by the King-Emperor or one of his generals. It showed ranks of French soldiers, a line of black paint for their *képis*, blue for their tunics, and white for their trousers. As for the Spaniards, they were yellow. The Emperor, or perhaps a lieutenant, was flourishing a long sword that, against the background of the blue regiment, looked like a skewer full of kingfishers, and in the background was the outline of a town that I still remembered clearly. Now, all these childhood memories came back to me, and I did not grumble too fiercely at the coachman who woke me up.

Three other travelers also dismounted, muffled to the eyes in their cloaks and broad-brimmed hats.

"Good!" said Alexandre. "They are genuine Almavivas. Get out your crayons, Giraud!"

"They don't seem lively table companions, anyway," commented Boulanger.

"Hush!" said I. "They may understand French!" So we silently followed these three figures into a long room, cold and bare, where there was a table big enough for a hundred guests, with absolutely nothing on it except plates, knives and forks,

108

and carafes of water. The mere sight of this big, vacant room and the long empty table made us feel depressed, cold, and hungry.

As we entered the *mozo* appeared, dressed in a short, light brown jacket and yellow trousers, his head covered with greenish white hair, a fancy-dress wig, I think, for never have I seen such hair. He was as wrinkled as a year-old orange, his legs trembled like reeds as he came forward and with a gracious gesture invited us to seat ourselves at table. His age was impossible to guess, and he would have inspired Hoffman to create a new fantastic character. Giraud and Boulanger, both blessed with a painter's eye for the unusual, were at once greatly amused by this singular figure, and so was Alexandre.

"Gentlemen," I murmured under my breath, concerned as I always am to maintain friendly relations. "Here we are deep in Spain. Do not, I beg you, laugh at things that seem strange to us, but are perfectly natural. We should offend the natives, whose taste may well incline toward tobacco-colored jackets and yellow trousers."

At this moment one of the Spaniards looked up, caught sight of the *mozo*, and burst into laughter. I was for a moment apprehensive, but his laugh was merely a friendly greeting, as he cried "Hullo, Jocrisse!" From the lively conversation that followed we learned that the first of our three "Spaniards" was a Parisian, a commercial traveler for a firm in Montmartre; the second was Italian born, now a nationalized Frenchman; and the third, born at Vaugirard, near Paris, but of Spanish blood, was visiting Spain for the first time. Thus the party at table was almost wholly French, and in a second we were all talking freely together. I must say, Madame, that the meal gave us something to talk about: saffron soup, boiled cow meat, and chicken that had apparently died of some chest trouble, served with a dish of *garbanzos* such as I described to you earlier, and some spinach that I will not describe at all. To follow, we had one of those impossible salads, swimming in water to dilute the stinking oil they put on in the hope of discouraging any lover of green stuff from touching it.

109

When we had disposed of these various items as though they were fit to eat, I turned to the *mozo* and asked in my poor Spanish: "Is there nothing more?"

"*Nada, señores, nada!*" he answered in pure Castilian, which means "Nothing else at all. Absolutely nothing!"

"And what do we owe for this wonderful dinner?" asked the commercial traveler.

The price was three francs. I have noticed—and this applies to every country I have visited—that no dinner is ever more expensive than a poor one, but we duly paid, Alexandre commenting, "I should certainly like something more."

"Gentlemen," said our Frenchman from the rue Sainte-Apolline, "in the coach I have a duck, bestowed on me as a parting gift by my host in Madrid, a very sensible fellow."

"And I have a basket on the roof of my coach," I said. "Now, Giraud, it's no use kicking me under the table. I have, as I was saying, a basket containing . . ."

"Very good!" said Giraud. "Your basket won't last long!"

". . . containing," I continued, "a Granada ham, two punnets of butter, three bottles of oil and one of vinegar, as well as sausages, olives, and other comestibles. Giraud, my friend, as general commissary of supplies . . ." Giraud gave a sigh. "If you will not see to your duties I'll send Desbarolles."

"Oh, no!" said Giraud. "I'll go. Hang it! I know Desbarolles. He is so absent-minded that he would eat the ham on the way."

Desbarolles was thinking about something else, and missed this accusation, while Giraud and the commercial traveler went out together, returning a moment later, one with his basket and the other with his duck.

"Ah!" we cried with one voice at sight of the bird. "It is roasted!"

I must tell you, Madame, that the spit is a kitchen instrument completely unknown in Spain. One does, indeed, find in the dictionary the word *asador* as its equivalent, but that proves only the richness of the Spanish language. In Madrid, dictionary in hand, I tried every likely shop, but nowhere could I find an *asador*. One or two of the better-educated ironmongers knew the thing by name, and one man, who had once visited Bordeaux, recalled that he had actually seen one. So I now asked, greatly impressed, "Did your host in Madrid possess a spit?"

"Oh, no," our friend replied. "He roasted this duck on a sword, a real Toledo blade!"

Quickly this delicacy vanished, and the ham, sausages, and other provisions for which Giraud had so nobly risked his life in the catastrophe at *Villa Mejor* duly appeared on the table before the astonished eyes of the *mozo* in the yellow trousers. At length, what remained was returned to the basket, and the basket to the coach, whereupon we were conducted to the padded planks that served as beds.

You will scarcely believe this, Madame, but at the very moment when we were about to slip between the sheets, Master Jocrisse appeared, calling, "Dress quickly, *señores!* The coach for Granada is ready to leave!" In blank astonishment we turned to Maquet, whose duties included keeping us informed of the time, and he assured us it was only 1 o'clock.

"Half-past one," cried that vexatious *mozo*. "Hurry, gentlemen! Hurry!"

"Ah, well. Let us dress again," said I. "At least we can sleep in the coach without being disturbed."

" 'Pon my word, I'm lucky," Giraud called from his room. "I shan't have the bother of getting up, for I hadn't undressed! I've been combing my hair." When Giraud wore his hair short, Madame, he gave it no attention whatever, but since leaving Paris he has let it grow until now it looks as though scissors have never touched it. This luxuriant growth has given Giraud the only touch of fatuous affectation I have ever noticed in him. Every morning and evening he spends an hour tending it, diverts money from our common fund to buy pomade, and steals every comb he comes across.

Ten minutes later, even the laggards among us were afoot, following my example. Punctuality ranks as a virtue with travelers, and I can truthfully boast that the terrible *pronto* of the Spaniards or the inexorable *fissa* of the Arabs never found

111

me behindhand. Suddenly we saw Maquet coming back upstairs, white with fury and incapable of speech. At last he managed to exclaim: "The mules are not even harnessed; the coach is in the middle of the courtyard, peacefully sleeping in the moonlight; neither the *mayoral* nor the *zagal* is astir, and that infernal rascal, Jocrisse, has played a trick on us!"

"I," said Desbarolles, majestically, taking out his long Spanish knife, "will find him and cut off his ears."

"Do!" said Giraud. "Cut them off by all means!" and Desbarolles, who had counted on our attempting to restrain him, found himself obliged to stalk out, ostensibly to carry out his threat. Ten minutes later, when he returned, his knife was back in his pocket and his hands were innocent of ears of any kind. He had searched in vain for the whimsical old man, who was doubtless enjoying at this very moment, in some invisible refuge of evil spirits, the sleep he had stolen from the just.

At this point, Madame, I took the trouble to find out the tactics adopted by the servants in Spanish inns, and they are not, I confess, peculiar to the *mozo* in the yellow trousers. Travelers go to bed after supper, at 11 o'clock, and have to take the road again at three. To wake them at a quarter to three, the *mozo*, whatever the color of his trousers, even if he is wearing only underpants, must be up at twenty-five minutes to three, though his duties do not begin in earnest until 5 o'clock. He therefore carries out his early morning tasks between 11 o'clock and midnight, then wakes the travelers, after which he goes off to his remote garret to sleep until 6 o'clock, safe in allowing himself the extra hour he has gained by doing his morning work the night before. Ingenious, don't you think? Even the curses of the travelers cannot disturb him, for those who travel in Spain are generally Germans, English, or Frenchmen who naturally swear in their mother tongue, which he does not understand.

We flung ourselves, fully dressed, upon our beds or into chairs, and at a quarter to three, dropping with weariness, we left the inn of Ocana after a serving maid had brought tiny cups of chocolate that warmed but did not console us. Then we were off behind eight galloping mules, at a speed that would have been some compensation if it had not proved an affliction. Speed, that luxury of travel, is no luxury unless the roads are good, and at this juncture I should tell you something about their condition in Spain. Within forty miles or so of Madrid the roads are quite fit for carriages, except when rain has washed away the surface, or the sun has dried it into large cracks, or when the road menders are at work. But beyond Aranjuez, workmen confidently rely upon the indulgence of the highway surveyor.

Ah, Madame! May Heaven grant me, in my old age, the boon of becoming a Spanish road mender, whose chief mission in life is to swathe himself in his voluminous cloak and watch travelers pass by in their coaches or on horseback, riding mules or journeying on foot, all with their own special interest. In his leisure moments, when there are no passers-by, the road mender collects from the nearby fields a number of stones (not more than a dozen), of a specified size (no larger than an egg), and carries them carefully in a little wicker basket to a place where the road needs repair. If a hundred of these little loads of stones are required to fill the hole, and the road mender has time to bring ten loads a day, the repair will take ten days, during which time every passing coach runs the risk of an accident.

Even if the coach does not capsize, it bounces high in the air at least twice before it can settle steadily on all four wheels again. Can you imagine the passengers? All unaware that they are nearing such a hole, they are dozing, chatting, lounging on the cushions, relaxing as best they can. Suddenly comes the first jolt; passengers, firearms, traveling bags are all hurled up to the roof, bruising and damaging each other, and at a conservative estimate there are four such holes per mile. Certainly the *mayoral* could avoid them and spare his passengers all these involuntary leaps and somersaults if he would slacken speed to a trot, but the Spanish postillion must always drive at full gallop to maintain his reputation, so trees and houses fly past and the very sky line rushes along like some fantastic streamer. After the open country come blue mountains, then more stretches of green ringed around by white mountains, where the snow lies like great silver blades against a glorious carpet of deep purple velvet.

This territory of La Mancha, where we awoke, is a harsh, forbidding place with arid wastes of shifting sands. How Don Quixote must have made poor Sancho suffer when they crossed these scorching deserts and his donkey sank knee-deep at every step. Don Quixote is in my mind, Madame (as he often is in any case), because yesterday morning we passed through Tembleque, where the windmills seemed to be defying fair Dulcinea's lover a second time; and because we stopped for lunch at the *venta de Quexada*, whence Cervantes' hero derived his name; and finally because we dined at *Puerto Lapice*, that celebrated inn where the king of knights-errant met those two delightful persons whom he took to be damsels. It goes without saying that we visited the courtyard where the noble paladin kept vigil over his arms and broke the head of the groom who came to draw water from the well for his horses.

Upon my word, Madame, we could have made the same mistake as Don Quixote, for this inn of *Puerto Lapice* still contained pretty girls. Two adorable smiling faces welcomed us as we arrived, a fair sample of those who waited on us. The landlord had eleven daughters, and Giraud, while eating quite a good lunch, sketched the two who first greeted us, Concha and Dolores.

Puerto Lapice is a picturesque pass between two chains of mountains. As for *la venta de Quexada*, it is a kind of castle, now almost in ruins, its two pointed turrets gnawed by Time, its main guesthouse served by a single door that looks out, like a melancholy eye, over a forecourt littered with dung and coarse straw. I counted two windows on the first floor; three irregularly placed openings lighted the lower room; and a fourth gave on to a little room, perhaps the very one where the knight kept his library, those books which the good *curé* burned as ruthlessly as the Caliph Omar burned the library of Alexandria.

"But," you will ask, Madame, "do you then believe that Don

Quixote actually existed? Do you not, like all the world, admit that he was merely an abstraction?" Ah, who knows, Madame? Many of my own characters, thought to be visions of my imagination, have lived, spoken, thought, as indeed they still do, and Cervantes may have known Don Quixote as I knew Antony and Monte Cristo.

While we were eating our lunch, and finding the room cold, we recalled that just outside the door was a broad open space drenched in sunshine, and the moment our meal was over we ran out to warm ourselves there. But the *zagal* was already in the saddle, the *mayoral* in his driving seat, so we perforce had to take our seats in the coach and start off, waving our farewells to the landlord's eleven daughters, who received them with the dignity of eleven princesses in *The Arabian Nights*.

As we traveled on, the plains grew less arid, the horizon less burned by the sun, as though, down there beyond the mountain, the gay, lovely land of Andalusia was coming to meet us, castanets in her hands and a garland on her brow. Soon the plains looked brighter and in some places seemed to be covered with a silken gauze. As we leaned forward to look at them through the carriage windows they reflected from the ground a light that varied from opal to the tenderest, most appealing shade of violet. We were in the land where saffron grows, and these lakes of color were lakes of flowers, the riches as well as the adornment of the plain. A few more turns of the wheels, and we entered the delightful little town of Manzanarès.

What exuberance of life surges in the peoples of the Midi! There is no end to the sound of singing and the throbbing of guitars. The lower room in every house is crowded with young girls taking the pistils from saffron flowers. Great heaps of purple petals reach to the ceiling and pile up against the walls, emphasizing the fresh complexions of the working girls. Against this delicate background their hair, black as it is, looks blue; their great velvet eyes, the bright crimson of their cheeks, their smooth white brows, all glow with a lovelier light. For an hour we strolled into ten or twelve such houses, and each time, when our interpreter Desbarolles had presented our com-

115

pliments, there broke out a peal of gay, girlish laughter, innocent and inoffensive. One could, in any case, take no offense when pretty mouths laughed so sweetly and showed such lovely teeth. It was all quite natural. We were French, and Spaniards consider French people most amusing. Perhaps they are more fond of teasing than we are, yet we invented vaudeville.

We were in the Square, listening to a blind beggar woman improvising flowery compliments in Spanish or Latin for the diversion of bystanders (I cannot comment on her Spanish, but her Latin was poor), when the *mayoral* brought us word that the coach was about to leave. Giraud was just starting a sketch but had to leave it unfinished, so if you would like to see a drawing of this place, and others we have visited, ask Dauzats, who has a whole portfolio of sketches he has made while traveling through the same part of the country.

Farewell, Madame. The *mayoral* tells me that tonight we shall sleep at *Val de Peñas*. Good! We shall at last be able to drink, in the place where it is made, this famous wine whose very name rings so pleasantly in Spanish ears.

17

❦ ❦ ❦

Granada, 27th October

We were rather disturbed to learn that a coach en route for Seville had left Manzanarès just ahead of us and would also stay overnight at *Val de Peñas*, for the proverb that "enough for one is enough for two" certainly does not apply in Spain. Alas, the news was only too true, and when we arrived at the inn we found the tables crowded with guests, if bare of victuals.

Though the first-comers frowned upon us, we all scattered to explore the possibilities of the place, and ten minutes later met again in the dining room to exchange information. I had discovered the kitchen and come to terms with the chef; Giraud had found the chambermaid and arranged about our beds; Boulanger had come across a store of chestnuts and filled his pockets; Maquet had discovered that there were no more letters awaiting him at *Val de Peñas* than there had been at Madrid and Toledo. Alexandre and Desbarolles, the last to rejoin us, had been opening doors at random and making other charming discoveries that I will not specify, adding simply that in olden days they might well have been changed into stags, like Acteon. We still needed to discover places at table, but by now the earlier guests were sufficiently reassured about us to move closer together and make room.

At supper we naturally asked for the celebrated wine, but the first to taste the frightful liquor brought to us hastily spat it out.

"Well . . . ?" said I, to Desbarolles, who for the past fortnight had talked of little else but this pleasure in store for us. With a gesture of his head Desbarolles summoned the *mozo*, who came running.

"Have you no better wine than this?"

"Certainly, sir!" The *mozo* vanished, coming back five minutes later with two bottles which he assured us were the best he could offer. On tasting, we found that this wine had been doctored and was worse than the first, so imprecations began to rain on Giraud and Desbarolles, who had promised us nectar.

"Come, come," said Giraud, rising from his seat. "This is no time to stand on ceremony. We promised everyone some real *Val de Peñas*, so we must look for it in the right place."

"Come along, then," replied Desbarolles, and they both went out, returning ten minutes later with an immense earthenware jar holding five or six quarts of a thick dark wine with which we filled our glasses. They had fetched it from a cabaret they knew of, and at last we enjoyed the real *Val de Peñas*, sharp yet exciting to the palate, popular with seasoned drinkers since it does not quench the thirst. Quite naturally we soon felt ready for bed and looked to Giraud, who had discovered the chambermaid.

She was a child of fourteen, no bigger than a girl of ten would be in France, yet her flashing eyes, her profusion of black hair, neatly braided, every gesture, every smiling pose proclaimed, "I am a woman! Admire me, love me or not as you will, but, above all, look at me!" We were content merely to look at this strangely alluring little creature who showed us to our rooms and brought us hot or cold water according to our needs as we prepared for the night. Without the slightest embarrassment she curved and twisted between us like an adder, cleverly anticipating our requirements and obeying our slightest behest, whether of word or gesture. Feeling sure we should not see her in the morning, we gave her a tip of two *pesetas* and dismissed her.

The *mozo* woke us at midnight, but we knew better than to take much notice, beyond replying: "All right! We'll be there!" At 3 o'clock our *mayoral* came in person to rouse us, and at his heels trotted the little chambermaid, complaining bitterly that the landlady had taken from her the two *pesetas* we gave her the night before. The play of her lovely eyes swimming with tears, her dainty, fluttering hands, her hair tumbling about her brown shoulders, all moved us so much that though we did not believe a word of her story we gave her another *peseta* and were rewarded by a wealth of smiles as we departed.

After traveling for two hours we saw the new day break and breathed the perfume of the land we were entering, la Sierra-Morena, a magnificent chain of mountains where oleanders and bay trees grow as freely as grass on a prairie. The boundary of Andalusia is marked by a pillar called Saint Veronica's Stone, and though in the Carlist wars this monument was riddled with bullets, its engraving of the face of our Lord was miraculously untouched. Nothing could be more fragrant, yet more desolate, than the road we were following. Everywhere we found flowers, fruit, perfume, yet here and there in this

118

immense oasis we came upon a deserted homestead, abandoned during the war of 1809. I cannot tell you very much about this mountain range, once famous as the haunt of brigands. I only know that we were starving when at last we reached Carolina, a little town colonized by Charles III, where our *Guide to Spain* told us we should still find traces of his German regiments in the language of the people, their customs, and their strict propriety. What we did find was that the doors were so low that Maquet nearly killed himself going into a house pointed out to us as an inn. Unfortunately, behind those dangerous portals we found nothing more interesting than a few cups of chocolate priced at six times their value.

On we went, through Baylen, where a French army under General Dupont surrendered to Spanish forces in the Napoleonic wars, and at sunset we approached Jaen, formerly the capital of a kingdom of that name, where we had our first glimpse of the Guadalquivir. The word, meaning "great river," is derived from the exclamation *"Oued-el-Kebir!"* uttered by the invading Moors in amazement at the sight of so much water all at once. Jaen is an immense tawny mountain baked by the sun and marked into zigzags by old Moorish walls. The African conquerors built their town at the summit, but gradually it has spread downward to the plain. We stopped at an inn that we were not due to leave until midnight, and my companions took advantage of this break to climb to the top of the mountain, while I preferred to spend the time in writing to you. They returned full of enthusiasm for the wonderful view of the country around, and of the gigantic cathedral, vying in size and dignity with the mountain on which it leans. Among the treasures of this cathedral, so the monks assured my friends, is the veritable kerchief that St. Veronica received from our Lord, marked with the sweat of His passion.

At midnight we resumed our journey. It seems that bandits keep different hours in different parts of Spain. You recall, Madame, that in La Mancha they were most active between midnight and 3 o'clock; in Andalusia it is between midnight and 3 o'clock that they take their rest. However, people assured us we shall meet particularly ferocious brigands between Granada and Cordova. We are not told precisely where, but when we approach the right spot we shall be held up. If that happens, I have publicly announced that we will certainly rob them.

At dawn we opened our eyes to see on the horizon the lacy outline of the Sierra Nevada, its snow-capped mountains pink in the morning light, while around us as we pressed onward the vegetation seemed more and more African. On each side of the road we passed gigantic aloes and huge cacti, while here and there in the distance a palm tree had sprung up in the midst of the plain. At last we saw Granada. Like no other town in Spain, this queenly city sends out her houses to meet and welcome the approaching traveler. A league from the gate there are dwellings whose gardens are the plain itself; nearer the town they crowd more closely until at last they form a solid mass; then one passes through the encircling wall and has actually arrived in Granada.

It is a town with low-built houses and narrow, twisting streets. The windows, square and plain, are enclosed by balconies of trellised ironwork, sometimes with openings too small for even a hand to pass through. It is under these balconies that the lovesick youths of Granada breathe their nightly serenades to the fair ladies listening above, for we are in the heart of Andalusia, where everything is still as it was in the days of Almaviva and Rosine, Figaro and Suzanne.

Giraud and Desbarolles took it upon themselves to arrange our lodgings. Neither of them had expected to see Granada again, and they exclaimed joyfully at every house they recognized. They led us to the place where they stayed on their last visit, kept by a man whom they nicknamed *le sieur Peppino*, for no reason that I can discover. He is the proprietor of a students' boardinghouse, such as there are in Paris near the Sorbonne, though I have no idea what his boarders may be studying. If I ever find out, I will tell you, Madame.

As soon as we entered the house we asked for baths. Master Peppino looked at us in amazement and repeated, *"Baños?*

120

THE PUERTO DE ARENAS—ROUTE FROM GRANADA
TO JAEN

COURTESY, THE METROPOLITAN MUSEUM OF ART, GIFT OF MRS. A. S. SULLIVAN, 1919

PEASANTS GOING TO THE FAIR

A BANDERILLERO IN DANGER

THE FANDANGO AT THE THEATRE SAN FERNANDO,
SEVILLE

Baños?" like a man completely unable to understand our meaning, so we did not press our indiscretion, and proceeded to settle into our new quarters. Peppino turned out three or four students to make room for us, and I now have a pretty little apartment all to myself where I am writing to you, while my friends are making themselves comfortably at home close by.

I must tell you, Madame, that our arrival was anticipated. M. Monnier, I think, had written beforehand, and consequently, when I had been here only an hour and was in the midst of this letter, I received a deputation of the editorial staff of the journal *El Capricho*, who brought me a charming poem of welcome, printed on colored paper in letters of gold. I took up a plain sheet of white paper, having no other, and responded to their compliments in a ten-line stanza which at least had the merit of being impromptu. Among these visitors was the Count of Ahumeda, a notable hunter who at this moment is examining and admiring the arsenal we have brought with us. He seems to me a most charming *hidalgo*, and I know that I shall regret that our acquaintance can only be brief. After the deputation I received a call from one of our compatriots, a M. Couturier, whom I certainly took for a Spaniard. He is a commercial traveler who came to Granada two years ago to sell daguerreotypes and has stayed here ever since. He has placed himself at our disposal as a guide, we have accepted with pleasure, and the first service I shall ask of him is to take me to the post office so that I can forward this letter to you with my heartfelt greetings.

121

18

Granada, 28th October

When you receive letters from Granada, Madame, you can believe yourself in communication with a soul still dwelling in a corner of the heaven you left a little while ago to come and live among us.

Granada, more lovely than a flower, sweeter than the fruit whose name she bears, was like a sleepy maiden resting in the sunshine on a bed of moss and bracken, ringed around with cactus plants and aloes. Beyond the sea the covetous Moors stood on tiptoe to view her beauty, and swooped across to claim her for their own, building a great wall around her and tempting her with two sculptured jewels called the Alhambra and the Generalife. In time the Spaniards won her back, but whether out of jealousy or avarice did little for her, and her richest jewels are still those given to her by the Moors. You shall come with me to see them, Madame, following my route step by step.

On the way we shall find a little house called *el Carmen de los Siete Suclos,* one of the most charming links in the chain that leads to the Alhambra. Yet it is only a little tavern, a simple, pleasant place where we found so much to enjoy that in gratitude I must tell you all about it. On leaving the Granada gate you walk for ten minutes under a sky of red hot steel and blazing sun. Then there rises before you, as if by magic, a broad, shady avenue whose trees link hands above your head. Shafts of sunlight, tempered by the foliage, brighten the road without disturbing its cool freshness, while all around is the perfume of flowers, the song of countless birds. For five or six hundred yards this avenue leads gently upward, then the sun blazes down in full force on a little white house with a brook running beside it and an arbor of trelliswork where, almost always, five or six natives of Granada sit lazily enjoying the warmth, the perfume, and the birdsong, smoking their eternal cigarettes. If you follow this path to its end, Madame, you will go to the Generalife; if, after glancing at this smiling little house, you turn sharply to the left and continue to climb, you will reach the Alhambra. We were going first to the Generalife, but at the angle of the two paths we paused to listen to the singing and the sound of castanets, watching the shadows of the leaves playing over the white walls, and the long cluster of red pimientoes hanging from one of the windows like some fantasy by Decamps.

Three steps led up to the garden, and under the latticework shelter stood several rough tables, each covered with a somewhat inadequate tablecloth, except one at which two Bohemians were sitting, and from which the cloth had been prudently removed. They were real Bohemians, Madame, I assure you, and looked most picturesque. Another table was laid for a party equal in number to ourselves, with plates and clear carafes of topaz wine, *hors d'oeuvres* inviting enough to transform appetite into raging hunger, everything shining in the sunlight that came flickering through the vine leaves. All eyes turned to Couturier, who confessed that he had arranged this pleasant surprise for us. Desbarolles was in ecstasy; his beloved Spain was at last showing us her true splendor. Alexandre, whose emotions always stimulate his appetite, sat down at the table; Giraud and Boulanger, who had just taken out their crayons at sight of the charming little tavern, put them away again without a word; Maquet informed us that the time was 11 o'clock; and I, bold as always, turned up my sleeves and went into the kitchen to see what was being cooked for us.

Madame, I was deeply touched by a sight that in some respects brought to my mind the patriarchs of old. In the room leading from the kitchen, amid the savor of roasting cutlets, the master of the house was solemnly dancing the simplest, most unaffected steps of the national *fandango* with his equally serious maidservant. From the ceiling, like great yellow stars, hung a store of pomegranates, each on its own string; and near the wide fireplace, where a *puchero* was boiling merrily, the mistress sat nursing her sleeping babe and smiling as she watched the dancers. Castanets were clicking softly, and a bright sunbeam wandered through the open door to illumine the dance and disturb the blissful *siesta* of a magnificent white cat.

When I appeared, the dancers stopped, but at a sign from me went on again, while my friends gathered around to enjoy this family scene, so common in Spain that only a foreigner would pay attention. At last the servant broke away, half-smiling, half-blushing, and her master came forward to greet us, taking off his castanets, obviously amazed that something he found so natural should give us such delight. We enjoyed our meal, too, with a light breeze tempering the sunshine and the two gypsies entertaining us with songs. (We had sent them a bottle of the same golden wine that sparkled on our table.) Couturier asked us if we would like to see a real Bohemian dance later in the day, on our way back from the Alhambra, a suggestion we acclaimed joyfully. He went over to the gypsies; their voices died away, the strings of their guitars trembled into silence as they listened to his proposal, and it was at once agreed that at 2 o'clock that afternoon the father, his son, and two daughters, all in their finest traditional dress, would be at the *venta de los Siete Suclos* to dance for us. You see how well our days are filled!

We left the inn and went on our way, coming after a while to a crossroads where stood a little white house, its open door a dark square. It looked like a farmhouse in Normandy, with hens scratching on the dungheap, farmcarts with their shafts in the air, dogs asleep with their heads on their paws. To the right, under a thick-set vine, women were laughing at their work while a baby was smearing his face with a bunch of black grapes clutched in his swarthy fingers. Nothing could be more unlike the entrance to a Moorish palace, yet this is the boundary of the Generalife; the women are its caretakers; the baby plucks the grapes from a vine whose roots mingle with the roots of

Boabdil's sheltering cypress. A few steps farther, and we are in the avenue that zigzags up to the palace, its every turn displaying fresh marvels of vegetation. It would remind you of English gardens, if the trees were not five hundred feet high, if the sky were not so deep a blue, if the flowers, the plants, the fruits, the perfumes were more familiar, less exotic. Never have you seen such violets, such velvet moss, such fairy rainbows arched over diamond cascades. You, who know me so well, know that I seldom notice such things, yet I assure you that this ascent to the Generalife will remain one of the sweetest, most intoxicating moments of my life.

After passing the third turn in the pathway, one catches sight of the Generalife, or, rather, the stone edifice that contains it as a casket holds a precious jewel. Again one's preconceived ideas are mistaken, for the outside is plain and homely. In front of it a vine forms a broad leafy ceiling and throws a dark shadow upon the low arched door of this mysterious retreat.

Before entering, we cast one final look around us. On our right, the view extended no farther than the thickly wooded hill overtopping the Generalife; but on our left, beyond the retaining wall, the ground fell away so sharply that at first we saw nothing but empty sky. Then our eyes traveled over Granada, asleep in the foreground; over the great plains cut by two rivers, sundered by two Sierras; to the far horizon sixty miles away. We felt reluctant to lose even a fraction of this glorious panorama until we noticed, in the left face of the building, a certain *mirador*, an observation window, crowned with high pointed arches. The Moors were men of keen perception, and since they had created this *mirador*, it was undoubtedly the best point from which to admire the view, so we passed through the low doorway into the Generalife.

Do you, like many people, Madame, imagine that the Alhambra and the Generalife are extravagantly Moorish in appearance, their walls streaked with blue, red, or yellow, and pierced with arched gateways, their roofs crowded with cupolas and minarets? The truth is very different. This whole exterior is conceived on lines of noble simplicity; there are no cupolas, no minarets, though here and there a palm tree or a cypress overhangs the roof; the walls, burned brown by the sun, are pierced by narrow slits that can scarcely be called windows. Would you like to know something of the interior? Then follow us.

Once inside, we could at first see nothing but a mass of soft verdure under a diffused and gentle light. Not one tiny patch of sky, not an inch of earth. Looking more closely, we realized this was a shady grove of yew trees, a dark-green bower forty yards long and twenty-five wide, divided lengthwise by a little stream running swiftly along its deep channel of brick. Seated beside this stream you forget the whole world, hearing only the murmur of the water, the song of the birds, the scratching sound a lizard makes, climbing on the sun-drenched wall. As your eyes grow used to the shade, you see lemon groves, orange trees, and jasmine girding the whole garden with perfume, while the boughs of the cypress sigh like the lovers who dwelt in this palace in days of old.

The glory of the Generalife does not lie in its staterooms, its baths, its corridors—we shall find all these in the Alhambra, finer and more carefully preserved—but in its gardens, its waters, its wonderful view. Nowhere else in the world will you find in such a small expanse such fragrance, such freshness, such a multitude of windows, each opening on a corner of paradise. The very breath of Arabia still lingers in the air. The interior walls, once carved into openwork like ivory fans, have been plastered with white so that now the pattern looks like vermicelli; the gardens, once so rigidly disciplined, have now grown free; but if you overlook these details you could believe the Moors were still around you, and that at any moment the lovely Zoreïde might come through one of these mysterious doors to sit under the gigantic cypress that still bears her name.

We passed two hours at the Generalife, and could, indeed, have stayed there all our lives without even thinking of seeing the Alhambra, for we found it wonderfully restful, deeply satisfying. Maquet wrote some charming verses which I will send you, but no one else among us did more than breathe the perfumed air and feast his eyes. At last we retraced our steps, saying "good-by" to the Generalife (alas! not "au revoir")—and making our way toward the Alhambra.

19

❧   ❧   ❧

Granada

As we passed the door of *los Siete Suclos*, we inquired for news of our Bohemians, and were told that the father was still very hopeful of collecting his family together before the time we had agreed on. Our day certainly promised to be well filled.

We walked on toward the Alhambra, up a pleasant road ending in a gateway crowned with a heart-shaped arch. It was built by King Yusef Abdul Hagiag in 1348, and bears two symbols that make it very interesting, not only to true believers but also to foreigners of inquiring mind. On the outside is carved a hand with the fingers thrust forward in the traditional Arab gesture for averting the Evil Eye; on the inside is engraved a key, to remind those who pass of that verse in the Koran which begins: "He has unlocked . . ." The significance of these symbols was too simple or too profound for the common people, who devised another explanation for themselves: "When the hand grasps the key, Granada will be conquered." The hand has never held the key. Nevertheless, to my profound regret, the Moors were driven from Granada.

Beneath this gateway is an altar, sacred to the Virgin, and here was celebrated the first Mass after Ferdinand's victory, at the very moment when King Boabdil, on the height beyond, was uttering that great sigh which has ever since been commemorated in the name given to that mountain, *el último sospiro del Moro*. Having passed through this gateway and entered the precincts, one sees, not the Moorish Palace (the Moors, Madame, conceal their women and their treasures), but a frightful palace erected by Charles V. Perhaps I am uttering a heresy; perhaps genuine architects would prefer this later edifice; but Charles V, whose kingdom encircled the world, could have chosen to build his palace in some other place, not in the spot where the Moors had already built their own. He would then have had no need to destroy half the Alhambra, a deed that brought ill luck to his own palace which has never been completed, and, please God, never will be.

The Arabs enclose their private lives, literally as well as figuratively, and in the whole Alhambra I do not think you would find more than three or four windows opening on the outside world. Even the gate by which you enter is almost invisible, once you are inside. It leads to a great courtyard known by three different names: "the Court of the Myrtles," "the Court of the Reservoir," and "the Court of the Baths." Once inside this court you have gone back five centuries in history, and are beyond question in the East, not the West. Do not ask me, Madame, to describe these marvels to you, one by one. That is a task for the brush, not the pen. Horeau or Dauzats will show you their drawings and engravings; or read Gautier, who will give you a more accurate picture than I myself would even dare to sketch.

Alas, Madame, though the Alhambra looks to be the work of genii, it was built by men, and the time is not far distant when it will crumble into dust. Even the Court of the Lions, that miracle of human creation, that dream brought to reality by an enchanter's ring, is on the point of collapse. Pray that it will still survive, or that, if it falls, it will never be restored.

Leaving this enchanted palace we called upon the Governor, who most courteously, though somewhat silently, showed us his terraced gardens where the tenderest tropical flowers blossom in profusion. Then I persuaded my friends to come away, reminding them of our treat in store at the *posada de los*

Siete Suclos, which they, like you, Madame, had completely forgotten.

A crowd had already gathered round the *posada,* for the host had let it be known that a gypsy dance had been arranged for the entertainment of certain illustrious foreigners. As we approached, a tentative clacking of castanets and a final tuning of guitars made it plain that everything was ready and awaiting our arrival. An upstairs room had been chosen for the performance, and all around it uninvited spectators had taken up their positions. The two gypsy girls, whom we had not seen before, were talking and laughing with their father, while a young lad of fourteen or fifteen years, clearly their brother, stood leaning against the wall, whistling a light air that yet seemed serpentine and inhuman in its modulations. I have thought of, and indeed seen, many evil characters, Madame, either in my wanderings in fiction or while exploring the real world, but, in sober truth, never have I seen a face so depraved, so sunk in vice, as the face of this boy.

His skin was livid, his cheeks hollow under prominent cheekbones, his half-shut eyes ringed with dark circles, all shadowed by his broad-brimmed Andalusian sombrero. He stood, as I said, leaning against the wall, with his hands deep in his trouser pockets, one leg crossed over the other, but this was far from the nonchalant elegance of pose we had so often admired since entering Spain. This was the debility that results only from debauchery, and to us this enervated creature, old beyond his years, seemed thoroughly objectionable, in spite of the wan smile that flickered now and then across his ivory features.

Though the girls were laughing quite spontaneously, in repose they looked sad. They had the characteristic sepia complexion of the gypsies, and great black eyes of velvet and mother-of-pearl; lovely eyes, but so closely neighbored by matted, unkempt hair that their beauty went unnoticed. Headbands of vivid red ribbon encircled their blue-black tresses, and each girl carried a bunch of ruby carnations and white marguerites, already wilting in shame at finding themselves in such sordid company. Imagine blue and white striped dresses covering wrists and ankles; scarlet sashes to match the hair ribbons; stockings, once white, now a dirty gray; large, broad feet in shoes that bore no relation to the rest of their costume; and you have a fairly accurate picture of these dancing girls. We had asked for real gypsies; now we had them.

Castanets began to trill, the guitar sounded its opening chords, the father broke into that monotone of song one hears everywhere in Spain, and one of the girls began a swaying movement in unison with her brother. At first, the steps were simple and unaccented, the conventional movement of the hips too vague to kindle a spark of fire in their eyes. But their glances grew more provocative; they danced in closer contact, linking hands, then lips, both wrought to passion by the lascivious dance, while their father mingled with his song various obscene exclamations that convulsed the audience and seemed designed to excite the boy still further and snatch the last shreds of modesty from the girl, leading up to the final pose of desire on the point of fulfillment.

As seasoned travelers and men of the world we are not over-squeamish about such exhibitions of passion, either in a play or as the climax of a traditional dance, but we prefer dancers with delicate hands, dainty feet, and a skin of white or gold. We found this family utterly distasteful—whenever the gypsy lad approached us we recoiled instinctively—and though we had offered them money to come, we would gladly have given them double to go away. Desbarolles, the most bashful traveler who ever left France, half-closed his eyes, either to limit his vision or to doze, while Alexandre's opinion was plain from his scornful lower lip and the longing glances he cast at the road outside.

Now the sisters prepared to dance together, and we began to hope that what we had seen was an exception that belied their normal habits. But their dance was just as licentious in its implications, if not in its actual steps, and when it was over the first dance began again. Giraud and Boulanger had started sketches they could not finish then, and it was arranged that next morning the Bohemians should sit, not dance, for us at

130

Couturier's house. So we parted, the gypsies very satisfied with us, while we were far from sharing that satisfaction.

As it was still daylight, on our way home we called on a certain *señor* Contrairas, who lived exactly opposite our friend Couturier. I had been advised to see his model of a court in the Alhambra, said to be a miracle of labor and precision. He willingly led the way to a little shed and showed us his handiwork, a reproduction of the Hall of the Two Sisters, some six feet high. There was little we could say, except to admire the perseverance of the man who had conceived the task and found patience to carry it out, but I noted his name and promised to make it known, hoping to procure some recompense for him, or at least some encouragement.

Do you recall, Madame, that I once asked you to bear in mind a certain green and yellow carriage that eventually capsized with us inside it? Well, this time I beg you to remember the house of the Contrairas family. In my next letter you will learn why.

20

❧ ❧ ❧

Granada

It remained for us to visit what is perhaps Granada's most curious sight, *las Cuevas*, the grottoes where the gypsies live, for they have their own particular quarter, as in all Spanish towns. It is difficult to explain the fierce antipathy between Spaniards and gypsies, which is felt particularly strongly in Granada, where the Bohemian quarter is right outside the town, beyond the Xénil. When we looked down upon this settlement from the height of the Generalife, it seemed impossible that twelve thousand souls could be living there. All one sees is the mountainside bristling with aloes and cactus plants, but in between are the ventholes of the caverns where these pariahs of the Western world have taken refuge. Here and there a thread of blue smoke rises vertically through the golden air and shows where a human habitation lies underground.

Having just seen members of this community at the inn of *los Siete Suclos*, we found it strange to be visiting their home. Foreign visitors, in contrast to Spaniards, are welcomed by these outcasts, who feel that strangers do not regard them with the crushing scorn shown by their Spanish fellow-countrymen. For Frenchmen such as ourselves, gypsies are peculiar, but still human, while for Spaniards, gypsies are dogs and less than dogs.

So, even before we spoke we were recognized as friends; children came and smiled at us; young girls carrying water paused, pitcher on shoulder, to watch us pass, while their parents crowded to the cavern mouths. Now and again our eyes pierced the gloom and discerned a man plaiting straw, or a girl standing combing blue-black hair that hung down to the ground. Everything seemed utterly strange, poor beyond belief, so filthy that one shuddered, yet below the matted hair, under the greasy rags, shone the loveliest black eyes and shapely forms that would inspire a sculptor.

Foreign visitors, especially Englishmen (for as a race they always love unusual things) are sometimes fascinated by these eyes, these magnificent bodies, but I am told that, notwithstanding the abysmal poverty of the whole community, there are none of those temporary unions so common in civilized society. Gypsies marry only within the tribe, and their strange, primitive rites place faithfulness between husband and wife above all other considerations. No stranger is ever admitted to these celebrations, which are consequently unknown, save by tradition.

We found our walk to *las Cuevas* most charming and picturesque. Mounting the right bank of the river, we had behind us a bird's-eye view of the low town of Granada, bristling with steeples and clock towers dating from the Renaissance. Beyond it lay the golden, sun-drenched plains, stretching away to the encircling purple mountains; before us, the snowy peaks of the Sierra Nevada were sharp against the azure sky. To our right, on the height beyond the valley, stood the glowing outlines of the Alhambra and the Palace of Charles V; while to the left lay this arid mountainside, honeycombed with burrows for human habitation, all hidden beneath thorny aloes and cactus plants. Here and there rose a stone cross, reminding us that we were still in a Christian country, more or less.

We went into one or two of these caverns, which are sold or rented just as real houses are, and we talked to an old woman who lived with her daughter in a simple hole in the ground, for which her yearly rent was one *peseta* (twenty *sous*). Though the sum was so small, she was in arrears and on the point of being turned out, but Alexandre sent for the proprietor, paid ten years' rent in advance, and placed the receipt in the poor woman's hands, the landlord generously overlooking the arrears under the circumstances.

We chatted, looked about us, and sketched until we were tired, then took a little path to the right, down through a cool, shady valley and up the flank of the mountain on the far side, where the high town, the Moorish city, was built. This side was as fresh and leafy as the opposite side was dry and bare, with springs gushing forth everywhere and tumbling in cascades over the rich earth and into the valley far below. We returned to M. Peppino's house, lost in wonder at all we had seen and swearing that we would come back and live in Granada—Boulanger, Giraud, and Desbarolles to paint, Maquet and I to write, Alexandre to enjoy himself doing nothing.

Awaiting us we found the program for tonight's performance at the theater. I must tell you, Madame, though my modesty shrinks from the task, that the mead of praise we poor artists seek, which is accorded us so grudgingly in France, is poured forth freely and lavishly as soon as we set foot abroad. While French critics tear to pieces everything we produce like hounds rending a stag, down here we are welcomed, feted, praised perhaps beyond our deserts. Ever since my arrival in

133

Granada became known, I have received visits from notable citizens, among them the Director of the Theater, who not only offered seats to all those in my party but also begged me to choose some special item for the program every day for as long as I stayed. This was a compliment I greatly appreciated, for it gave me the opportunity of seeing characteristically national productions instead of the ordinary repertoire. My choice for this evening was a ballet composed of Andalusian dances and two *sainetes*.

I have already praised to you Mme Guy Stephen's interpretations of Spanish dances, so I will now add only that Calenderia Melindès rivals her very closely. The *sainetes* are especially worth seeing for their portrayal of national traditions, and every facet of the Andalusian character is mirrored in these delightful trifles. The actors, too, gave an inspired performance, very different from the mediocre standards they reach in plays by Scribe or Bayard, when they are handicapped by having to depict customs that are completely at variance with their own.

The Hall was packed, and when the performance finished at 11 o'clock we went out into the freshness of a quiet, starlit night, crossing a delightful square where, before a statue of the Virgin, adorable in her maiden modesty, five or six candles of varying size were burning steadily. Whose hands lighted these candles? What boon did the worshipers crave from this madonna?—They were lighted in all sincerity, Madame, by the women of the streets, praying that business should be brisk. Indeed, I was told that at the house bearing this statue one can obtain the addresses of these pretty ladies, but we did not verify this detail for ourselves.

We were strolling slowly on toward our lodgings when from a nearby house we heard the merry noise of castanets and guitars. Clearly, a ball was in progress, and we were reminded of the *Villa Mejor*, but now, surrounded by friends and in the heart of a city, we had no need to fear the same *dénouement*. So we paused and gave ear to these entrancing sounds; only Giraud seemed more preoccupied in scanning the house itself than in trying, like the rest of us, to decide whether the fragments we could hear belonged to the *jalco* of Xérès, the *fandango*, or the *cachucha*. As we listened, our desire grew to find some way or other to join the dance, and Desbarolles was instantly instructed to seek out the host or hostess and convey our compliments and this request. But, to our amazement, it was Giraud, who does not speak a word of Spanish, who took upon himself this hazardous commission. He knocked at the door, which opened and then closed behind him, while we waited outside for his return, planning to rescue him should this become necessary, as well it might. Ten minutes later Giraud reappeared and triumphantly signaled us to follow him. The house itself looked poor, and a stairway led from the alley beside it to the first floor where the dance was being held. On the upper steps stood two or three young people, holding a lamp to guide us. Such a ceremonial welcome amazed us, for the Spaniard is cold, grave, and undemonstrative, especially as a host, but these reflections did not prevent our noticing a lovely Andalusian girl smiling to greet us.

"Come in," said Giraud. "We are among friends." This was clearly so, and we obeyed. As we entered the ballroom, the first thing that struck us was a fine pastel drawing of a young girl on the very point of death, sinking back on a pillow strewn with roses. The second thing was the remarkable likeness between the girl in the picture and the girl now standing smiling at us. We were quickly given the key to this mystery, which also explained our warm reception. Six weeks earlier, Giraud was in Granada sitting sketching a beggar in front of this very house, when a weeping woman ran out. Her daughter was dying, and she implored Giraud to come and draw her, so that after her child's death some token of her would remain with her broken-hearted mother. Giraud instantly agreed to do his best, and made from nature the pastel sketch that had attracted our attention.

But Youth abhors nothingness; Youth fought Death, and gained a new hold on life. In two weeks her strength revived; in four her cheeks regained their color; and in six she was the shyly smiling queen at this party given to celebrate her recovery. Hence our cordial welcome, as friends of the man who prepared for a grief-stricken mother a consolation that, God be praised, proved needless.

The dance ended at midnight, and ten minutes later the door of our lodgings slammed behind us, waking unaccustomed echoes in the *calle del Silencio*. Next morning at seven we woke from dreams of the Alhambra and rushed out like a troop of schoolboys to see more of Granada, for no place we had yet seen had so fascinated us.

You will recall, Madame, that we were to visit our friend Couturier to finish sketching the Bohemians who had danced for us, so punctually at 11 o'clock we knocked at his door in the *plaza de los Cuchilleros*. Exactly opposite was the house of the Contrairas family, where I had seen the model of the Alhambra that I mentioned in my last letter. Both houses had balconies at the same level overlooking the square, a detail of some importance in view of what occurred later. Couturier had spread a canopy over part of his balcony to provide shade where we could sit, Giraud, Boulanger, and Desbarolles sketching the gypsies as they posed in the sunshine, Maquet and I bringing our notes up to date, and Alexandre trying to write verse. The gypsies made a picturesque group, the father smoking as he strummed his guitar, his daughters sitting at his feet, and his son standing stroking a dog—all of them with their backs to the Contrairas house, while we were facing it.

Suddenly one of the girls gave a cry. A stone had hit her shoulder while another struck a few inches from Desbarolles' head. They could only have been thrown at us from some neighboring vantage point, but all the windows we could see were shut and every balcony empty. However, the angle from which the missiles came strongly suggested we were being attacked from the house opposite, so the boy watched it through a hole in the curtain. Ten minutes later he gave a signal of warning, and almost at the same instant Alexandre leaped from his chair and rushed down the steps, while Maquet threw down his notebook and followed.

LADIES OF GRANADA LISTENING TO ITINERANT
DWARF MUSICIANS

"Whatever has happened?" I cried.

"I don't know," replied Boulanger, "but it seemed to me that Alexandre had blood on his face."

The gypsy lad picked up a piece of brick, about the size of an egg and obviously just prized off a whole brick, and assured me he had seen three men on the balcony opposite. Each had thrown a stone, and hearing from the commotion among us that they had scored a hit, they had vanished. I guessed that Alexandre, struck in the face, had dashed down to execute vengeance on his unknown adversary, and Maquet had gone to calm him or to back him up. Leaning over the side of the balcony I saw Alexandre already in the street, hammering at the door of the Contrairas house, so I also ran down, in through the still open door, and up to the first story, four steps at a time, brushing aside people who had come out of their rooms to find the reason for the sudden uproar. At last I reached a kind of garret where I found Alexandre and Maquet at grips with three men, two of them wielding chairs while the third held a slender file, sharp and pointed as a dagger.

Alas! You, Madame, like all my friends, know that I possess considerable muscular strength, a valuable gift in a primitive people but sometimes a dangerous one in a civilized community where everything must proceed under cover of Justice. I forgot that I represent a thirty-two millionth part of a civilized nation, and seized two of the men by the throat. It seems I must have squeezed with some force, for they both dropped what they were holding, but it did not occur to me to do likewise. Alexandre knelt on the third man while Maquet ran to the head of the stairs to confront the other tenants of the house, who appeared disposed to lend their friends a hand, but, unfortunately for these auxiliaries, the rest of our French colony, all except Couturier, had invaded the house and were holding the bottom of the stairs. At the street door an old woman was shouting "Murder! Assassins!" at the top of her voice, and a crowd was beginning to collect in the square.

Desbarolles came up and suggested an honorable retreat. We could get away now; in five minutes it would be difficult and in ten impossible. So we released our three stone-throwers, who made not the slightest protest, gathered up items of evidence such as a brick with its corner missing and the file, which still held red fragments where it had been used to break the brick, and went down. The waiting tenants stood in line to let us pass, some of them even saluting us, and at the bottom we met the Civil Guards and the *corrégidor*.

The whole crowd with one voice accused us of having broken into a peaceful house and assaulted three children asleep in an attic, an incredible charge, yet dangerous since it seemed to be believed. We brought forward our evidence of the true facts; the brick, the piece that perfectly fitted the broken corner, the file with its incriminating fragments, and, above all, Alexandre's bleeding cheek, which spoke strongly in our favor. We found the *corrégidor* of Granada as just a man as the *alcade* of Aranjuez. He declared that we had been at fault in entering the house, but that the prime offense lay with those who had attacked us and thus provoked our invasion. He announced that a full inquiry would be made, and advised us to withdraw pending that inquiry, whereupon the *garde* opened the door for us to leave. We had only to cross the street to regain Couturier's house, but in that space were at least three hundred people, all glaring at us with threatening eyes and grinding their teeth. We thrust our hands into our pockets and passed through the crowd, I leading, Desbarolles bringing up the rear. No one molested us, and we were soon safely inside the shelter of our friend's home.

The gypsies had not moved from the balcony, fully understanding, poor devils, that had they appeared they might well have been made the scapegoats for the whole disturbance, so we set to work again, while the uproar in the street steadily mounted. After a quarter of an hour we were honored with a visit from M. Monasterio, the Granada chief of police. We received him somewhat anxiously, but were quickly reassured, finding him a thoroughly unbiased man who listened to our story, accepted it, and promised us complete satisfaction. Indeed, the marks the stones had made on the balcony were still there for him to see. He advised us, however, to stay where we were until the crowd had dispersed, to avoid any further disturbance.

Toward 3 o'clock the street was fairly clear, so we left and returned to our lodging, where we found our rooms packed with *escribanos*, lawyers' clerks, all busily engrossing various documents. When we suggested they should leave, they took flight like crows—all except one, who claimed he had the right to remain.

Farewell, Madame. That, thank God, is quite enough for today; tomorrow, if Messieurs the chiefs of police, the *corrégidors* and the *escribanos* leave me time enough, I shall have the honor of telling you the rest of this sad affair.

21

Granada

My last letter ended with the officious visitations of the *señores escribanos*, who all set a different valuation upon the damage caused by the little red stone to Alexandre's left eye. The least pleasant, most crafty of them all has settled himself in with us in spite of all our hints, even our threats. There he sits, nailed to a chair in front of a table, writing, writing, writing without stopping except when he pushes his green spectacles up to a point midway between his yellow hair and his nonexistent eyebrows, and informs us:—

"Gentlemen, the Contrairas family is guilty of a crime against every Spanish law simultaneously. Perhaps if you were to intercede for them very vigorously the delinquents might not be sent to prison, but they cannot escape paying an enormous fine,

139

a colossal indemnity. This is a good case, a good case! The Contrairas family will be utterly ruined in a fortnight."

This assurance, given with complete conviction, makes us shiver from our toes to the roots of our hair and look at each other with a secret longing to strangle him and burn his body, surely the most combustible we have ever seen, in a great bonfire of his documents, as the quickest way of finishing off the matter once and for all. We simply cannot tolerate the idea that we have come to Spain, seen all her glorious scenery, her ancient monuments, only to become involved in a lawsuit against three young fellows. The more our stream of visitors talk about this immense boulder and the ruffians who hurled it at us, the more disposed we are to consider it merely a grain of sand tossed by some sportive cherub. Think of our happy days in Granada, Madame—the wonders we have seen, the memories we have gathered! Now a wretched *escribano* will efface all this joy with a stroke of his crow's quill. We are so much at ease in our traveling clothes. Can you imagine us struggling into conventional black to be interviewed by judges? Your obedient servant, flanked by a disarmed Desbarolles, standing on his dignity as a father and an ambassador, while that key witness, the young M. Dumas, displays the rainbow under his bruised left eye? Giraud drawing the plan of the two balconies, and Boulanger charting the parabola described by this grenadine brick from a Spanish hand to a French eye?

In truth, Madame, we found the position intolerable and appealed to Providence, who responded, as always. This time Providence appeared before us in a sheepskin jerkin, holding a turned-up hat with two pompons, carrying the whip of an *arriero,* and answering to the name of Lorenzo Lopez.

"*Señor,*" said this incarnation of Providence, "I have collected the mules you ordered. They are ready in the stable and we will leave as soon as you like in the morning."

The *escribano* raised his head, getting wind of an escape. "Does Your Lordship propose to leave Granada?" he asked anxiously.

"And why not?" I demanded.

"Because it is impossible for you to leave Granada at the moment, Don Alexandro."

"Get along! You're joking! Am I a prisoner, by any chance?"

"No, but you have a lawsuit on hand, and one never goes away when one has a lawsuit, especially a good one like this."

All this was said in Spanish, a language we followed only with some difficulty, but there are words, gestures, tones of voice that are always understood. I signaled to Maquet and Boulanger to take Lopez out of the room, and asked Desbarolles, who was anxiously twiddling his thumbs, to go and help them settle a price with the muleteer. He picked up his gun and went. I thought the sound of his steps would be deadened by the mats on the floor, but the *escribano* heard them and reflectively scratched his ear with his quill. Ten minutes passed before Maquet and Boulanger returned, looking incredibly innocent. The *escribano* turned to watch them enter, and smiled to see that they were alone.

"Is everything settled?" I whispered very quietly to Maquet.

"Yes, near enough. Desbarolles and the muleteer are arguing about the last ten francs."

"Did you tell him not to breathe a word about our departure in front of the *escribano?*"

"No, but I'll run and tell him now."

Alas! At that very moment Desbarolles reappeared with his arms crossed and a sparkle in his eye.

"That's all settled!" he cried, in a voice of thunder.

The *escribano* jerked around as though he had touched a galvanic battery, and the bravest among us grew pale. Our interpreter had given everything away. In vain did he try to retrieve his blunder. The *escribano* understood the position perfectly, folded his parchment carefully, wiped his pen, and took leave of us with the most elegant politeness in which we felt a vague threat.

Scarcely had the door closed behind him when a stream of abuse swamped poor Desbarolles.

"Couldn't you see my eyes?" cried Maquet.

"Didn't you guess why my finger was on my lips?" said Boulanger.

"Oh! What's the matter with you all?" asked Desbarolles, wildly. "I was talking French. How would the Spaniard understand?"

"He understood all right," I replied, while Desbarolles' expression sank from bewilderment to despair. "Still, never mind," I continued, "we must put up with it. What did you agree with the muleteer?"

"I booked all his eight mules."

"I don't want a mule," cried Alexandre. "They're too slow!"

"I foresaw that," said Desbarolles, "and reserved a horse for you."

"I don't want a mule, either," said Boulanger. "They're too fast for me."

"I had thought of a carriage for you," continued Desbarolles, "but in certain places between Granada and Cordova the road is practicable only for mules, and, besides, there isn't a single carriage for hire in Granada."

"Then I'll walk," retorted Boulanger. "I'm no horseman."

At this moment the door creaked on its hinges and M. Peppino, our landlord, announced: *"M. le corrégidor."*

This official, clad in a black frock coat and carrying a scroll, crossed the threshold and advanced three paces into the room, bowing to us. I called Desbarolles to my side and cautioned him to forget every language but French and Spanish, for this *corrégidor* was a full-blown orator. Here, Madame, is the substance of his discourse:—"I have not hesitated, gentlemen, to present myself before an illustrious writer, a brilliant planet escorted by shining satellites. By means of a stone, an injury, a tort, an aggression even, has been made against you while on a balcony overlooking the *plaza de los Cuchilleros*. I have examined the stone, which is red; and I perceive by the light of the candles that the eye of your son has a green bruise."

"Blue," interrupted Alexandre.

"Blue always looks green at night," said Giraud. "Don't interrupt the gentleman for such a trifle."

"—which is green," resumed the orator. "Gentlemen, Spanish justice will see that you are fully avenged. Will you be good enough to sign this complaint, which I have had prepared to save you the trouble?"

"But, monsieur," I responded, through our interpreter, "I have not complained, and my son declares himself sufficiently avenged."

Le corrégidor vouchsafed us a smile. "You cannot judge your own case, *señor*," said he.

"Well, *señor corrégidor*, since Justice is so kind as to assume my prerogatives, I beg her, with all respect, to forget the matter."

"That is impossible. We will never suffer an illustrious Frenchman such as the *señor don Alexandro* to be insulted with impunity, attacked, injured in the person of his son. We pay proper respect to our guests at Granada."

"That may be so, but I assure you that I will never sign a complaint that could ruin a family, *señor corrégidor*."

"Upon my word, *señor don Alexandro*, the Contrairas family have no such scruples, for they have signed a complaint against you for violating their domicile, claiming damages and interest to such a tune that if you do not ruin them, they will ruin you, and all the more easily," continued the magistrate with a searching glance, "if you show any intention of leaving the city."

"Leaving the city?" I echoed. "Whoever told you that?"

"An estimable *escribano* who left you a short while ago, and to whose insistence you owe my visit."

Five pairs of eyes, sharp as daggers, pierced the unhappy Desbarolles, who for the first time fully realized the extent of his error. I saw that it was a moment for decisive action.

"Well, yes!" I replied. "We are leaving. The Contrairas family must ruin us if they so choose, but we will sign nothing; we will not appear as witnesses; above all we will not spoil our

143

memories of such an adorable place as Granada with the tedium of a wretched lawsuit."

"Can it be possible, *señor*, that you would rob Justice of her freedom of action?"

"Injustice seems preferable, under the circumstances."

"Your mind is fully made up?" asked the *corrégidor*, in a tone that advised us to beware. "Irrevocably? Very well, then," and he took leave of us with much solemnity.

Scarcely had the door closed behind his heels when I cried: "Gentlemen, if it is possible for them to ruin us, let it be at a distance. While there is still time, let us flee away from all *alcades*, *corrégidors*, and especially all *escribanos*."

A general murmur of agreement arose, Boulanger adding: "Certainly let's be off, but how?"

"We have a horse, we have eight mules, and Moorish stirrups."

"Pardon," interrupted Desbarolles, "I never said anything about Morrish stirrups. Don't for Heaven's sake make out that I said more than I did." He seemed most disturbed, and Boulanger moaned.

"Come, Boulanger," I continued. "What does it matter whether they are Morrish stirrups or not, provided they'll take your foot? What the devil! If the Cid could sit his horse after death, surely you can keep on a mule while you're still alive?"

"Ah, well," returned Boulanger, good-humoredly, "I'll try, provided that there are stirrups of some sort."

"But," persisted Desbarolles, "that's just the trouble. There are no stirrups of any sort, Moorish or otherwise."

"Then where do you put your feet?" demanded Boulanger.

"You let them hang. It keeps them warm in winter and cool in summer."

"Feet hanging?" Boulanger protested. "But your balance! Where do you get your balance?"

"From your center of gravity," returned Desbarolles, majestically.

Now that the point had been brought up, I recalled that ever since we entered Spain, such riders as we had seen were all

144

dangling their legs, so, hoping to reassure Boulanger, I commented that the comfort of the Moorish type of saddle was proverbial. But again Desbarolles broke in. There might be such a thing as a Moorish saddle in Algeria. We should see when we got there. But certainly there were no Moorish saddles in Spain, nor English saddles either. The muleteer would tie a piece of blanket across the mule's back, and that would suffice. For anyone who craved the futile luxury of stirrups he might be persuaded to throw over the mule's withers a cord with a running knot at each end. Incidentally, there were no bridles either, merely halters, but these were perfectly adequate, mules being the easiest animals in the world to drive.

"I shall go on foot!" cried Boulanger, thoroughly resolved. In vain we pointed out that he would have to walk thirty, forty, sixty miles a day, and that in any case only muleteers walked behind mules. He was adamant. Then Maquet spoke, the most cool-headed, far-sighted man among us.

"Why should we do without saddles, stirrups, and bridles if we need them? Can't we buy some at a harness-maker's?"

"It would be completely out of character," said Desbarolles, scornfully.

"Never mind. You can ride without them if you like. No one will stop you. Come along, Maquet," said Alexandre. "We'll go and find a harness-maker."

But Maquet took out his watch.

"Gentlemen," he said, "it is just on midnight, and I would remind you that all the shops are closed by nine in the evening. Besides, a Spanish shopkeeper already finds it too much trouble to be gracious to customers in the daytime. I should not advise trying to buy from him at night. I realize now that my suggestion was ill-timed and may have raised false hopes. Please forgive me."

"In any case, there would not be time to go shopping, pack our bags, pay our bill here, and get some sleep before our mules arrive at four in the morning. We simply must have at least a little rest," insisted Desbarolles, to whom sleep is all-important.

"I have an idea," said Alexandre. "Instead of starting out at

145

4 o'clock in the morning, let's go at noon. The shops will be open at eight, which will give us ample time to see to our trunks, pack our drawings properly, pay our bill, and buy a saddle and bridle for Boulanger. For the others, too, if they wish."

"Suppose the police try to stop us tomorrow?"

"Then we'll fight our way out!" and Desbarolles ran to his gun.

"Madness! We six against a town? What does Maquet say?" I asked.

"I think," he replied carefully, "that since you came to Spain as the guest of royalty, the authorities would be very reluctant to resort to force. We are threatened with a lawsuit, but are not yet actually involved. We have signed nothing, and received no citation, no order, no official communication, consequently we are at liberty to leave Granada at any hour of the day or night we choose. But if, on the other hand, we had been officially convened . . ."

At that moment a heavy knock fell on the outside door.

"Oh! Oh! Who can be coming at midnight?" asked Giraud.

"Do you think you are being besieged already?" returned Maquet. "Probably it is one of Peppino's boarders. You know they daren't come home till we have settled down for the night." But we listened with considerable uncertainty.

We heard on the flagstones of the *patio* the tread of someone in unfamiliar surroundings, then steps upon the stair. Soon Peppino himself came into our room, nightcap in hand, smiling radiantly.

"A letter," he said. "From His Excellency the Commandant. The messenger is downstairs waiting for your reply. My word! You have some very important friends, gentlemen."

"Yes, indeed. But tell him we have retired for the night, and that you will give us his letter as soon as we wake up. Now don't protest. Just do as I say." Peppino bowed, and went out.

I felt a sinister foreboding as I grasped the letter, as though it were a new Pandora's box, and by opening it I should let loose a whole swarm of misfortunes. Yet I opened it, and since it was in Spanish I passed it to Desbarolles to read aloud. It was very short, stating simply that *le capitaine général* invited M. Alexandre Dumas to call upon him at 11 o'clock in the morning.

We swept into concerted action, forgetting saddles and bridles, our personal dignity, even sleep. Our empty trunks were filled as fast as canoes in a flood. Even Eau-de-Benjoin bestirred himself to seem helpful. Maquet arranged about paying Peppino; Boulanger packed our drawings; Giraud gathered up all that remained of our former glories in the matter of provisions; Desbarolles stacked up our firearms; and Alexandre slept with a hardihood few could have shown in such an uproar. I, Madame, have retreated into a corner to finish this letter to you. It is now twenty-five to four, our luggage is all piled up in readiness, and my companions are snatching a few moments' sleep like soldiers in a bivouac. We are due to leave at four, so I have twenty-five minutes in which to try to follow their example.

22

❦ ❦ ❦

Cordova

You lost sight of us, Madame, in the students' boardinghouse in Granada, at the moment when my five friends were sleeping as fast as they could in the hope of catching up on their normal complement of rest, and I was about to do likewise.

At precisely 4 o'clock an energetic clip-clopping of hooves on the stones beneath our window woke all of us except Alexandre, and when we looked out the warm dampness of a wet morning pervaded the room. The corps of *escribanos* must be an extremely influential body, Madame, to be capable of inventing a lawsuit, setting aside an *alcade*, spurring on a *corrégidor*, setting in action a *capitaine générale*, and now calling down on us from the skies the first rain we had seen since leaving Madrid. Our resolve to leave remained inflexible.

The road outside was only six feet wide, and you can imagine the uproar created in it by eight restless mules, a whinneying horse, two vociferous *arrieros*, four street porters anxious for good tips, and our zealous host hovering around to render us every service until the last moment. Add the banging of trunks down every stair, the questions of neighbors awakened by the din; reflect that only twenty yards away was a police barracks whose supreme head was anxious to interview us, while we hoped to slip away as silently as shadows; and you will have some idea of how we suffered during the hour and a half this clatter lasted. To crown everything, for half an hour longer we were surrounded by a dozen of the friends we had made in Granada (Couturier was conspicuous by his absence), who suddenly descended upon us with copious good wishes and resounding *adieux*.

The church clock was striking six when we finally tore ourselves away and strode briskly off, gun over shoulder and hunting knife at hip, along a tortuous path leading to the Cordova Gate. Near this gate is a great round stone building at the end of an open space planted with young trees, and in one corner a superb palm tree is growing behind a white wall, waving its gracious plumes with every breeze. Here we had arranged to meet our mules, but they were not yet in sight, their normal walking pace being much less rapid than that of a man anxious to avoid an interview with a *capitaine général*. We were, in any case, not particularly desirous of mounting them until we were outside the city, so we went on through the soft, warm Spanish rain as the darkness gave way to a gray twilight, looking back now and again to see whether the mules were coming, and also, I confess, to make sure we were not being pursued.

The road ahead was cut by a charming little bridge, coquettish like all Spanish bridges, which for half the year span dry river beds and look like half-open mouths smiling at passers-by, and as we turned back to admire it a second time we saw, on the graying road, our long file of mules walking nose to tail, Eau-de-Benjoin perched on the best of them; then came the two *arrieros*; and in the distance behind them followed three figures of ill omen. At three hundred paces they were barely distinguishable in the gloom; at two hundred one could discern their martial bearing, their uniform of blue with yellow accoutrements; at a hundred they were clearly gendarmes with stiffened tricorne hats, and each of them carried a gun.

It was Maquet who exclaimed, "Here come the gendarmes!" and like well-drilled troops we all instantly pivoted on our heels. I had already seen them. (Do you recall admiring my keen sight one day when we stood on my balcony in Saint Germain and I read for you the time shown by the station clock more than half a mile away?) Thus, when Maquet spoke, I had for ten seconds been considering the various probabilities, recognizing that these worthy representatives of the law were almost certainly on our trail. Having missed us by five minutes at our lodgings, they had stepped out smartly in their leather gaiters on the road to Cordova, the next town we were known to be visiting.

It had been embarrassing enough to rush away from Granada so early in the morning, more hurriedly than is customary among honest travelers who have paid their debts. It would be much worse to return under police escort, possibly wearing handcuffs, just when the public was beginning to open its eyes, and its shops! That would be quite intolerable! Desbarolles, the most soldierly man among us, was the first to answer Maquet.

"Bravo!" he cried. "We're going to have a fight!"

I looked at the others in turn, and saw that though they were not so eager for battle as Desbarolles, each of them, as things were, felt disposed to accept the challenge. Naturally I assumed command, my cavalry being Alexandre, Giraud, and Desbarolles; my infantry Maquet and Boulanger; and my reserves the two *arrieros* and Paul, on whom it would be imprudent to place too much reliance. I surveyed the terrain, arranged our positions to the best advantage, and then, since there was still time, invited everyone to express his opinion.

Desbarolles, our oldest member, waved his gun and cried "War!" Giraud commented that he had not yet painted a battle scene, never having been present at one. The experience would enable him to estimate more accurately the skill of Salvator Rosa, Lebrun, and Horace Vernet in depicting such matters; besides, since this battle would be fought for the greater glory of France, he, as an eyewitness, might well be commissioned by the government to paint a picture of it, to be enshrined in Versailles. So, on the whole, he would stand by his friend Desbarolles and vote for war.

Boulanger declared that his conscience was clear (apart, perhaps, from having advised young Contrairas that his cardboard Alhambra would look better if the colors were softened). He had committed no crime, caused offense to no one, and if, in spite of his serene equanimity these gendarmes proposed bothering him, he would certainly bother them, so he, too, voted for war.

The gendarmes were advancing steadily, and Maquet spoke. He considered war a tiresome extremity, a senseless futility from a social point of view. Historically, it threw a glorious brilliance over the growth of empires and the lives of heroes, and consequently had certain advantages, in spite of its disadvantages. Under present circumstances, in a land so uncivilized that quarrels between kings, peoples, and individuals were still settled by war, war was preferable to shameful submission. He concluded by observing that when the Bey of Algiers struck M. Duval with a fan, the consequence was the conquest of Algeria; the stone hurled at Alexandre by one of the Contrairas family could equally well lead to the conquest of Granada, in which case I should become the natural successor to the late King Boabdil, Alexandre the presumptive heir to the crown, and the rest of our party ministers of state—an entertaining prospect that fully occupied our attention for several seconds.

"Let Alexandre speak next," said I, with a gesture meant to curb his normal exuberance, not always the best of counselors. He thanked me and drew from his pocket a large paper, to use when loading, we thought. But we were wrong. It was his passport, issued at Paris on October 2, 1846, by the Minister of Foreign Affairs, Guizot, and he read it aloud to us, stressing that all civil and military officers of France and her allies were enjoined to allow him to pass freely, according him aid and protection in case of need. "Now," he went on, "each of you has a passport similar to mine, and though we are not in France (at the moment I wish we were), we are certainly in a country allied to France, moving peacefully from place to place as our passports permit, and the gendarmes therefore owe us not only free passage but aid and protection as well, against any who would hinder us, even against themselves. Therefore I propose that, before coming to blows, we should each show the gendarmes our passports and put this point to them. If they then refuse us the aforesaid aid and protection, they will be in the wrong. We will thrash them and be well within our rights. Incidentally, on the back of my passport is a notification, signed by the French Ambassador at Madrid, that I am carrying a double-barreled rifle and a hunting knife, obviously to use against anyone who interferes with my free passage, gendarmes included."

"Bravo!" cried Giraud. "Alexandre, you have spoken eloquently. Desbarolles, pass me my gun." Desbarolles did so, frowning fiercely, twirling up his mustache, pulling his sombrero well down, and muttering that soldiers and gendarmes were all the same to him. Meanwhile, the gendarmes were coming nearer and nearer.

"Gentlemen," I said, "they will be on us in five minutes. Reluctant as I am to open the hostilities, we must not let them take us by surprise. As soon as they pass the little inn you see there on the right, if they come on in our direction our cavalry will ride forward to meet them. They will probably challenge us in some such terms as: 'Gentlemen, you have overlooked the invitation issued to you by M. *le capitaine général*.' You will reply, 'It is true, *señores*, that we received this invitation, but it specified 11 o'clock. At present it is only 6 o'clock, so we still have five hours in which to keep it.' "

"But if that fails to satisfy them?"

"You will show them your passports. If they still try to force us to return to Granada, well, we are six and they are only three, so we will arrest them and march them on to Cordova."

"Hurrah!" chorused Alexandre, Giraud, and Desbarolles.

"Silence in the ranks! Now they are coming up to the inn. Interpreter, get ready to parley."

"They're observing us pretty closely," said Giraud.

"They're conferring with each other," said Maquet.

"They're getting the guns ready," said Alexandre.

"They seem uncertain," said Boulanger.

"Impressed by our military bearing," added Desbarolles.

Every eye was fixed upon them, as the first one stopped before the inn door, swung his gun from his shoulder, bent double, and slipped inside. The second adopted identical tactics, then the third, and the door closed behind them. No more gendarmes!

A great weight was lifted from my breast as I realized their objective was the inn, not ourselves. Though, like the others, I had voted for war, like Maquet I considered war a brutal extremity. I much preferred to leave this lovely town, where I had been so well received by many, if badly by others, without the need to strike a blow. However intrepid one may be when facing the unexpected, when gendarmes are concerned it is always cheering to know one need have nothing to do with them, so we lifted our heads and joyed in breathing the air of freedom. Only the little arched bridge, with raindrops trickling down on each side, seemed to weep at losing the historical importance it would have gained from a battle.

Our mules had profited from our strategic halt to browse here and there in the wet grass, and among them strayed the melancholy horse destined for Alexandre—a horse such as I have come across everywhere in Italy, Germany, Africa. He was a dark bay, or rather he had been, for the shining coat he doubtless displayed some ten years ago now remained only in scattered spots. The mules, gray or brown, and shaved from withers to rump in the Spanish fashion, had, as Desbarolles predicted, no harness whatever, but plenty of character from an artist's point of view. A coarse blanket, thickly folded and fastened by a strong girth to each animal's back, provided a comfortable-looking seat, while an Andalusian mantle, decrepit yet still glowing with color, hung in symmetrical folds over the mule's shoulders, adding a typically Spanish touch of floating elegance that delighted Giraud's eye and would have rejoiced Boulanger's also, had there been any sign of a stirrup.

Three mules were loaded with our luggage, leaving five and the sad-looking horse for us to ride. The biggest mule wore a black and yellow headband made from a scrap of old cloth; her blanket was less tattered than those of her companions; her air more coquettish and purposeful. Obviously she was wearing her Sunday best, and she gazed at me in a regal manner that I found most striking. She had chosen me, so I chose her, though Boulanger, noting something skittish and perverse in her manner, stroked his beard thoughtfully.

Alexandre vaulted upon his horse, whose spindly legs doubled under it; with the aid of a leg-up Giraud managed to bestride his mount; Desbarolles, like a real *contrabandista*, flung himself horizontally on his mule's back, kicked like a swimmer for a few seconds, and successfully regained the perpendicular; Boulanger shamelessly climbed on a boundary stone to reach his seat; while Maquet and I, the tallest in our party, merely raised our right legs to hip level, thus creating an angle equal to that of the mule's back, and hopped into position with a facility that aroused the admiration of our *arrieros*.

Mounted, I surveyed my party, all of them firm and resolute. Even Boulanger, whom I glanced at rather dubiously, wore to my surprise and delight an expression of calm good humor. The mantle over his mule's withers had been cleverly tied by the *arriero* to form, not exactly stirrups, but a pair of foot-muffs which completely engulfed his legs, keeping them warm and dry as well as providing the sense of balance he so much desired.

"I *told* him," cried Desbarolles, enthusiastically, "that riding a mule was the most comfortable way of traveling!"

Desbarolles has an unfortunate habit of accompanying his remarks with gesticulations, and this time he happened to be carrying, not his gun, but a large umbrella which suddenly opened as he waved it in the air. At sight of this unknown object hovering above her head, his mule reared in fright and fell on Boulanger, who pitched forward, his fist coming into vigorous contact with the mule's nose, a well-chosen point for attack. The animal wheeled, sidled from Giraud to Alexandre, who administered two more punches, overturned the *arriero* who rushed up to catch her, jumped over his prostrate body, and shot off at full gallop along the road back to Granada.

For five minutes we watched him diminishing as he approached the horizon, according to the laws of perspective. Then, completely master of his mount, controlling her simply by a halter, he came galloping back, belaboring the animal soundly with the umbrella to accustom her to the feel as well as the sight of the object that had so alarmed her.

This incident, which Giraud recorded in a sketch, fully restored our good humor, and we collected our scattered mules to start on our way, but with no initial success. Even Desbarolles' mule, having shown us her possible paces, refused to move at all until the *arriero*, fortunately unharmed by his tumble, came to our assistance.

"Gentlemen," he said, "kindness will achieve more than severity. Your mules all have names. Use them." So we, as instructed, called: "*Arre*, Pandiego," or "Gaillardo," "Pajarito," or "Redondo." Alexandre called "*Arre*, Acca!" and immediately the well-trained beasts lowered their heads, jingled their bells, and set off at a good round speed.

23

✢ ✢ ✢

Cordova

I am writing to you, Madame, from a charming balcony
giving on to a *patio* all planted with orange trees, belonging to
a hotel that seems like a private house. It is 5 o'clock in the
afternoon, and the November sun, bright and warm as ours in
September, is gilding the top of my page as I greet you.

You left us journeying on at a good pace, and we had covered some few miles when, after a final scurry of rain, the sun
broke through, the mist cleared, and we could see the gray-
green plain rolling away to the distant blue mountains. All
around, wagtails strutted, piping cheerfully, and larks, still
heavy with dew and rain, rose about us into the sky to pour
forth their clear morning song. The keen air raised our spirits,
woke our appetites, and tempted the sportsmen among us to
try their skill. After a mouthful or two of dry bread and a few
draughts of sweet white wine from the wooden cup that
served as a stopper for the leather bottle on Paul's mule, we
spread out over the plain, free and happy in the sunshine, our
guns ready for any game we could find there or on the nearby
mountain with birds of prey circling over its bald, rocky
crown.

Alas for our dreams of a wild boar or a mountain lion! Except for two partridges at which I fired and missed, we saw
nothing larger than sparrows, so we pressed on to a fair-sized
village buried among willows and magnificent mulberry trees
—I think its name was Tino—a pretty little place where a blue
stream ran sparkling through the woods with their two shades
of green. Maquet, leading the file on Pandiego, was the first to
cross a little bridge where several children stood watching the
arrival of our imposing cavalcade. They were fine children,

bright and happy—quite unlike the solemn little ragged skeletons we had seen in the two Castiles and La Mancha—and they ran before us with shouts that may not have been cries of welcome but which bore witness to their healthy vigor.

Once over the bridge we saw, through the fine rain that was now falling, a long line of houses. "Ah!" cried the hunters. "Now we shall be able to wash our hands." "Ah!" said the others. "Now we shall have a meal." Desbarolles and Giraud looked at each other without a word: they had traveled this way before.

"We'll stop at the best inn, of course," said Alexandre. "Where is it?"

It is useless, Madame, to ask a muleteer such a question. For him the best inn is the one he prefers to stop at himself, and in reply to Alexandre Juan pointed out the last house in the village.

"It's the same in Spain as in France, then," I commented. "The house one wants is always the last in the road. Since a road has two ends, one would expect chance to favor the nearer end sometimes, but it never does."

Rain was falling heavily as we approached the inn, where a dark opening in the white wall led to a broad arcade which we entered, followed by several sinister-looking men, hard-featured women, and untidy children. Firearms always interest Spaniards, and they had come to gaze at our rifles with covetous eyes.

It was a typical Spanish *venta*, an open space paved with sharp cobblestones that bruised the feet, girt round with white, windowless walls, furnished with three benches, a fireplace, a circular rack for the mules, and, hanging here and there, strange accessories such as a string of red pimientoes, a long-necked amphora, a goatskin bottle, a guitar. Our arrival caused a din that in France would have brought innkeeper and servants running to serve us; here, no one stirred to hold a bridle or help us to dismount, or, indeed, to show us the slightest welcome. Peering into the shadows, we saw two figures sitting before the dying embers of the fireplace: our host, blissfully smoking and spitting while his wife peacefully watched him. Eau-de-Benjoin, a miracle of activity compared to these living mummies, did his best to stir them out of their shadowy refuge, while the rest of us watched our streaming mules crowding together, and hastened to wipe our guns. Every voice was raised for water to wash our hands, but we might as well have called for it in a desert, so I peered around seeking for some utensil. Paul had already made three attempts to rouse the innkeeper, without avail, so we decided to help ourselves, and I pointed out a sort of cauldron hanging on the wall. Paul unhooked it, plunged it in the bucket our *arrieros* had been using to water the mules, and bore it to me triumphantly, while we all started to roll up our sleeves.

Whether the host had a particular dislike of clean hands, or whether he considered his Spanish cauldron would be polluted by any contact with French skin, he leaped from the fireplace to Paul's side, snatched the utensil from his hands, and with fiercely rolling eyes poured away the water to the very last drop. Then he resumed his seat by the fire.

I had a strong impulse to flatten him between two of his own benches, but Alexandre saw the flash in my eye, and knowing how swiftly, with me, thunder follows lightning, he seized one of my arms while Giraud held the other.

"This is more than we will put up with," I cried. "You know it was agreed that at the first insolence . . ."

"An innkeeper may be churlish toward us, father," said Alexandre, "but never insolent."

"This young Dumas," remarked Giraud, in his own inimitable manner, "has far more common sense than his father."

"Let's get away from here, then," I rejoined, slinging my gun over my shoulder.

My companions followed my example, and leaving the mules to the *arrieros* we marched out, Paul bringing up the rear with a final expostulation which the host and hostess heeded no more than they did our departure.

The Spanish innkeeper is a singular species, Madame, that should be examined by physiologists. He lives in a house lying open to the road, and over the door he writes *venta, fonda, posada, parador,* or some other word with the same meaning—to wit, a hostelry. But if this notice attracts some poor wayfarer who dares to venture over the threshold, his intrusion arouses the proprietor's fiercest wrath. Money itself is powerless to appease his flaming eyes, his threatening gestures, the bristling indignation of his hair. Yet he never effaces the notice above his door.

We retraced our steps through the village, and halfway along we read over an entrance the words: *Parador San Antonio.* Inside we found the same paved yard, the same pimientoes and guitars, the same shadowy gloom and dying fire. Once more we saw host and hostess seated around the embers, but this time their faces were bright and cheerful, hers framed in lovely black hair, his with a cap of russet wool. On seeing us they rose and came forward in welcome, while Giraud murmured "Hosanna!" and Desbarolles "A miracle!" for, staunch champions of Spanish customs though they were, they had never before met with such obliging manners at an inn in Spain.

In an instant our rancor was forgotten, our good humor fully restored, and preparations for a meal were well in hand. Maquet, with streaming eyes, was slicing onions; Giraud was preparing a bushel of potatoes; Boulanger carefully broke a score of eggs; while Desbarolles supervised the execution of a couple of fowls, making sure they were not plunged into boiling water immediately after death, as is the Spanish custom. As for Alexandre, his first concern on arriving anywhere is to find somewhere to sleep, and while he dozed off I set about looking for a table, searching everywhere until our hostess ventured to ask me what I required. Then my puzzle was solved; I had overlooked the table because Alexandre was sleeping on it.

Tables, in Andalusia, are stools, rather lower than the normal ones in France, for Andalusia, in 1846, is still purely Arab, and one sits on the ground to eat from these stools. If you insist on eating in the French manner, you must sit on a stool and eat from a chair, or from a cloth spread over your knees. Desbarolles was dispatched to find three or four more tables of the same height as the first, a cloak was thrown over all, and in less than an hour this improvised dining table was spread with two fried chickens, a ham omelette, fried potatoes, and one of my celebrated salads dressed with lemon and new-laid eggs. Our hostess stood watching us enjoy our meal, her arms akimbo, her satisfaction mingled with astonishment. A Spaniard is always astonished to see anyone eating.

Meanwhile the village, noticing clouds of smoke rising from the kitchen chimney, watching the basket of eggs brought in and the servant fetching a large pitcher of wine, listening to the fowls cackling before their necks were wrung—the village, I say, realized that a feast was in progress at the *parador San Antonio*. The rumor spread until it reached the inn where they had refused to let us wash our hands, and so began our revenge.

Alas, Madame! Man is so made that he is quite willing to earn nothing, provided his neighbor does likewise, but if his neighbor makes any money, he is jealous. We sent Paul back to the first inn to see whether the mules were ready for us, and to sustain him on the way he carried a large dish loaded with helpings of everything served at our table. Our first landlord could thus see that we must have spent at least three *douros*, of which two at least represented a profit for the host of the *parador San Antonio*.

While we were eating, a Frenchman came to see us and enjoy a few moments' conversation, for the poor man had not spoken a word of his mother tongue for two years, except to his dog. He was a poor devil of a knife grinder who had brought his wheel to Spain, hoping to make a fortune sharpening *cuchillos* and *navajas*, but from the look of things his venture had not turned out well. There was nothing I wanted ground, but I left him a dozen *réals* which he warmly appreciated. In exchange, he warned us that five smugglers had been held up by bandits and robbed, a league beyond Buena, and one who resisted was killed. We should pass over the same road the day after tomorrow to reach Castro del Rio, and we should be wise to take special precautions.

For the rest of the day it rained, and we forded swollen streams that engulfed our mules to their barrels. Most of the streams had bridges, but these had decayed in boredom at never seeing a drop of water, their middle arches had collapsed, and their remnants stood at each side of the river bed like elephants with raised trunks. Toward 4 o'clock the rain stopped for a while, so we dismounted and spread out by the roadside. Since morning we had seen only a few travelers, or, now and then, a ragged herdsman standing motionless on a granite boulder overlooking the plain. Now, we caught sight of a head in a pointed hat rising above a distant crest of rock; a body followed; then a pair of legs that began to run toward us. An arm waved to bring us to a halt, while the other arm seemed to be holding an animal of some sort. When the figure was a hundred paces from us we recognized the man as a poacher and the animal as a hare. Our visitor had doubtless spotted that we were foreigners who might not share his compatriots' prejudice against the hare as food, so he hoped to sell it to us at a good price.

"Splendid! A hare!" said I. "Pshaw!" said Desbarolles, who, I suspect, does not like hare. "A hare is not to be despised!" said Boulanger. "Especially when papa prepares it," added Alexandre. "Why bother about a hare?" said Desbarolles. "We shall sup at Alcala Real, a town of fifteen thousand people. Of *course* we shall get a good supper there." Desbarolles is incorrigible with his illusions about Spain. "Let's take it, anyway," said Maquet, so we sent him to bargain with the poacher, a transaction he managed so well that he came back with a fine hare, three-parts grown, which cost us one *peseta*. We should have paid six times as much in France.

We resumed our march over very broken country; mountain rising behind mountain, and at each new summit, when the drifting fog allowed, we glimpsed marvelous views that would have been even more wonderful under sunshine. Yet we were content, for they were still some of the loveliest we had seen.

It grew colder as we breasted the escarpment, Desbarolles ten yards ahead, carrying his gun and making vigorous passes with the big umbrella in an effort to keep warm. Then came Maquet and myself, eagerly looking to right and left, anxious not to miss a single point of interest. Alexandre was riding Acca up and down the line to discuss the merits of certain artists with each of us in turn, giving his horse so much additional exercise that the muleteers prophesied it would not last three days at that rate. Boulanger, his feet warm and dry, was smiling blissfully and letting his mule choose its own path, while Giraud tried to remain alongside him to talk about color and the gradations of light. Last in line came Eau-de-Benjoin, occupying himself with eating, drinking, sleeping, and falling off his mule.

Paul's life is one long meal, and except when he is drinking our wine he always has in hand a loaf, some ham, sausages, or hard-boiled eggs. As digestion proceeds he naturally grows drowsy and curls up for a nap on top of the luggage. Provided that the mule does not stumble, gravity maintains him in position, but as soon as the mule makes a false step the balance is disturbed and Paul slides to the ground. Then he picks himself up, climbs back on his mule, and goes through the same cycle again.

How does he manage to fall so constantly without breaking any bones? Madame, I do not know. As soon as I get back to Paris I shall ask the School of Medicine to give Paul a thorough examination. He must be made of rubber. He is certainly the right color, and when he falls one never hears a sound. He bounces up again with a smile that shows thirty-two perfect teeth, and that is all.

"Well!" he exclaims. "That's the second fall I've had today," or "the third," or "the fourth." He never complains; he simply counts his falls, and he can count very well—up to a hundred.

Consequently, we are now only relatively disturbed by these falls. Every time we hear our *arrieros* burst out laughing we turn around, and there is Paul, picking himself up from a rut, shaking out his black burnous with its red tassels, uttering his ritualistic phrase and climbing into his seat again, helped by

Juan or Antonio. I said "relatively," however, for he is apt to lose his private flask, or our wineskin, sometimes our percussion caps or our powder and shot, or a volume of poetry handed to him for safekeeping. We have therefore adopted the practice, whenever Paul falls off his mule, of going back to search the place where he fell, but we never find anything. Only in the evening do we discover how much we have lost during the day. Of course our *arrieros* are honest men, incapable of an evil thought, but nevertheless our goods are steadily vanishing. The gnomes must be robbing us.

Let me give you an example, Madame. Toward noon on this first day out of Granada, hoping to shoot some game for supper, I dismounted, and finding myself inconvenienced by something bulky in my trouser pocket I put in my hand and drew out a pistol. (It was a repeater, and you may recall, Madame, that when we started out I had a pair.)

"Has any kind gentleman an empty pocket?" I called, and six or eight pockets were at once offered to me. Reflecting, however, that my friends might well find it as inconvenient as I had myself, I told Paul to take care of it and dismissed the matter from my mind.

As night fell it grew colder. In France, perhaps, we should have thought it merely chilly, but here, in comparison with the temperatures we had recently known, it seemed glacial. The *arrieros* thrashed their arms across their chests, while Maquet and Giraud walked sharply on ahead with the twofold object of warming themselves and arranging lodgings for us in Alcala Real. The rest of us trailed wearily on, under an icy rain that soaked us to the skin. At last we began to make out the cone-shaped mountain at whose foot the town is built, and the twisting road, full of holes, rocks, and quagmires, led us to a kind of boulevard and through an arched gateway. Inside, the street was made of sharply pointed cobbles, and at once we had to dismount, for they were covered with a sheet of ice on which even our mules lost their footing. Never have I known any path so slippery. Paul stubbornly refused to walk, and fell off his mule twice within a few yards, bringing his total for the day

162

to a dozen. The inn on the far side of the square was as welcome as a haven to storm-tossed sailors, yet, frozen as I was, I paused a moment at the door to admire its beautiful façade, covered with heraldic shields, sculptured crosses, and carvings of leaves and flowers, like the entrance to a palace.

I entered, and saw that Maquet and Giraud had used their time to good purpose, for we had a courteous, smiling welcome, due to the gift of a good Havana that the host was enjoying. Eau-de-Benjoin was rushing hither and thither in a fever of activity that filled me with apprehension. When I called him he pretended not to hear, but I insisted, and he came slowly to my side.

"What have you lost, Paul?" I demanded. He hung his head, and I repeated my question.

"Sir, two hundred yards from the town my mule stumbled . . ."

"And you fell over its head?"

. "No, sir. This time I fell to the side."

"What on earth does that matter?"

"Indeed, sir, it matters a great deal. When I slide over the mule's head I land sitting down; when I fall to the side I land on my head. And then, sir, everything falls out of my pockets."

"Wretch!" I exclaimed. "You have lost my pistol!"

"Ah! I knew you'd understand, sir!" he responded, cajoling me to his own complete satisfaction. "Yes, that's how I lost it."

"What? He's lost your pistol?" cried my friends, while Paul bowed modestly and spread out his empty palms.

"Where did this happen? Do you know?"

"Certainly, sir. I missed it ten minutes after I fell off for the ninth time."

"And you didn't go back to look for it?"

"Oh, sir! It was raining, and besides, it was so cold!"

"Wait a bit," said Maquet. "There may still be a chance of recovering it. As Paul says, it is a dark, cold, wet night, and all Alcala is asleep, so no one will have picked it up."

Eagerly I called Juan and Antonio, explained the matter and offered an encouraging reward, whereupon they each snatched up a lantern and dashed off into the night. Half an hour later they returned, having found nothing.

"Astonishing!" murmured Paul. "Simply astonishing! I'm certain that is where I lost it."

The loss itself is serious enough, Madame, but the consequences could be even more serious. This type of firearm is completely unknown in Spain, where they are still using the same sort of blunderbuss as Gil Blas. Some unlucky Spaniard has found it, or will find it tomorrow; not realizing it is a pistol he will experiment with the mechanism; and in all probability he will blow out his brains. With such a dreadful vision before my eyes I feel quite unequal to talking about our entertainment at the inn, so I must leave that until tomorrow.

24

❧ ❧ ❧

Cordova

As this conversation about the loss of my pistol was carried on in French, no one else took any notice of it. Even our host paid us no attention, though when I approached him, smiling, he seemed anxious that we should make ourselves free of whatever comfort his inn could offer.

Around the blazing fire in the huge, old-fashioned hearth a dozen grim-faced ruffians sat smoking—muleteers, beggars, peddlers. As we came in, soaked to our very bones, stiff with cold and dropping with fatigue, some of them moved away, either because they had had their fill of warmth, or, as I prefer to think, out of Christian charity, and my friends quickly occupied the empty places. In five minutes most of them were asleep in various picturesque attitudes, and Maquet was on the point of following their example when I advised him that we should be wiser to see to our supper.

Paul, still energetic in compensation for his carelessness, was walking up and down the staircase like a black shadow, skinning the hare as he did so, and ending up with the hare in one hand and its skin in the other.

"What is there for me to do?" asked Maquet. "I shall be asleep in five minutes unless I have a job."

"There are the birds to pluck," I replied, indicating the couple of dozen larks we had shot during the day, and he uttered a cry of distress. I did not know, until then, that Maquet has a horror of touching feathers, just as I myself cannot bear to touch velvet, but he heroically sat down beside me, shuddering visibly, repugnance adding such agility to his fingers that he worked more quickly than I, and in an hour the birds were ready.

Paul reappeared, empty-handed, and announced, "Gentlemen, your rooms are ready."

"Rooms?" I inquired, unable to believe my ears.

"Yes, sir. I found them for you," he replied, exuberant with self-satisfaction.

"Are they real rooms?"

"Well, more or less. You can dine in the one where I've lighted a good fire and put everything ready: flour, onions, a frying pan, a *manteca*. I did not venture to prepare potatoes, knowing that M. Giraud likes to do those himself . . ."

"Potatoes?" asked Giraud, wakened by the word. "Where? Look at these lazy fellows sleeping while we're doing all the work! Come along, Desbarolles! Wake up, Boulanger!"

"All right, Giraud," replied Boulanger, still half asleep. "Is supper ready?"

"Not quite," I replied, "but if you will follow us . . ."

"What about young Dumas?" asked Giraud.

"Let him go on sleeping."

"Alone, at the mercy of all these bandits? Come, you poor unfortunate, abandoned by your father! Come along!" and with Giraud's hand on his arm Alexandre, quite unaware of danger, followed the rest of us like a sleepwalker, up a steep staircase into the room where we were to dine. We were delighted to see a clear fire in the hearth, until, wondering why it was burning so fiercely, we realized that the draught from the window, which had no fastening and lacked two panes, was blowing hard enough to turn a windmill. Opposite the window a door with no lock and no bolts rattled in the icy blast coming from the mountain. Maquet stuffed the window with his cloak; Alexandre and Boulanger fell asleep in the chimney corner; Desbarolles, trying to seem awake, stayed on his feet, but walked on the birds that Maquet and I had plucked with such pains and placed on the floor on some white paper; Giraud decided that this time we would have potatoes baked in the ashes, and marched up and down the room attending to them.

Every time anyone shut the door, the window flew open; every time we closed the window, the door swung ajar as if drawn by suction, letting in all the air that had been cooling off in the corridor. Still, supper went on cooking, and soon we drew up to the table. Shall I try to describe to you the sort of room one is offered in this town of fifteen thousand inhabitants, a town that pompously calls itself "Royal Alcala"? There was a worm-eaten table; two or three wobbly chairs which we distrusted so thoroughly that we had benches brought up from the kitchen; two open doors, one leading to a corridor and the other to an attic; a window flapping with all the winds of heaven; a floor with wide gaps and a fowl house below, where cockerels, mistaking the light of our candles for the dawn, crowed vociferously, and clucking hens provided a sociable accompaniment to our conversation.

Our supper was none the less cheerful. Those sitting near the fire were roasted, those away from it were frozen, so Maquet set his chronometer on the table and every five minutes we all changed places, making sure of being cooked and chilled in equal portions. Having finished our meal, and refusing to sleep in the room where we had dined, we sent Paul to look for another room. He discovered a sort of dungeon with no windows and only one door (so we should at least escape draughts), and here he had collected every available mattress. There was no question of sheets or blankets, and perhaps it was just as well.

Going from our dining room to this dungeon we acquired a remarkable insight into the sleeping habits of Andalusians. On the stairs and in the corridors we stepped over peddlers, journeymen, muleteers, all scattered around, fast asleep in corners, or against walls, or flat on the floor. Less fussy than ourselves, they did not bother about a room, and our own arrangements seemed all the more acceptable by comparison.

We passed a better night than we might have expected. There is one thing in favor of these Spanish inns; their white-washed walls may seem stark, but the eye learns to appreciate their color, and, moreover, can instantly spot any insect likely to disturb a traveler's sleep. It goes without saying that the local insects get on better with local men, and I have never seen a Spanish mule driver disturbed by a native flea.

Weariness had given us a truly Castilian imperturbability, and we slept well until 5 o'clock in the morning, when our *arrieros* sternly roused us. In vain we argued that the day's journey should need only twelve hours, and that we need not arrive in Castro del Rio before nine in the evening. All they would reply was "*Vamos, señores, vamos, vamos!*" Time, that reveals all mysteries, may reveal this one, too.

Our mules seemed quite refreshed by their night's rest, and after replenishing our store of wine we started off once more, leaving it to Providence, that yesterday sent us the hare, to provide whatever else we might need.

⚜ ⚜ ⚜

25

Cordova

So we set off at five in the morning of Sunday, November 2nd. The storm had passed and the starlit sky was clear save for a few transparent clouds. The track we followed was almost indistinguishable from the scorched red earth of the plain that spread all around as far as we could see, and, our troubles of yesterday quite forgotten, we went forward lightheartedly. We saw the dawn begin to break beyond the mountain ridge, and as the rim of the sun rose the air was filled with the song of countless birds, from the partridge in her cleft of earth to the lark disappearing skyward in her vertical flight.

Only Alexandre's horse remained dejected, his eyes dull, his head drooping low as he lagged behind the mules, and though Alexandre managed to spur him on to take the lead, the muleteers, undeceived by this short burst of speed, shook their heads with foreboding. Seeing this gesture, I suggested to Alexandre that he might enjoy looking for some game, so he and Maquet dismounted and strode off with their guns.

"Don't stray far, *señores*," called the *arrieros*. "We must reach Castel del Rio by daylight." I had already inquired the reason for this urgency, and had been put off, so I did not ask again.

Nothing can give you any idea of these great Spanish plains, Madame. They seem to have been deserted since the dawn of creation, and for six hours we saw nothing but mountains, rocks, sand, and thistles. Though it was November, the heat was stifling, and every other minute we had recourse to the pitchers slung upon Paul's mule. Today, to avoid falling, he had persuaded the *arrieros* to tie him securely in place.

At about 11 o'clock we saw, on a little plateau, a line of five or six houses built at right angles to the road, opposite a fountain with a drinking trough. We took it for granted that we should halt here for a meal, and were amazed when the muleteers, having watered their mules, urged us on again with cries of "*Vamos!*" We flatly refused to go on until we had eaten, so we stopped before the most likely-looking house and sent Desbarolles to parley with the natives, that is, with the five or six men and women who stood at their doors gazing at us in amazement. Our burnous and traveling hoods called forth roars of derisive laughter. It seemed we were taken for monks, and I am certain that only the fact that we were obviously well-armed saved us from being pelted with stones, so fierce is the hatred that Spaniards feel at the moment for anything resembling the garb of a monk. When we inquired for an inn and some food they laughed even more scornfully, but eventually Desbarolles prevailed upon one woman to allow us to use her kitchen and cooking utensils, though victuals were quite out of the question.

We hoped our hunters had bagged some game, but they rejoined us empty-handed and starving. Boulanger, by dint of his utmost persuasiveness, managed to obtain a loaf and six eggs. Desbarolles hoped to find something to make a salad, but after three attempts had to give up. No one had ever heard of such a thing. Then Providence saved us again, and a herdsman in a pointed hat brought us another hare. Only the all-seeing eye of Providence could have discovered game in such a wilderness, and we did not cavil at the monotony. Maquet quickly hushed our cries of delight in case they should cause the price to rise, but Providence charged us the same as before, one *peseta.*

The hare was skinned, jointed, and cooked, while our muleteers boiled with impatience, declaring darkly that we should never reach Castel del Rio that night. At about 1 o'clock we set off again, and three hours later reached a small village where the *arrieros* drew up before an inn, assuring us that the mules were too tired to go any farther, so we had better stay there overnight. I expostulated, they offered unconvincing excuses, and I was beginning to take firm command when Paul glided up,

169

his open hands palm upward at shoulder level, asking for a word with me privately. He had overheard the muleteers talking together, and learned that they were fearful of passing through a certain *malo sitio*, a bad spot infested with the robbers that the knife-grinder had warned me about. By daylight, they felt brave enough to face it, but not at night. Juan and Antonio supported Paul's explanation with vigorous nods, so I called my friends together and discussed the position. All were eager for adventure, especially Alexandre, who exclaimed, "Oh, please, papa! Do show us some real bandits. I'll be such a good boy if you will!"

Questioning the men, I learned that it would take us three hours to reach the *malo sitio*, and that the moon would rise at 8 o'clock.

"Very good," I said, "we'll rest here for an hour or two, to give the moon plenty of time, and we will pass the *malo sitio* at nine." Desbarolles interpreted my orders to Juan and Antonio, whose jaws dropped in utter amazement at the mere idea of encountering brigands voluntarily, by moonlight, but I was *l'amo*, the boss, and they had no option.

Accordingly, we rested our mules and the tottering horse, ate an omelette, looked to our guns, and renewed their powder and shot, while the whole population stood watching our every movement and waved to us encouragingly as we departed.

26

Cordova

It was a delightful evening, the twilight closing peacefully around us as we rode forward, discussing animatedly, as artists will, the beauty of Nature, the work of great painters, the place of Art in Life. We had just crossed a torrent running swiftly between deep banks when our guides conferred together and brought us to a halt.

"There is the *malo sitio,*" said Juan, pointing out a dark stretch of road ahead of us, in the shadow of a wood. All conversation ceased, and in ten seconds everyone was armed.

"I'm ready," said Desbarolles, cocking his gun.

"You're always so rash," complained Giraud. "Now you cannot unload, and will have to fire, probably into our legs. You had better act as *avant-garde* and keep well in front."

"Quiet, gentlemen. Not a sound," begged the *arrieros*, and in silence we scrutinized the terrain. Never have I seen by moonlight a lovelier spot; to our left, on the higher bank of the silver stream, stood a low, thick wood, with here and there a tall tree rising above the rest; to our right lay the open plain; beneath our feet was a carpet of pine needles, and far away in the distance rose the outline of a mill. Nothing could have appeared less sinister, and we all felt more disposed to laugh than to tremble, but Juan and Antonio were trembling enough for the whole party. I glanced at Paul. Imperturbable as ever, he was sitting on his mule, securely lashed on top of the luggage, eating some bread wrapped around a joint of hare.

"Why not get down, Paul?" I asked.

"It would waste too much time, sir, to untie me and fasten me up again later. I'd rather stay where I am."

"But if the robbers fire on us, they might use you as a target."

"Oh, sir, they won't see me. I'm black!" and he laughed with that characteristic, silent merriment which expresses his delight in his own cleverness. So we left Paul happily ensconced and took up our own agreed positions.

Suddenly we heard a strange sound which set us shivering in spite of ourselves—an inhuman noise like nothing we could identify, except possibly the long cry of a man whose throat is being cut, but it lasted too long for that, and repeated its rise and fall every five seconds. Neither of us could explain it, and our *arrieros,* petrified with fright, could only stammer, "Let us turn back, sirs. For God's sake let us turn back!"

"Ah!" said Boulanger at last. "I know what it is! Good old Sancho Panza and Don Quixote! Immortal Cervantes! It's a *noria,* my friends. One of those immense water wheels that we've heard a hundred times. What fools we are!" We all burst out laughing, and this moment of fear gave place to complete self-assurance.

"Come along," said Giraud. "Pick up your muskets and march, left, right, left, left!" Our muleteers were stupefied at our hilarity, but although we seemed to be treating the matter jauntily, our plans were soundly conceived. Each of us was to walk with his mule between him and the wood, so that his body was adequately protected, and to some degree his legs also. We moved in single file sixty yards distant from the edge of the wood, Desbarolles in the lead, while the muleteers, bent double to shelter behind their mules, passed down the line enjoining us to preserve complete silence.

Possibly Alexandre misunderstood. At all events he started to shout at the top of his voice: *"Olé,* you bandits of Castel del Rio! Where are you?" The muleteers stopped dead, as though their feet had taken root.

"Now you've done it, my young friend!" said Maquet. "Still, they won't understand French. Come on, Desbarolles, try again in Spanish!" and Desbarolles repeated the challenge in the local dialect, while our muleteers were stunned by the realization that in that land of madmen, France, travelers actually invite robbers to attack them.

The robbers seemed equally stunned, and though we proceeded to hurl defiance at them till we reached the limit of the danger area, not a shot was fired at us, no bandit showed his face, no sound was heard except the shriek of the mill wheel, which grew more doleful as we drew nearer.

"It wasn't worth the fuss," said Alexandre, remounting his horse, which sagged visibly.

"Just a moment," Giraud exclaimed. "Desbarolles, fire your gun! No, it's no good saying you'll unload it. With you, that's more dangerous than firing it!" Several other voices gave the same advice, and Desbarolles sighed deeply as he brought the butt to his shoulder.

"You'll see how gentle his gun is," said Giraud to Alexandre. "A real lamb!"

Desbarolles pulled the trigger, and somersaulted backward. "*Sacré tonnerre!*" he muttered. "The wretched thing gets stiffer and stiffer." The shot went vertically, and a long streak of fire split the dark blue night, while the sound echoed and re-echoed like thunder among the mountains. Five or six dogs at the mill set up a furious barking, the miller and his men came out in force, so our *arrieros* went over to explain, while the rest of us continued on our way. Soon Juan and Antonio came galloping after us, crying that the bandits were still in the wood, and the night before had stolen a cow and two sheep from the miller. That was why he and his servants were keeping guard, and on hearing our shot had rushed out, thinking to repulse a new attack.

"They're taking their bandits very seriously," said Giraud. "I wonder whether they really are in the wood. Still, all men are happier with illusions," and with this axiom we resumed our march, while the barking of the dogs and the screeching of the mill wheel gradually died away behind us. So we came at last to Castro del Rio without mishap, and learned that the swift stream we had crossed near the *malo sitio* was the source of the great Guadalquivir, king of Spanish rivers.

❧ ❧ ❧

27

Cordova

If ever I come to Spain again, Madame, I shall have a team of donkeys, for they are much better than mules or horses, and far easier to feed. Spanish donkeys are the finest in the world, except perhaps in Arabia. Ever since the time of Cervantes (and Sancho Panza's love for Dapple), the Spaniards have been steadily improving the strain. I shall also bring a tent, so that I never need stay at even the best of Spanish inns, still less the sort of place we had to put up with at Castro del Rio. It is a pretty little town, charmingly situated, but best visited by day.

We rode out into a chill, misty dawn, through much the same country as before, rugged and desolate, with no sign of human habitation save that, now and then, from the top of a mountain the ruin of a feudal castle overlooked our path. I have noticed a curious thing about our mules. If they stumble, it is nearly always on a good road where they amble heedlessly along; when the going is rough they pick their path carefully, stiffen their legs, and become surprisingly sure-footed. But it was otherwise with Alexandre's wretched horse, which seemed so near collapse that in two or three particularly rocky places I urged my son to go on foot. But you know Alexandre, Madame, and his deference in obeying my fatherly advice. He stayed in the saddle, but before long I heard a sudden disturbance, shouts, oaths, and on turning saw that Acca had fallen into a boggy cleft. With great difficulty he was dragged out again, and stood panting, his legs trembling under him, so instead of mounting again Alexandre took his gun to hunt what game he could find, and I went with him. There was no great need, however, for we should arrive at Cordova soon after midday, and we had with us a supply of bread, wine, and chocolate.

Once when I went to the mule bearing these stores I noticed it was coughing violently, and drops of blood were falling from its mouth, so I called one of the muleteers, who understood at once what was the matter, and called Juan to help him. One of them opened the animal's mouth, and the other thrust his arm into its gullet and pulled out a leech. Then he pulled out another, whereupon the mule stopped coughing, though more drops of blood fell. Juan explained to me that all the springs, brooks, and rivers of Andalusia are full of tiny leeches, as fine as a hair, which are swallowed when an animal, or a man, drinks the water. They attach themselves wherever they can, and then grow to full size, to the great discomfort of their involuntary host. One way of avoiding them is to strain all drinking water through a handkerchief. Paul says that a much better way is to drink nothing but wine.

The heat became stifling as we rode on for another three hours, anxiously looking out for Cordova, which we should have reached by noon, but it was after 2 o'clock when at last we caught our first glimpse of our longed-for goal. There are towns one dreams for a lifetime of visiting—Athens, Rome, Constantinople, Granada, Cordova—yet when one actually arrives the romantic illusion vanishes, and one sighs, "Is that really the place?"

Cordova, in spite of its position on the last slopes of the Sierra Morena, beside the Guadalquivir, under a Moorish sun, lacks dignity. It is a mass of houses with no shade, no gardens, no monuments except its cathedral. One's first sight of cities, as of men, can be deceptive, and it is true that, like all good things, Cordova improved on acquaintance, as you shall hear later, but it is equally true that when we saw it from the ridge we were disappointed. After a moment's pause, with the sun beating straight down upon our heads, we started off again, but an incident brought us to a halt. Acca refused to move, despite all the urging of the *arrieros*. Slowly he sank to his knees, gathered his hind legs under him, stretched out his head with his mouth open and his tongue hanging, sighed deeply and lay down, so that Alexandre found himself standing. In sight of his journey's end the old horse had died. The muleteers shrugged significantly, but without surprise; they took off his saddle, loaded it on a baggage mule, and left him to the crows, deeming even his hide worthless.

"Ah, well!" said Alexandre, philosophically, "I shall at least know what to be at. All the time I had that horse I was constantly having to walk. I was like the dragoons, never knowing whether I was in the cavalry or the infantry. Now the point is settled."

Cordova was still some distance off, but after covering several miles we found ourselves on the bank of the Guadalquivir, which at this point was as broad as the Marne, where, to our surprise, we found not a bridge, but a ferry. The bridge at Cordova is as famous as the one at Toledo, so I turned to our guides for an explanation, and learned that the charge for our party would be about three francs cheaper by the ferry than by the bridge. To save that paltry sum they had brought us a league farther around. Their intention was good, but the road to Hell is paved with good intentions. For the past two hours we had been dying of thirst, promising ourselves that, having crossed the whole of Spain to find a river containing water, as soon as we reached the bank we could drink our fill, now that we knew how to cope with the leeches. What a mistake!

When we got there we found that between the banks of the Guadalquivir rolled a flood, not of water, but of liquid mud with the color and the consistency, if not the taste, of milk chocolate. We stood scratching our ears for a moment in perplexity and disappointment, then we piled into the ferryboat with the dogs, horses, and mules of another caravan that the ferrymen had forced to wait for ten minutes until we arrived to complete the load. After a moment of confusion we cast off, feeling as though we were in the Ark, except that we lacked any females of our species, and five minutes later found ourselves on the opposite bank, in a pleasant little olive grove. Above the trees we could see the arrow of the steeple of Cordova cathedral, so we walked in that direction, leaving the

176

arrieros to settle with the ferrymen and follow on behind. Paul was still perched on the luggage. Ever since he had the idea of being tied on top of our trunks, his serenity has been complete. There he sits cross-legged in the blazing sun, looking like one of those divinities that travelers bring back from India to present to museums.

Still longing for water, we came to a house encircled with a canopy of trelliswork that cast on it a lovely blue shadow. At any other time we should instantly have sketched it, but now we rushed to knock on every door and window crying: "*Agua! agua!*" The house was deserted, or the inhabitants had all died of thirst (we never found out which), so we continued on our way. Some of us chewed vine leaves, for the grapes had all been harvested. Others tried to eat fresh olives. May God show them mercy in the next world, for they certainly suffered in this! At last we found a shady path that led to a plain, and beyond stood the ancient Moorish wall that still girds this town of the Caliphs, its gateway an arched tunnel that looked cool, being in shadow.

Outside the gateway stood a covered stall crowded with hordes of children, a few men and women among them. As we approached, armed and travel-stained, they all took fright and fled screaming, leaving only the proprietress, who stood her ground with that calm composure in the face of invasion which belongs only to a beautiful woman, or one exceedingly plain. Our heroine was certainly plain and seemed resigned to any eventuality, but Desbarolles explained politely that our greatest ambition at the moment was to buy the watermelons with which her stall was loaded.

Ah, Madame, you should have seen us enjoying those melons! We had each eaten three or four by the time our caravan caught up with us. While Paul was still some distance away we saw, to our surprise, that he was sucking something with great gusto, and as he approached we realized it was a huge melon. He had bought it for a trifling sum from the party that crossed the ferry with us. Ours were half the size and twice

177

the price, but when we pointed this out to the vendor she retorted scornfully that Paul's melon was secondhand. Note, Madame, that without disturbing himself at all Paul had managed to quench his thirst half an hour before we could, and at a fraction of the cost. But, there, he is a member of a privileged race.

Rested and refreshed, we walked on toward the gate, growing somewhat perturbed as Giraud and Desbarolles warned us that the Customs Office at Cordova was known as the harshest in all Spain.

"That will take a good two hours," said Alexandre.

"Our simplest plan," said I, "will be to let Paul have our keys and remain with our baggage. We will go on to the *hôtel de la Poste*, recommended to us in Granada, and the luggage can follow later." So we went up to the gate and passed through.

Inside, a crowd stood waiting for us. The fugitives from the melon stall had announced our coming, and, diversions being rare in Cordova, curious sightseers had gathered from all over the town. We showed our passports at the office of the *Civil Garde*, while our baggage mules halted at the Customs House directly opposite. The officer in charge took one look at my passport, barely glanced at those of my companions, bowed ceremoniously, and waved us through.

"Pass, gentlemen," he said. "We have been expecting you. We knew that M. Alexandre Dumas was in Spain, and felt certain he would not leave without visiting our town."

I thanked him cordially, and as we went on I noticed our mules following close behind.

"Paul!" I cried. "What about the Customs Office?"

"Oh, sir," he replied, "the officer saw your name on the trunks, asked me if you were the author of *Monte Cristo*, and then said 'Very good! You may pass!'"

"Without searching our luggage?"

"Without even opening anything."

I retraced my steps and thanked the customs officer as I had already thanked the officer of the guard. I should be diffident about telling you of this incident if my five companions had not been with me to witness it. Do you know anyone more polite and more literary than the soldiers and customs officers of Cordova? A quarter of an hour after this triumph we entered the *hôtel de la Poste*.

28

Cordova

After such a journey our first cry was for baths, but we might as well have talked in Hebrew. To bathe is not unheard of in Cordova, but bathtubs are completely unknown. In some places there exist huge jars, like those used by Ali Baba's forty thieves, and when anyone insists on taking a bath, such a jar is half-filled with water. One gets in by climbing up and then down a double ladder, crouches down until only his head protrudes through the neck of the jar, and then can proceed to wash without interrupting his conversation.

Unfortunately, there were no such jars in the hotel, and we had to make do with great earthenware dishes in which we looked like tritons splashing about in seashells. We were still occupied with our ablutions when two visitors called to see me to offer any service in their power. The first, M. Martial de la Torre, was profoundly shocked at the state in which he found us, and fled with all speed. The second, a French professor named M. Eugène Perez, less modest or more familiar with personal cleanliness, stayed and talked to us while we dressed. We had gained a poor impression of Cordova, with its narrow, dirty streets; its houses low, gray (an unusual color in Spain), and barred from top to bottom like prisons; its cobblestones painfully sharp to the feet; all dominated by the only building of importance, the cathedral. M. Perez assured us we should become used to the cobbles, and behind those bars such lovely eyes would shine for us that we should come to like Cordova. (The town, possibly, I think, but never the bars.) Perez will spend all his time with us, except for the two or three hours daily he spends in the college. As for his private pupils, we will all help him teach them. It will enable us to visit their homes, and find out what conditions are like behind the bars we dislike so much.

We are very comfortably installed in this hotel, Madame, with a drawing room as well as our bedrooms. There are, of course, no fireplaces, but the sun still provides ample warmth in November, and outside our windows is a great orange tree that fills our rooms with perfume. One thing that pleases us all is that the chef is French, for if my companions are not tired of my cooking, I am certainly tired of having to do it. Having bathed and changed our clothes, we went down at 6 o'clock for dinner, which proved to be quite a good meal. Even in Paris it would have been tolerable.

In view of the hard usage our guns had received on our journey, we arranged for a gunsmith to attend to them, and they were all stacked in the *patio* ready for him to collect. Word of this had spread, and when we went down, all the marksmen in Cordova were in the *patio* examining our weapons, passing them from hand to hand, loading and unloading, trying the springs, testing the balance, fingering the triggers, all so engrossed in their study that they were not disturbed in the slightest as we passed through their midst and took our places at table. We sat at one end of a long communal board which, except for us, was empty, the general hour for dinner being 1 o'clock. Soon, however, several of the men who had been examining our guns came and sat down, giving us a friendly smile but keeping at a certain distance, not even calling for the smallest refreshment to excuse their presence.

While we were dining an Arab came in, selling scarves. He really was an Arab (I had him questioned by Eau-de-Benjoin), but his scarves were Spanish. They were not particularly attractive, and I could see a much nicer one around the waist of a man sitting at our table, so I pointed to it and asked if he had one like that. He had not, but the owner of the scarf immediately rose, took it off, and ceremoniously offered it to me as a gift. I declined, for I knew how readily Spaniards offer you anything of theirs which you admire, but Perez whispered in my ear that the owner would feel insulted at a refusal, so, as he repeated his offer, I accepted, adding jokingly to Perez that, since it would not go with the rest of my clothes, I should have to get a new coat, waistcoat, shirt, and trousers.

Immediately a young man of about my own build offered me his jacket, assuring me he had put it on for the first time only an hour or so ago. I let him see my embarrassment, but he begged me in excellent French to take it. He had lived in Paris and knew me well, he said, though I did not know him, and he would be honored by my acceptance. Another man implored me to accept his waistcoat.

"This is most awkward," said I to Perez. "They'll be offering me a pair of breeches next."

"In that case it would be excusable to decline."

I turned to the men who stood waiting, each with his offering in his hand, and said: "Upon my word, gentlemen, I will accept your gifts, for this is a singular occasion. You must let me know your names so that I can thank you personally. Now, if you will wait a few moments, you shall see what use I make of your presents."

I went out to buy a hat, and since I had already bought breeches and leggings in Madrid I returned in ten minutes in complete Andalusian dress, to receive a vociferous welcome. In my absence Giraud had produced a sketch of the incident, with my three new friends putting on me the gifts I had accepted, while in the background a fourth man was hurriedly divesting himself of the garment I had declined. The resemblance was remarkable and we all drew lots for this little *chef-d'oeuvre*, which was won by Juan Paroldo, the man who gave me his jacket. The whole evening, impromptu and in unexpected company, could not have been more enjoyable.

At 10 o'clock, however, all the company rose to depart, and when I tried to dissuade them, Perez whispered that it would be wise to let them go. They were on their way to *pelar la pava*, which means "to pluck the goose," a term I will explain, begging your indulgence for my Spanish friends. You recall those barred windows, those balconies I spoke of earlier with their closely woven grilles? On moonlight nights the young men stand wrapped in their cloaks in the darkness (for the streets are so narrow that the moonbeams cannot reach the ground) and wait for their fair ladies to appear at these balconies. If his loved one lives on the ground floor the lucky swain may have the joy of kissing a tiny hand slipped through the bars; if her balcony is on the first floor her lover can only gaze in adoration, unless he has a rope ladder or can climb on the shoulders of a friend to blow a kiss through the bars. This form of courtship is carried on much more earnestly than one would imagine from the term used to describe it. The streets of Cordova are more thronged at night than in the daytime, and everywhere is the sound of soft whispers, gentle kisses, sighs from fond hearts. If it is happiness to love one's neighbor, Cordova must be the happiest place on earth.

29

Cordova

The next day, Madame, we set out to explore the town with our new friends, Perez and Paroldo, carrying our sketchbooks and crayons. First we visited the only mosque that survived the earthquake of 1589, and admired its great courtyard girt around with palms and cypresses, lemon and orange trees now loaded with ripe fruit, and the marble basin at its center, where a fountain played unceasingly to cool the air. When we entered, the full rays of the sun were shining on the wall facing the door of the mosque, and here Spaniards were lounging and smoking in complete relaxation, watching velvety-brown children paddling around the basin, listening to the song of countless birds. Everywhere outside was melody, perfume, sunshine, but as we passed inside we found a strange contrast.

Have you ever, in a dream, Madame, found yourself in an immense building whose vaulted roof rested on thousands of slender columns; where the dim, cool shades were pierced here and there by faint sunbeams falling to rest on the flagstones; where unknown figures glided in and out like ghosts through unseen doors? So it was with us as we stood inside the threshold, feasting our eyes on sculptured figures of Christ, the Virgin, or one of the apostles, or on some vast golden mosaic bearing a page of the Koran, bruising our knees on the marble tomb of some Arab chief. The temple encloses a seemingly infinite space, with nineteen naves, each three hundred and fifty feet long and forty feet wide, running from north to south, and nineteen others running from east to west, all defined by columns of jasper or of lustrous marble gleaming red, yellow, or blue, creating a different effect according to which of the six doors the visitor has entered. On one of these columns is a little iron grille where a lamp shines upon an inlaid figure of Christ on the cross. The story goes that, in the time of the Moors, a Christian slave was chained to this pillar, and, with no tool but his fingernail he created this mosaic as an act of devotion.

In the midst rises a great chapel, built there in 1528 despite the opposition of the town, for though the chapel, in itself, does not lack beauty, to build it many of the columns of the mosque were removed or encased in stonework. As Christians we cannot regret the rise of Christianity, but as artists we grieve that the mosque was defaced in this way, instead of being preserved as a monument unique in Europe. Cordova, for the rest, having cast off the turban, was not content with a

Christian halo but aspired to a martyr's crown by waging fanatical warfare against the Moorish religion, until such crusades were forbidden by a special council of bishops.

Leaving the mosque, we visited the Circus, one of the smallest in Andalusia, and the most renowned for bullfights, for the smaller the ring, the greater the danger, and the more enjoyment for the spectators. On this occasion it was quiet and empty, but still a pretty, gaily painted little place. Then Perez suggested taking us to see the ruins of a fabulously beautiful retreat, almost a city in itself, built by Abd-Er-Rhaman II for his favorite, the lovely Zehra, but it was two miles outside Cordova, at the foot of the mountains, and we preferred to return to our hotel for dinner.

Perez and Paroldo were our guests, and the conversation at table turned to the weapons that the gunsmith had just returned to us. Alexandre exclaimed that ever since he came to Spain he had found nothing more exciting to shoot than birds. Was the wild boar of the Sierra Morena nothing but a myth? If it really existed, would it not be possible to go hunting for it in those mountains? Perez, Paroldo, and some of their friends who had joined us looked at each other questioningly, and then inquired if we were seriously interested in Alexandre's suggestion. Six of us assured him in chorus; Desbarolles' voice shook with excitement; and Alexandre urged that we should make all arrangements at once.

"Then I see no difficulty," said Paroldo, "though the Sierra is not always safe to cross."

"Some of your little bandits?" I inquired. "We're always hearing about them!"

"Hum!" returned Paroldo. "I've been held up by them myself, in the Sierra."

"And I!" broke in several Spaniards sitting at our table.

"Listen," Paroldo continued. "You are our hosts, and we can vouch for you. I think I might find a way to manage it. Perhaps we could engage them as beaters."

"Who? The robbers?"

"Aha!" smiled he. "I have not specifically stated that there

184

are any robbers. But leave it with me. Go to bed, sleep well, while we go to the casino, try to contact our friends, and arrange everything. Tomorrow morning we will tell you whether we have been successful."

30

❧ ❧ ❧

Cordova, 7th November

There has been a gap of three long days since my last letter, Madame, and you must feel sure something extraordinary has been happening down here, beyond the Pyrenees. Indeed it has. We have just come down from the highest peaks of the Sierra Morena after an experience no traveler has ever had before, for we spent three days in close and friendly contact with the men who dwell on these mountains.

We arose early on the morning after my last letter, and learned that Paroldo had indeed sent a messenger to the sierra, but it would take at least twenty-four hours to receive a reply and make the necessary arrangements. Much would depend on whether I was known to the outlaws, as I had been to the civil guards and the customs officer at Cordova. When men take the desperate step of going to live in the Sierra Morena, it is because of a strong urge to cut themselves off from civilization. In this lonely mountain range there are no bookshops or public reading rooms, and it would be quite understandable if people living there had never read *The Three Musketeers* or *Monte Cristo*.

We devoted the day to helping Perez teach French to some of his private pupils, and visiting some of the finest houses in the town with Paroldo, who is well known in Cordova society.

Everywhere we received a frank and friendly welcome, and I noticed none of that hatred said to exist between our nations —which, indeed, I have found only among the lower classes.

I knew that among Cordova's historical relics was Seneca's house. Seneca was not a great tragic writer, but Rome had no one to surpass him, and in his poem *Medea* he foretold the discovery of America, so I felt I would like to see his house. Every time I mentioned this to Perez, Paroldo, and Hernandez (a third friend who joined us), they began to laugh, but when I persisted with all the obstinacy of a tourist, Perez finally said: "Very well. We will take you there tonight."

"Why tonight? Isn't it open in the daytime?"

"Oh, yes. It is open all the time, but we prefer not to be seen visiting it. If, however, you really insist . . ."

"Why not? Our purpose in traveling is to study the customs of the places we visit, and the customs one can observe at night may be none the less interesting, though travelers never seem to talk about them."

Perhaps I should tell you of an experience we had at Granada, which had given us some insight into customs of the latter type, and I feel less hesitation in mentioning it since we emerged from it, as from similar ordeals in Spain and Africa, as chaste as Joseph. One evening we were exploring Granada by moonlight when we lost our way, and called to inquire at a house where a light was burning. The woman who opened the door, possibly failing to understand our imperfect Spanish, led us into a little room which she called the *salon*, but which in France would have been considered a garret.

The walls were whitewashed, and the furniture consisted simply of a couch of woven straw spread with a cotton coverlet, and four straw-seated chairs. Here we remained for a quarter of an hour undisturbed, and then there entered a princess for each prince in our party. In describing them, I would give them credit for retaining simplicity among the virtues they still possessed. Some, in my opinion the most elegant, wore their national costume of a mantilla, brightly embroidered swirling petticoats, and a fan. A high, tortoise-shell comb held up the mantilla, and in front of it lay a rose, real or artificial, whose deep red color shone like a flame through the delicate black lace. The others were dressed in a French style, with a simple muslin dress, a little shawl over their shoulders, and upon their heads a small bonnet or hat. Perhaps these would be considered more elegant than the others, in Spain.

A detail you would not know, Madame, is that in France such gay ladies live in the caravanseries where travelers are entertained. It is different in Spain. Princesses live in their own family circle, and, just as kings' daughters of old filled their time with needlework, so these spend their days in dressmaking, working at artificial flowers, or sewing the gold and silver spangled embroideries worn by Andalusian dancers. Only, since all these activities are very trying to the eyes, in the evenings they adopt another profession in which they merely risk their souls, more easily spared than their sight. This profession, in Spain, is not regarded with the social prejudice it evokes in France, and the princesses I spoke of continue to mix sociably with their acquaintances and enjoy the company of their friends. No one calls them to account for their activities between 6 P.M. and midnight. Besides, who would have any right to? They never go out alone. Always their father, their mother, or their brother accompanies them. True, these escorts remain outside the threshold, but they are there, and who would dare call a girl's behavior into question with her father or mother so close by? Indeed, these Spanish princesses have excellent manners. They enter a room quietly and sedately, seat themselves without saying a word, and wait for their visiting prince to engage them in conversation—to woo them, in fact! I do not say this wooing is as protracted or as decorous as the courtships conducted through the latticed grilles I spoke of earlier, but, at least, appearances are preserved. By and by a lady rises, takes her escort's arm for a turn or two around the garden, or up and down the room; they vanish for a while, re-appearing so calm and unruffled that you might well imagine they had spent their time studying astronomy or a chapter of *Don Quixote*. Never can the evening degenerate into an orgy, for there is no question of eating or drinking, and at 10 o'clock the princess prepares to depart, explaining that her mother or her brother has been waiting to escort her home, and cannot be detained any longer. She rises, graciously allows you to kiss her forehead, sweeps you a curtsey, and withdraws. Tomorrow, should you wish, you may see her here again, subject to the same conventions, but if you attempted to visit her home you would be indignantly rebuffed, or taken for a drunkard who had mistaken his door. Incidentally, I might add that during all the time we were in Spain we saw only one drunken man, and then the whole population was following him to observe the phenomenon.

Seneca's house, which we visited that evening, had nothing fresh to offer, except, perhaps, to a student of archeology. I cannot even tell you where it was, for the night was dark, with driving rain. We went through a wide gateway into a courtyard, a kind of garden, surrounded by walls that seemed to me of Roman construction, but these walls, and the mistress of the house, were the only relics of antiquity I noticed. One quite true-to-life detail complicated the occasion with an unfortunate embarrassment. We had had what seemed the good idea of going first into a nearby café and ordering a bowl of punch to be prepared to our instructions and brought to us at Seneca's house. Unfortunately, the waiter who carried it in to us from the café, doubtless a king's son in disguise, turned out to be the sweetheart of the prettiest of our princesses, so we did not prolong our stay.

Before closing this letter, Madame, I will add that during the evening Paroldo's messenger returned with the message that we were expected in the Sierra Morena next day. We were eager to make preparations at once, but our friends declared they would see to all the arrangements, and our mounts would be waiting outside our hotel at 4 o'clock in the morning.

31

Cordova

At 4 o'clock we were awakened by the noisy arrival of a cavalcade of mules, donkeys, and drivers beneath our windows. Instantly we were afoot, and were fastening the last buckle of our gaiters as Paroldo came into our room, looking splendid in the rather ostentatious costume of an Andalusian *majo:* short jacket, tasseled hat, wide breeches, and elegant gaiters, all worn with a delightful air. Giraud and Boulanger longed to paint his portrait then and there but were overruled, though before we went down Giraud dashed off a quick sketch of Paroldo lighting his cigar.

Torches flickered in the paved courtyard and around the huge fruit-laden orange tree in the garden, showing us the waiting donkeys, each bearing a brightly striped but tattered rug; the muleteers and guides swathed in their cloaks, their heads bound with gaudy handkerchiefs, their legs bare, their feet thrust into sandals like those of their Arab forefathers. Near the gateway were our two leading huntsmen, Ravez and Count Hernandez of Cordova, riding sturdy, deep-chested Andalusian horses which they placed at my disposal, but I preferred to accept Paroldo's offer of his own personal mount, a magnificent white ass with a regal bearing, and a proud twitch to her ears. Someone had found a saddle and stirrups for Boulanger, the rest of us bestrode our mules or donkeys barebacked except for a rough blanket, and we moved off into the darkness, a compact group with the horsemen and myself in the lead.

You may recall, Madame, that the mules we hired in Granada wore halters. The donkeys of Cordova are less sophisticated and wear no harness at all. The rider does not sit on the animal's back in the usual way, but on his rump, which gives a broader seat, and steers him with a long white stick, hitting his right ear to make him turn left, and his left ear to turn right. To go forward one belabors him at the rear. These simple methods of control work very well and the donkey makes good headway, throwing his rider no oftener than once every two or three miles. Even that presents no difficulty, for, the moment he is unburdened, the ass stops to crop the nearest thistle and so is easily caught and remounted.

Here and there along the road to the mountains, men on horseback came across fields or along bypaths to join our party, some in the national costume of Andalusia, heavily embroidered jackets and breeches; some wearing velvet-trimmed leather coats and trousers, the traditional hunting dress of Cordovans; others, apparently from La Mancha, clad in sheepskin with the fleece turned outward, and a foxskin cap. Each had a gun slung behind his saddle and, thrust through his belt, a long dagger with a horn handle, shaped to fit inside the gun barrel and serve as a bayonet. All of them wore one of those voluminous traveling cloaks peculiar to Cordova, made of a rusty-gray blanket with a yellow and red border and a central hole through which the wearer's head passes. Some wearers have the luxury of a button and buttonhole at the opening, but generally the hole itself suffices. All these newcomers, young men from the neighborhood, were introduced to us as they arrived, and by the time we reached the first slopes our party had increased to fifteen, not counting Eau-de-Benjoin, who had secured the quietest and sturdiest ass and assumed command of the mules laden with provisions.

As the eastern sky lightened with the coming dawn, we were climbing the first slopes of the Sierra, where the faint path, narrow and rock-strewn, skirted precipices two thousand feet deep. To our left rose frequent crosses bearing inscriptions—so many that at last I asked Paroldo what they were.

"Go and read the next one," he replied.

It bore the date August, 1845—only a year or so ago—and

the words, in Spanish, "On this spot Count Roderigo de Torrejas was assassinated. As you pass by, pray for his soul." Ten yards away was another inscription nailed to a tree and surmounted with a wooden cross; "On this spot, on the same day, his son, Hernandez de Torrejas, was murdered. Pray for his soul, too." Before us and behind, as far as our eyes could see, similar crosses stood in an endless line.

Calling my friends together, I said, "Gentlemen, this is much more definite than the *malo sitio* of Castro del Rio. Are our guns ready? I should be sorry to leave behind this sort of record of our visit."

"Don't worry," replied Paroldo, "the bandits aren't on this side of the mountains today. Besides," he added, laughing, "even if they were, we are vouched for, and shall be safe enough."

When I am told anything by someone who should know, I believe it unquestioningly, so I slung my gun over my shoulder again and cried: "Very good! Come along, then!" The Spaniards of the party, passing all these crosses without a second thought, were already so far ahead that we had to trot to catch up with them, but my friends and I, if not alarmed, were so depressed by the sight that we tried to concentrate our attention upon the vast panorama, more magnificent than anything we had yet seen.

Beyond the precipice yawning at our feet, beyond the granite spurs of the Sierra, lay the tawny plain, broken by silver-gray olive plantations, with Cordova sharply etched into light and shadow by the first rays of the rising sun. The Guadalquivir shone like a river of flame, its farther bank marking the edge of the desert we had crossed so recently in raging thirst, while the mountain ranges lying toward Granada, seen from our present height, seemed no more than gentle hills, now veiled in a lavender mist.

As we took the road again, still climbing, the Sierra engulfed us. Here there are few large trees, and the tallest forests are merely thickets eight or ten feet high, covering the ground like a series of green waves. The bushes bear a fruit that looks like a large round strawberry, called in Spanish *madrono*. We crossed a plateau, plunged into ravines, and scaled their farther slopes, coming at last to a shady valley shut in by mountain peaks, the first lush verdure we had seen since leaving Granada. Paroldo urged his mule alongside mine, and remarked: "This is where the brigands held me up, four years ago."

"And was that cross already there then?" I asked, pointing to an impressive memorial standing near the path.

"Yes, and I assure you it made the matter seem all the more serious."

"And it cost you . . . ?"

"Everything we had with us. Fortunately, we were traveling light and were not held to ransom."

The path led on to an open space encircled by *maquis*, to borrow the Corsican term, and dominated by a hill that was itself crowned by a great dwelling like a fortress. In the midst of this clearing an abundant spring flowed into a trough, and around it stood thirty armed men with fifty hounds coupled in leash. They were an impressive sight, especially when we thought of all the crosses marking their handiwork, but for today these brigands were our huntsmen, standing hat in hand to receive us.

Ravez rode on ahead to exchange a few words with a middle-aged sentinel stationed between the bandits and ourselves, then signed to us to come forward. Our welcome, though courteous, was somewhat reserved, and to infuse a more friendly warmth I suggested we should begin by enjoying a meal together, an idea that was very well received, though Paroldo quietly advised that everyone should drink sparingly since we were soon to use guns. The word *déjeuner* had broken the ice, cloaks were spread out on the ground, and under Paul's direction our provisions were arranged upon them, poultry, pasties, olives, and goatskins bulging with the light wines of Montilla. The bandits, for their part, were well provided with haunches of venison and smoked hams of wild boar, the natural products of this mountain region, and a store of wines from Malaga and Xérès, the fruits of their intercourse with smugglers.

As Paul carried across my box of cutlery, Paroldo whispered to me: "Surely you haven't brought your table silver?"

"Certainly I have. Why not? I take it we are in good company?"

"Yes . . . yes indeed, but with such a crowd . . . ?"

"My friend, I wager there won't even be one little spoon missing."

"Oh! Then I'll say no more. Such odd things seem to happen nowadays!" said he, sharing a laugh with Hernandez and Ravez.

"Paul," I cried, "put all the knives and forks in a pile on one of the cloaks, so that anyone who prefers not to eat with his fingers can help himself."

"Very good, sir. But am I to be held responsible . . . ?"

"No, Paul. As long as we are in the mountains you need not answer for anything."

My trustfulness created an excellent impression among our new friends, who grew more cordial, and we all set to with zest, for the mountain air gives one a tremendous appetite. The hounds, tied to trees at the edge of the clearing, strained fiercely at the leash, their blazing eyes fixed upon us as though they would have devoured us as readily as our repast. A few loaves were divided sparingly among those terrifying, half-wild creatures to sustain their strength without dulling their hunger, for such hounds hunt to satisfy themselves, not their masters.

Before we had eaten our fill, the brigand who had acted as sentinel when we arrived, and whom we had at once christened Leatherstocking,* warned us that the sun was climbing rapidly and the first *battue* was a good hour's march farther on. Accordingly, we packed the remainder of our provisions, Paul tied the chest of silver, all complete, upon his donkey, and we

* The novels of Fenimore Cooper were widely read in France at this period, and of all his characters Leatherstocking was the most popular.

set off again, striking deeper into the mountains, while our thirty huntsmen marched in single file to left and right of us, the howling pack at their heels.

32

✤ ✤ ✤

Cordova

An hour later we halted at the foot of a great peak shaped like a broad-based sugar loaf, rising fifteen hundred feet above us and covered by a mass of four-foot-high shrubs. We were to encircle the base of the mountain while our new companions climbed the peak and drove in our direction whatever game they found. We watched our beaters climb with the firm, unhurried tread of true mountaineers until at length they gained the summit, hailed us and waved their guns, let slip their hunting dogs, and began the descent. We were stationed at intervals and given instructions not to make a sound; not to shoot at any small game such as partridges or rabbits; and particularly not to fire in any direction except straight ahead, for the huntsmen concealed in the thickets to left and right of us must not be wounded, even by noble strangers. Each of us crouched in his appointed place, and was not to leave it until it was time for a general rally.

In view of the probable danger I offered Alexandre a good deal of prudent advice, but he paid little attention and wandered off with Paul, which surprised me somewhat, though later in the day I learned why. Boulanger had brought nothing except his album and pencils, and seldom have I seen anyone more astounded than our guides when they realized his intention was to sketch, not shoot, whatever wild creatures came his way. He is completely oblivious of danger, and I took the precaution of keeping him as near to me as possible. Desbarolles, whose weapon we all mistrusted, had been given one of the distant butts, and for some time I watched his Andalusian hat and the gleam of his gun barrel above the bushes until they vanished, and I imagined him settled in place. Ten minutes later I caught sight of a little black spot and a sparkling pinpoint almost on the horizon. It was poor Desbarolles. Every time he approached a butt he was urged to go farther on!

For us all, nothing could have been finer or more novel than the opening of this hunt. Once in our agreed positions, we lopped the upper branches of the surrounding bushes with our hunting knives, spread them on the ground, and lay comfortably on this improvised bed, awaiting a signal of some sort and savoring the unfamiliar perfumes that filled the air. All around us in the sunshine, to the very sky line, spread the silence and solitude of the age-old *maquis*, where our brief passage would tomorrow be forgotten. This mountain, so often disquieted by the screams of dying men, bearing among its trees and shadows the proofs of so many murders, covered everything with its own eternal silence, its pitiless serenity. I mused upon the insignificance, the insolence, of man-made noises in the face of God's great silence; I longed to live here, filling my lungs with this pure air, gazing every day at this vast prospect bare of human life, like St. Augustine, Madeleine, or St. Jerome, those saints chosen by the Lord and suddenly imbued with a yearning for solitude.

Not only my bodily eyes, but also the eyes of my mind, had lost all sight of the Paris we left a short month ago, and to me it seemed impossible that even beyond the horizon there could be anything other than what I now saw. Suddenly the sound of a gunshot brought me out of my reverie. The poet vanished. Only the hunter remained, and I leaped for the carbine at my feet, my eyes and thoughts fixed only on the little puff of blue smoke rising to my left, in Alexandre's direction. I took cover and waited.

"Is it the fearsome boar or the timid stag?" whispered Boulanger, who came across a volume of Delille two or three days ago and has been quoting phrases from it ever since.

"Quiet!" I returned, and he went on sketching in silence. Hearing no more and seeing nothing, I sat down again, and then caught a slight sound, faint as the rustle of silk, between the branches. There before me stood a hind, her ears pricked to catch a hint of counsel from the wind. She was out of range, and, besides, I have an aversion to firing at a stationary creature. For me, hunting must seem like a battle, and it would be inexcusable to shoot a deer standing mildly at gaze. The only contest then is one of generosity between man and animal, and though my pride as a hunter is strong, I have often, when no one else was by, allowed a roe to pass unharmed.

"It is the timid deer," said I to Boulanger. "Look!"

He took up his field glasses to supplement his spectacles, gazed at her beauty in silence and then remarked: "May we enjoy a feast of her tender flesh tonight!"

The deer, catching some unwonted sound, bounded up the hill on my right, slipped through a sunbeam like a shadow, and vanished. A minute later, another shot woke the echoes, and the hind fell dead. We should find no further sport here, and in response to a rallying cry we rose from our hiding places and gathered to learn details of our next move. In the distance I could see Desbarolles coming slowly forward to join us, but on looking over the group by my side I grew increasingly anxious. Paul was missing. In view of his color I had, from the start, been worried lest someone might mistake him for a wild boar. Still more disturbing, Alexandre was missing too. Probably, I thought, they are together somewhere, and at the top of my voice I shouted "Alexandre! Paul!" but my call died away over the mountain with no response.

"What the devil is the matter with you?" asked Boulanger.

"I'm getting anxious," I replied. "We heard two shots, but we only know where the second one went."

"You're crazy," retorted Boulanger. "Alexandre is somewhere on the mountainside—climbing, probably—and has not heard you. That's all!"

"Let's go and find out," said I, starting off in the direction my son had taken, constantly calling his name as I went, while my friends followed my example, and French or Spanish voices shouted "Alexandre" or "Alexandro" until the whole mountain re-echoed. At last we reached the place allotted to them for the hunt, and there lay Alexandre, stretched at full length on a very comfortable bed of branches, so deep in sleep that even the noise we had made had not disturbed him. There, too, lay Paul, flat on his back with his lips parted in a blissful smile, his face, handsome in repose, lightened to bronze by the sunbeams dancing through the leaves.

I shook Alexandre awake (it was impossible to wake Paul), and told him of my anxiety, but he seemed to think their slumber perfectly natural, and, to turn my annoyance, invited me to take some refreshment.

"Refreshment? Here?" I inquired in astonishment.

"Yes! If you keep quiet a moment I can offer you some bread and a drink of Montilla." Kneeling beside Paul, Alexandre drew from one of my faithful servant's pockets a fine Andalusian loaf, and from another an enormous gourd filled with wine. Paul stirred uneasily as the gourd left his pocket, but it was back again, empty, before he waked.

"So that's why you stay with Paul," I exclaimed, "though now his gourd is empty and the bread is finished there's nothing more to gain."

"Don't worry," smiled Alexandre. "I don't know how he manages it, but in an hour his pockets will be loaded again."

As he waked, Paul first made sure his gourd was safe (bread was evidently less important to him, for he did not try his other pocket), then rubbed his eyes, yawned prodigiously, and was instantly ready to fall in behind us as we strode off to overtake our friends. Half an hour later we had flanked the mountain to take up our new positions, and only by very careful observation did I discover that Paul, the last in line, van-

197

ished for several minutes on the way. He was duly at our heels again as we approached the second *battue*, a hilltop commanding a long narrow valley along which the beaters would drive the game.

Maquet made himself quite a nuisance at this juncture, for he was wearing a scarlet jersey and black cap that made him stand out against the green *maquis* like a giant ladybird. We were forbidden to speak or show ourselves, yet, either through a misunderstanding or sheer obstinacy, there stood Maquet in his flaming jersey. In vain did Alexandre and I gesticulate to him to get down out of sight, and at last we gave up and took cover ourselves, whereupon Maquet followed our example, and not a moment too soon. Following each other down the hillside facing us came five deer, moving like silent shadows through the undergrowth. Alexandre, hasty as all young hunters are, had already leveled his sights at the leader when I breathed, "Hold your fire! They're six hundred yards away!"

"The maker assured me this gun would hit a target at eight hundred yards!" he returned.

"Wait until they're nearer," I whispered. "Then perhaps we can each bag one." But it was too late. Already the hinds were in headlong flight, and, looking around to discover what had startled them, I saw Maquet standing in all his brilliance. You can imagine Alexandre's disappointment! Then, to our right, I heard a shot and saw, a thousand yards away, one of the deer staggering to a halt, trailing a broken hind leg. So ended our first day's hunting.

Twenty minutes' march by devious tracks brought us to a spot where our beaters already had a good fire blazing. As always happens after a hunt, those who had not used their guns felt bound to fire at something, and bets were made as to the rival merits of French and Spanish weapons. A sheet of paper, the size of a hat, was fixed to a stick a hundred yards away from us. Hernandez, the first to shoot, broke the paper, while cheers rose in the Spanish camp. Then Alexandre stepped forward, saying in an aside to me: "This is the bullet you stopped me from firing. See whether I should have missed!" He raised

198

his gun, took careful aim, pulled the trigger, and nothing happened! Three times he tried, while all the onlookers, French as well as Spanish, were convulsed with mirth.

"But," cried poor Alexandre, in bewilderment, "it came from Devisme, the best gunsmith in Paris!"

"It's a lovely gun," said Paroldo, his voice shaking with laughter. "Perfectly balanced! Beautifully engraved! What a pity it won't work!"

"Your turn next, Desbarolles," urged Giraud. "Come along now! None of your excuses!"

"Must I, really?" returned Desbarolles. "I'd much rather not. I doubled the loading today, to shoot boars. Oh, well! If you insist . . ."

A tremendous explosion woke every echo in the mountain, and we never knew where the bullet went. Desbarolles dropped his gun, clasped his cheek, and began to spit blood, while Maquet, always equipped for any emergency, passed him a flask, Giraud held his head, and Hernandez promised him his horse for the rest of the day. Now it rested with me to redeem our French prestige if I could, and I blush to tell you of the congratulations showered upon me when my bullet pierced the very center of the target. Then, with the songs and laughter of all returning hunters, we made our way back to the plateau where we had met that morning.

Several of our new companions had gone ahead of the main party, and preparations for a feast were well in hand when we arrived. Huge, bubbling saucepans fringed the blazing fire; on the ground lay an immense cloth on which a rich profusion of succulent dishes quickly appeared while we lay in a circle around it. Here, within the perimeter of this little plateau, were light, happiness, and human companionship; beyond, the great panorama, empty of humanity, stretched as far as eye could see, and the sun, like a pasha reclining on golden cushions, rested on the western horizon. As the leaden dusk fell and the firelight gleamed more brightly on the swarthy, bearded faces of our hosts, we ate our fill without benefit of knives or plates, tearing roasted chickens apart, passing gigantic hams around the table from one to another, while jars of wine were no sooner emptied than re-filled. One of the strangest touches, to me, was the way our horses and mules, free of their saddles, wandered grazing in the background, now and then even filching some tidbit from our repast until, at a gesture from us, they trotted a tired step or two before halting amid the bushes.

At last, when we could eat and drink no more and were exhausted with laughter, the cloth was removed, cigars were lighted, and our revels began in earnest under the starlit sky. Never have I heard the traditional song *los Toros* sung with such an intoxicating rhythm, or seen a *fandango* danced with such wild abandon as it was by our bandit-friends. Then they insisted that we should perform our national dance—as though a country as prim as ours still possessed such a thing!—and after much persuasion, while Desbarolles played a guitar, Boulanger, Maquet, Giraud, and Alexandre did their best to dance a quadrille. They had more zest than skill, and I was heartily glad the night was dark, but they were given riotous applause—especially the "ladies," Boulanger and Giraud.

Then our hosts, who seemed to have renounced all idea of rest, began a mock bullfight, with a former *torero* acting as the bull. Every detail of a real fight was faithfully portrayed: the three *picadors*, borne on the shoulders of sturdy comrades; the music, the passes with the capes; the yells and wild excitement; until the bull had brought all his opponents to the dust and even the spectators were prostrate with weariness. It was 1 o'clock in the morning as my friends and I retired to the straw huts prepared for us; the bandits slept where they lay, while Hernandez and Paroldo sat quietly chatting over their last cigar. Hours later I was awakened by a horse munching my roof, and as I drove him off I took a last look at the sleeping world, where all lay quiet and still. The fire had sunk to a handful of gray ashes, and the moon, rising in a cloudless sky, was bathing the whole mountain with her mysterious light and silvering the distant peaks of the Sierra.

33

❧ ❧ ❧

Cordova

At 6 o'clock we awoke, made our hasty toilet, snatched a quick meal, and started out. The hunt began under much the same conditions as before, and with no better luck. Speaking for myself, the only game I set eyes on all day was an immense boar, well out of range, but I was more than compensated for the absence of sport by watching the play of light and shadow on the distant plains, the infinite splendor of the wooded crests around me. Our mountain-dwelling friends, anxious that we should carry away a good impression of the sierra, swore they had never known such a run of ill-luck, and their enthusiasm changed to an angry determination as *battue* succeeded *battue* with but poor result, the day's bag totaling only a wolf, two wildcats, and one boar.

Toward 4 o'clock we returned to camp and set about cooking our evening meal, roasting cuts of venison, scrambling eggs, frying the delicious liver of deer and wild boar. Our intention had been to leave immediately after supper and arrive back in Cordova by midnight or soon after, but the meal lasted longer than we expected, a comfortable lethargy overcame us, and we noticed the rising moon was ringed with mist, so we decided to pass another night in our straw huts and set out two hours before dawn. This decision precluded any such revels as we had enjoyed the evening before, and, dropping with fatigue, we completed our preparations for departure and went early to bed.

At 3 o'clock we were once more astir, and learned that during the night Ravez, with other keen hunters of the party, had decided to stay one more day in the hope of better sport, but the rest of us gathered to take our leave and thank our hosts for their unstinted hospitality. I was turning aside to take from my purse two or three gold coins to be shared among them when Paroldo seized my arm and warned me to desist.

"Why?" I asked in surprise. "Don't beaters get paid in Spain?"

"Not these, anyway. They would refuse, and you would spoil all their pleasure at having entertained you. Give these good fellows your hand, if you are not too proud, but nothing more."

They begged us to stay another day, and bowed regretfully on hearing I was due to leave Cordova on the morrow for Seville. It surprised me that Alexandre did not suggest joining Ravez for another hunting expedition. On the contrary, he expressed an urgent desire to be back in Cordova before 8 o'clock in the morning, and I listened carefully to the reasons he gave, feeling sure they were not the real ones. I know nothing sadder, Madame, than such a leave-taking. For two whole days we had hunted, eaten, slept with these men as though we should know them for years. Now, the first bend in the road would separate us for all eternity. They, too, must have felt a similar pang, for while two of them accompanied us down the first slopes the others seized burning brands from the fire and held them aloft like torches, so that we could look back through the night and see that friendly glow.

After two hours' march through the silent majesty of the woods and mountains we saw the first streaks of dawn; from the peaks the growing light showed us the desert, then the Guadalquivir, then Cordova; the precipices that had flanked our right three days ago now yawned on our left; once more we looked on the long rank of crosses and read their inscriptions; at 8 o'clock the last foothills lay behind us, and at nine we re-entered Cordova.

The moment we arrived, Alexandre changed his clothes and disappeared. The rest of us passed the day in shopping and making final preparations for our journey. One serious difficulty was that seats could not be reserved in advance. There were seven of us, including Eau-de-Benjoin, and, though Spanish coaches are rarely crowded, we could scarcely hope to find seven seats in the same vehicle. It might, however, be possible that the diligence and the stagecoach, between them, would have room for us.

We made it known in the town that our friends who had stayed in the mountains for another day's hunting would be returning early that evening. Such expeditions always arouse great excitement, for the Sierra Morena, so near their gates, is for most Cordovans completely unknown country. Our own return, being unheralded, had gone unnoticed, but when we went out to meet Ravez and his party we found the gates thronged with waiting townsfolk. Twilight was falling when two or three gunshots announced the approach of the hunters, and the crowd replied with a great shout and the notes of a horn. Soon the little procession came in sight, in the midst of it four donkeys laden with the spoils: two stags, a hind, two boars, and two wildcats as large as young tigers, the carcasses covered with branches to conceal the fact that portions had already been consumed. Out ran the eager children and sober townsfolk cheering the sportsmen and escorting them back in triumph through the narrow gateway, along the congested streets, and so to our hotel. Our friends paid us the compliment of offering us the choicest game, but since we were leaving in the morning we could not take advantage of this for our own pleasure. We contented ourselves with having one of the boars carved up, and sending joints to the four or five houses where we had been entertained. Then we sat down with the starving hunters to enjoy our last meal together.

After dinner, contrary to all custom, Alexandre disappeared again and I saw him no more last night, though toward 1 o'clock this morning I was wakened by a tune from his musical clock, and thought to myself: "Good! Alexandre's back safely!" I have not seen him this morning, though it is already noon.

Good-by, Madame. I am writing these last lines in the midst of leave-taking. We have just learned that there are four seats available in the diligence and one in the stagecoach, with, at a pinch, another in the box where the guard sits. That will just suffice, for Paul is so adaptable that he can be tied on anywhere. I called Alexandre so that he could add a line at the foot of this letter, but he has vanished once more. I fancy there must be some mysterious love affair behind all these disappearances, but I shall doubtless learn more about it later. Once more, *adieu;* my next letter will reach you from Seville.

34

❧ ❧ ❧

Seville

Ah, Madame! In your prayers remember any who travel on the road from Cordova to Seville. The one part of my body I can still move is my right hand, and that only because I took special precautions to avoid breaking my promise to write to you. How Maquet, Giraud, Desbarolles, and Alexandre fared I cannot say, for their diligence left Cordova an hour and a half later than the stagecoach that brought Boulanger and myself, and is not due in Seville for some hours yet.

Boulanger nobly insisted that, since he is seventeen days younger than I, he would occupy the lonely little box where the guard usually sits, leaving me the more comfortable inside seat where I had the company of two fellow travelers. One of them, Poutrel, was a French merchant whom I had met at that celebrated dinner in Madrid where we smoked five hundred francs worth of cigars and were entertained by Strauss. The other was a nobleman of Seville, returning home from Italy. As the last to arrive I would have taken the middle seat, but each of them pressed me to take his corner seat (I have since had the unworthy thought, Madame, that their courtesy was not entirely disinterested), so I finally settled myself in Poutrel's corner and the coach started off.

The first turns of the wheels made me suspect what sufferings were in store. Traveling at top speed, the stagecoach bounced over the cobbles like a rubber ball, and the upholstery was much too thin to cushion passengers against the jolts. I hoped, in vain, that the going would be smoother when we left the paved streets for the open road, and above my head I could hear Boulanger's cries and groans as he was tossed around his nutshell of a box, but when I turned to my fellow-travelers to protest, I saw that they were managing very comfortably, swaying gently, but avoiding all contact with the sides of the vehicle, the Spaniard by gripping the only curtain strap, and Poutrel by holding on with both hands to the luggage net hanging from the roof.

This was serious. Except on those rare occasions when the conversation is absorbing, it is my invariable habit to sleep when traveling, but though I wrapped my head in every kerchief I could find and drew my hood over them, I soon realized it was impossible to rest against the panel of the coach. Conversation flagged, the countryside was dull, and to crown everything it began to pour rain. I swear the deluge that floated the Ark was a mere shower compared with the torrent that lashed down on the road from Cordova to Seville yesterday, November 7th! Never have I seen such lightning or heard such terrifying thunder! It occurred to me that Boulanger might well be drowned in his box, his cries for help unheard above the noise of the storm, and I had the coach stopped to reassure myself. Fortunately, the water could stream freely out at the bottom, so I passed my cloak up to him and the coach moved on again. On their little platform the coachman and the guard held on for dear life to the iron supports of Boulanger's perch, the water pouring into their sleeves, down their necks, and out at the bottom of each trouser leg. It was a night to sear the memory, Madame, and you can imagine our relief when, at dawn, we found ourselves at Alcala, only three leagues from Seville.

At the gate, someone inquired whether M. Alexandre Dumas was on the coach, so, hiding the swollen bumps on my forehead as best I could, I presented myself, and learned that on the two previous days the Marquis of Aguila, one of the noblest gentlemen of Seville, had sent his own carriage to await my arrival, so that my entry into the town should be suitably dignified. Alas! Our trip into the sierra had delayed us for three days, so we had to complete our journey in the stagecoach, but the gracious gesture pleased me very much.

The first thing one sees on approaching Seville is the Giralda, a tower built by the Moors in the year 1000, when Christians were on their knees expecting the end of the world. Its height was then about two hundred fifty feet, topped by a platform roofed with shining tiles of different colors. In the sixteenth century Francesco Ruiz removed this roof and built three more stories, the first a belfry, the second an observation platform, and the third a cupola surmounted by a gigantic figure symbolizing Faith, serving as a weather vane—which struck me as odd, though I must agree that this golden figure with outspread wings is a marvelous sight as it swings in the sunshine. Around the city the vegetation has a tropical luxuriance; the great aqueduct to the left of the road adds a special feature to the scene, and the roads are thronged with country-folk, muleteers, gypsies, *contrabandista*, all laughing, singing, playing guitars or mandolins. Even when our coach thrust them rudely aside they still smiled happily and threw flowers at the driver—not stones, as in France—and called jestingly after us until we were out of earshot.

When we entered the town my first impression was of far too much yellow. I know it is Spain's national color, and very attractive on oranges and lemons, but most unsuitable, in my opinion, for houses and soldiers' uniforms. We reached our hotel, the *Europe*, stepped thankfully down, and managed to catch Boulanger as he jumped from his box declaring that one more stage would have driven him mad. Good-by, Madame. I see our host's name is Rica. Probably he's Italian. The cooking should be good!

206

35

Seville

After twelve hours' sleep I woke at 11 P.M., more refreshed and less bruised than I should have thought possible, to find that Maquet and Giraud had arrived at five and were already asleep. All I could learn was that Alexandre was still missing when the diligence was due to start, so Desbarolles, true friend that he is, declared he would wait until he could bring Alexandre with him.

Feeling wakeful, I wandered out through the open door of my room (Do you shiver, Madame, at the thought of doors standing open in November?), into a little gallery overlooking a tiny garden filled with orange trees. There I lay on a couch, watching the moonlit sky and the colored tiles of the house next door, shining like the silver scales of a gigantic fish; savoring the perfume of jasmine and lemon trees; listening to the mysterious sounds of the night, now and then a little cascade of merry notes shaken from a guitar below a balcony, and, at intervals all the clocks in Seville striking the hours, no two of them coinciding. (You remember, Madame, the trouble that mighty ruler of empires, Charles V, had when he tried to regulate his twelve clocks to strike simultaneously? It nearly drove him mad!)

There they found me sleeping when they came at 8 o'clock to tell me a M. Henri Buisson had called to see me. I recalled that our good friend M. Monnier of Madrid had given me a letter of introduction to this gentleman, and had doubtless also written direct. Have you ever met someone completely unknown to you, Madame, and felt at once as though he were an old friend? So it was with us, and you, too, shall meet him one day, for he has promised to visit me in Paris. Buisson is a

Frenchman, settled in Spain for business reasons, but he abandoned his business, his family, his friends, to devote himself entirely to us.

He brought us, too, a splendid piece of news. Montès and Chiclanero, the rising and the setting suns of tauromachy, had traveled in the same coach as Maquet and Giraud, and now sent word that if I would stay in Seville until Sunday they would arrange a special bullfight in my honor—a most flattering compliment, since it ran counter to all custom. Spain does not hold bullfights after October, for the weather becomes too uncertain and bulls lose some of their ferocity as winter approaches. This proposed event was the talk of the town, and my popularity soared.

We wished to be the first to buy seats, and Buisson offered to take us there at once. At our door was a carriage drawn by two mules, which Buisson begged me to use as my own during my stay—an unheard-of luxury in Seville, where everyone goes on foot and only five or six streets are wide enough for a vehicle to pass. I thanked him warmly, we got in, and after half an hour of bewildering detours we reached the quay, ten minutes' walk from our hotel. The route we had taken, however, allowed us to see the *Cristina* and the Gold Tower. The *Cristina* is the fashionable promenade of Seville, with the peculiarity that here and there are posts around which are twisted smouldering ends of rope to light the cigars and cigarettes that Spaniards consider such a vital necessity. The *Torre del Oro*, an ancient Moorish tower of three receding stories, stands so near the river bank that the Guadalquivir washes its base. Tradition says that it was given its present name when the first gold brought back from America by Christopher Columbus was stored here.

The circus, closed three months ago, had just been opened when we arrived, and wore an air of bustling preparation as workmen tidied away loose stones and pulled up grass from the arena. At some time or other a discriminating storm had demolished half of a monument, leaving the lower steps intact and making a breach in the circus wall through which we had a magnificent view of the Cathedral, dominated by its gigantic sentinel, the Giralda. Boulanger and Giraud at once set up their easels, and you will see their paintings of this circus with its jagged wall and the beauty beyond.

Two hours later, when they returned to the hotel, I was already on excellent terms with our host, M. Rica, a native of Milan, where Italian cooking is at its best. He feared his artistic touch might have suffered from his long sojourn in Spain, but our presence was a challenge that inspired him, and the lunch was excellent. With us at table we found a compatriot, M. de Saint-Prix, who frankly told us he had lost his heart to a fair Andalusian maid. Every night he visits her balcony, hoping either to regain his heart or at least to win hers in exchange. This story has somewhat reassured me about Alexandre's continued absence, which was worrying me. I have heard nothing from him, or from Desbarolles, and have written to ask Paroldo for news.

Our French contingent is growing visibly. Today two Parisians arrived, and recognized me immediately from the frightful lithographs displayed all along the boulevard. One of them, M. de Monthérot, is attached to the Embassy at Lisbon, the other, M. de Nugeac, is consul at Oporto, and in view of current affairs in Portugal I think they would both prefer to be going somewhere else to eat their oranges!

I have just had a visit from the editors of the only literary journal printed in Seville, *La Giralda*, charming young men who brought me some complimentary verses inscribed in letters of gold, to which I replied as best I could. They also, on behalf of the director of Seville's theater, begged me to choose the program for as long as I stayed in the town, and brought me a list of their repertoire, which included every national dance known in Spain.

I received, too, a letter from the Count of Aguila, placing his box at the theater at my disposal. (My first care, on arriving in Seville, was to call and thank him for sending his carriage to meet me on the road from Cordova.) The stars at the Seville theater are three young dancers, Anita, Pietra, and Carmen, and no trinity, Brahmin, Egyptian, or Catholic, has ever, I swear, been worshiped so fervently. You should see their eyes, Madame, flashing brighter than stars! And their tiny feet! Two of them could easily go into Cinderella's slipper! All Andalusian beauties joke about the shoes that French or English women wear, large enough, they say, to make leg-guards for *picadors*, or boats to sail on the Guadalquivir! Their own are so small, yet they walk with such assurance, even on the crippling cobbles of their streets.

When, hoping for a closer view of such lovely eyes, I visited backstage, I was received like a sultan, which encouraged me to kiss Anita's hand in greeting. She screamed and jumped back six feet or so, and when I glanced around to discover the cause of this alarm I saw that half the onlookers were laughing and the other half shocked into silence, so that I realized I had committed a grave misdemeanor. I must tell you, Madame, that all these young ladies are ferociously virtuous. For whom do they guard their charms? It really is quite pathetic, and now it is the Frenchwoman's turn to laugh! Each of these dancers is courted by a *novio*, or *fiancé*, generally some journeyman tailor or shoemaker who has managed to insinuate himself into the theater to sell waistcoats or gaiters, and in making my Parisian gesture of courtesy I had filched a favor that a *novio* would wait a year and a half to win.

As I stood, deserted and embarrassed by my faux pas, I saw a pretty little hand extended toward me, and heard a trembling voice say in Spanish, "May I have the honor, monsieur?" At first I did not understand, but as the words were repeated I took the tiny hand in mine and kissed it with tears in my eyes.

"Thank you, Carmencita," I murmured.

"You know my name?" she asked.

"You certainly know mine!"

"Oh! I've known yours ever since I learned to read."

Carmen is younger and wiser than the others, Madame, and has no *novio*. That is why she dared to give me her hand to kiss, and stood in the background smiling at me as Pietra and Anita came forward again to receive my compliments.

Buisson joined me and said: "My dear friend, these young men would like to arrange a ball for you tomorrow night, if the young ladies will agree to dance." Anita and Pietra needed some persuasion, but Carmen agreed at once and threw her arms around her mother's neck with a warm kiss. So tomorrow evening there will be a ball, with only three ladies and all the young gentlemen in the town, plus ourselves, our French friends, and Alexandre and Desbarolles too, if they have arrived by then. After this interlude I returned to the front of the theater, where I was received by the Count of Aguila, his wife and her sister, who, to my great relief, spoke fluent French. The show did not end until midnight, and the director of the theater begged me to attend the next performance, when he hoped the house would be equally crowded. Tomorrow is so fully engaged, Madame, that I hardly know whether I shall have time to write.

36

❦ ❦ ❦

Seville

At last, Madame, they have arrived! Yesterday I was waiting hopefully at the coach office as the diligence drove in at 4 o'clock, when I saw Desbarolles' gun barrel sticking out of the window, and Alexandre was in my arms almost before the carriage stopped. He told me a garbled tale that I still cannot understand, about a tailor, a dog, and the celebrated knife he bought at Châtellerault, which seems to have been worth its weight in gold, but beyond that I've heard nothing, not even from Desbarolles.

There were four other Frenchmen on the coach, so we are

now fourteen at table. We spent the early part of the day sight-seeing, visiting the Alcazar and Pilate's house, built as a replica of the one in Jerusalem, to a plan brought back by the crusaders, so tradition says; learning something of Seville's history in the last thousand years; hearing legends of those two great conquerors who still dominate Seville as Nero dominates Rome: Peter the Cruel and Don Juan de Marana.

The cathedral, built in the fifteenth century, has no equal in the world. In the choir we saw what we took to be the mast of an enormous ship, and an hour later realized it was an immense paschal candle. It weighs, we were told, more than two thousand pounds, and stands in a candlestick like the base of an obelisk, made of bronze. Every year the cathedral uses twenty thousand pounds of wax candles, and the same amount of oil in its votive lamps; mass is celebrated six times a day at each of the forty-eight altars, and over every altar is a painting by Murillo, Velasquez, Zurbaran, or Alonzo Cano; among its other treasures are eighty-three stained glass windows, the work of such masters as Michelangelo, Raphael, Albrecht Dürer. It would take at least a year to see this glorious church as it should be seen.

Seville possesses another landmark of a very different type, a huge tobacco factory which makes three-quarters of all Europe's cigars. It is amazing to see its thirteen hundred pretty young workgirls, the famous *cigareras*, as characteristic of Seville as our *grisettes* are of Paris, all smoking in the streets like veterans, or chewing tobacco like old sailors. In addition to their wages of five or six *réals* a day they are allowed to use as much tobacco as they like in working hours, and if some also finds its way into their pockets, that may explain why no *cigarera* is ever without her escort of a young subaltern or a handsome officer of the merchant navy.

Buisson hinted that our hosts at the ball would feel especially honored if we attended in national costume, an idea which delighted us, for we have quite lost our hearts to Andalusian dress and have already bought all we could carry. (I also ordered six pairs of gaiters and a whole set of Spanish mule-harness, pom-

212

pons, little bells, and all! I hope to startle Longchamps with it!) Formerly it would have been essential to wear full Andalusian costume, including velvet-trimmed breeches, slashed gaiters, and embroidered stockings, but nowadays our hideous fashion of plain trousers and polished shoes has even invaded Seville, and the present custom is to be French from the soles of one's shoes up to the waist, and Andalusian from there on, with a brilliant sash, embroidered jacket, and waistcoat, crowned by the pompon on the inevitable hat. An unsightly mixture, that makes the most distinguished man look like some frightful cab driver!

The ball was arranged in the upper story of a café, in a large whitewashed room with a floor roughly tiled in squares of red. The lighting came from four smoking lamps, and the orchestra was a solitary gypsy, sitting with his guitar on his knees and the butt of a cigar in the corner of his mouth. When I arrived the room was already full of spectators waiting in the gloomy half-light, the first row sitting in a ring on the floor, others kneeling or standing behind them, forming a funnel of heads that reached to the ceiling. The only brightness was reflected from the white gauze skirts, silver-embroidered bodices, and spangled headdresses of Anita, Pietra, and Carmen, as they stood, cloak on shoulder, surrounded by their mothers, brothers, sisters, and *novios*, awaiting the moment to begin.

The first chords sounded, and into the eight-foot circle stepped Carmen, the youngest and least practiced of the troupe. Her performance was no more than a prelude, and she gained only moderate applause. Then Anita rose, and a chorus of voices called for "*L'olé.*" This, Madame, is one of those dances which the Spanish censor has banned from the theater, and as I watched it I reflected that censors love to ban anything truly original or really beautiful. What offended them, I think, was not any particular steps of the dance, but its whole atmosphere of proud yet voluptuous abandon, provocative beyond description; its accompaniment of songs with piercing whistles, the passionate enthusiasm it arouses in Spaniards, for whom it expresses the very essence of their national traditions. Every

213

time they see it, it completely intoxicates them. Judge, then, of its effect upon strangers, to whom it is new!

I know nothing more dreary, Madame, than our French dancers mincing timidly upon the stage, a meaningless smile forever pinned to the corners of their mouths, their stilted movements eloquent of anxiety and fatigue. In Spain, dancing is a joy to the dancer herself. She delights in every toss of her head, every flicker of her hands. Her feet spurn the ground, she whinnies with excitement, and the magnetic current of her passion streams out to galvanize every man who watches her. People talk of the glorious dreams of opium-smokers, the frenzied exhilaration that hashish can give, but I, who have studied both, assure you that neither can for a moment compare with the delirious joy of fifty or sixty Spaniards applauding a dancer in the upper room of a café in Seville!

Now Pietra came forward, cutting short Anita's triumph, while here and there someone called for "*Le vito*" and other voices, mine among them, took up the cry, though I had no idea what it might be. The first notes of the guitar, the first steps of the dance, gave me the answer. Its first movements express the nonchalance of a woman bored with life; it quickens as she grows impatient, and culminates in such convulsive fury, such a frenzy of stamping, that a dancer might well fall lifeless at the finale. The whole dance is indescribable; no pen could convey the color, no brush could paint the swirl of movement, no one but a daughter of Andalusia could achieve it. Pietra must have been thrilled with her success, and I expressed my thanks to her as best I could, as I had previously thanked Anita, though one hardly knows how to thank an artist when one may not even kiss her hand!

To refresh us all, two or three dozen bottles of excellent Montilla were brought in, and three or four of us drank from the same glass in the friendliest fashion. Anita took one sip, then sent her glass to me by the hand of a friend.

"Drink it!" breathed Buisson in my ear. "She is paying you a compliment!"

It seemed she had forgiven me for my *faux pas* of yesterday, so I bowed to her and drank. Five minutes later Pietra's glass was brought to me in the same way, and her lovely eyes signaled her pleasure as I drank to her. Then I looked around for Carmen, and meeting my glance she sipped her wine and brought the glass to me herself, blushing red as a cherry. I took it (and squeezed her hand a little, too), drank, and returned the empty glass. Quite simply and seriously she said: "Now I shall keep this glass all my life!"

Three tables were brought in, one dancer to preside at each, and we sat down to supper, though, since in Spain eating is a duty, not a pleasure, the food was very simple. Yet the meal was gay and boisterous. Some sang to guitar accompaniments, others declaimed verses, odes, sonnets in praise of the three ladies who had entertained us so charmingly, and who would receive no reward except applause and adulation. Suddenly twenty voices called to Anita: "*Le vito!* Again! On the table!" Anita needed no second request, and once more we watched this amazing dance performed without a fault. Then, as the crowning finale of the evening, Anita and Pietra were persuaded to dance the *fandango* together, a dance normally performed by a man and a woman.

Imagine two bees, two butterflies, circling each other, their wings now touching, now wafting them apart; or two sylphides rising from a lake to dance on the reeds. After a thousand flights, a thousand meetings, their lips join and the sylphides swoon in ecstasy, sinking back below the surface of the lake.

Two things struck me forcibly during this memorable evening: the complete exhaustion, the apathy of each dancer when her dance was over; and the respect shown to them by their audience, for no man, even during moments of delirious excitement, as much as touched the dress of Anita, Pietra, or Carmen. The ball ended at 2 o'clock, when each dancer donned her cloak, took her mother's arm, bowed, and walked home. I went slowly back to my hotel, broken with emotion, thinking of two very different evenings which I shall never forget. The revels after the hunt in the sierra, and the ball in Seville.

37

Seville

General consternation in Seville, Madame! There will be no bullfight today, Sunday. It rained all last night, and after one look at the mud Montès and *le Chiclanero* shrugged their shoulders and took the steamer to Cadiz. Since we now had time to spare, it occurred to me that I should greatly value some souvenir of last night's ball, so with Buisson and Giraud I visited Carmen's house, hoping she would pose for a sketch in her dancer's costume.

The child blushed crimson as we entered. She, her mother, and a younger sister were busily working on a costume for tonight's performance, but she agreed to pose for an hour, and went upstairs to change. As we waited in the poor, white-washed room, four chairs its only furniture, the mother told us that her husband was dying, and the family was living on what the girls could earn. Carmen worked at sewing and lace-making for three or four *réals* a day, and had also managed to gain entrance to the theater, where she is paid—do not smile, Madame, for I found it pathetic—fifty sous each time she dances. With four dances a week, she thus earns forty francs a month, out of which she must provide her own costumes.

One unaware of their circumstances might well have laughed when Carmen returned in the dress that had looked so fine last night, for by daylight it was tawdry. Yet she posed with a charming smile, doubtless puzzled by the sadness that had come to our eyes during her brief absence, for we found it heartbreaking that, at an age when a girl should be thinking only of beauty and happiness, she was already carrying life's heavy burdens. As Giraud sketched, he asked for a crumb of bread to rub out a line, but they had none in the house and had to obtain a little piece from a neighbor. In an hour the portrait was finished—to my great delight Giraud had succeeded admirably—and we rose to depart. I wondered how to express my gratitude to this little family without offending their pride, but when Carmen bestowed her little lace headdress upon Giraud, who had admired it, I ventured to give her the jeweled cuff links I was wearing, to use as earrings, and she was as overjoyed as if they had been valuable.

At our hotel I found the Count of Aguila. Knowing my disappointment at the canceled bullfight, he had come to offer me a substitute. He and his friends would arrange to "pic" a whole drove of bulls for my entertainment in the open country near Seville. Imagine the lavishness of their hospitality, Madame! That ten or twelve of Seville's noblest gentlemen should become *picadors* on my account! I accepted gratefully, preparations are already in hand, and the *course* is fixed for the day after tomorrow.

Alexandre disappeared again yesterday, and has not come back. Seeing that I was now seriously troubled, Buisson confided to me that Alexandre cashed a letter of credit with him for a thousand francs, and asked him to tell me not to worry. He would catch up with us again, somewhere or other, if we would leave a trail for him to follow. This was all very well, but soon we shall receive word that our ship is awaiting us at Cadiz, and then we must sail at once. I wish I knew where he is, or in what corner of the world we shall meet again.

Good-by, Madame. Probably I shall not write again till we are at Cadiz.

38

Cadiz

It is 7 o'clock in the evening, and we are installed in the southernmost tip of Europe, having left Seville at ten this morning.

Yesterday morning at 9 o'clock a carriage drawn by seven mules awaited me—not outside my hotel, for not even a one-horse carriage could have penetrated that narrow street, but in the nearby square. It was a most elegant equipage, with its trappings of red and yellow silk, its pompons and plumes, bells and tassels, its *zagal* and coachman. M. Ecala, the gentleman who traveled with me from Cordova, had also sent his coach, so that we were able to offer a place to M. Buisson and another to M. de Saint-Prix. A hundred yards outside the town gate, where these two carriages caused a good deal of excitement, the Count of Aguila met us at the door of a little inn where the custom is to drink a glass of sherry, a good wine, served in glasses of a pleasing shape. With him were some twenty riders in Andalusian costume, bearing *picadors'* lances. There were spare horses for us to ride if we wished, an offer which Giraud and Desbarolles accepted at once, though they declined the lances.

Off we went across the rough ground to a rendezvous lying between the bank of the Guadalquivir and the wall of a noble-man's park, a large square of short grass, its third side formed by a hill where stood ranks of spectators, and open on the fourth side, where the bulls would enter. We could see them in the distance, grazing in scattered groups of five or six, now and then lifting their heads and stretching their necks to bel-low. The Count with twelve or fifteen other horsemen rode out to encircle the bulls, as beaters encircle game, and the beasts grew restive, turning their heads from side to side, snorting angrily and lashing their flanks with their tails. Then their leaders moved away from the riders, others followed, stragglers fell in line at the prick of a lance, and a herd of some sixty bulls trotted into the arena, looking from the stone wall on one side to the crowd of spectators on the other, and sensing the third barrier, the invisible Guadalquivir. They were all four or five years old, and bred for the bullring. Today's *course* was planned to test their ferocity. The brave ones would be reserved for the field of battle, the weak or the cowardly would go to the butcher.

The Count opened the *course*, chose a bull, touched it with his *pic*, and, as the animal fled from the pain he galloped beside it and, leaning over, struck it between the base of its tail and the top of its haunch. It somersaulted three times, came to rest with all four feet in the air, then settled itself on the ground, right way up, looking extremely bewildered. The Count waited a moment to see whether it would rise and return to the combat, but as it still lay pensive he consigned it to the butchers and chose another adversary. Twenty similar contests were already taking place all around, and two or three bulls, thrown in the same way, turned on the *picadors*, one of whom was so closely pursued that the Count intervened to save him and sent the bull rolling. Again it charged, and now the Count gave proof of his superlative horsemanship, avoiding every attack, forcing the bull to weary itself with ineffectual turns until, after ten minutes, it sank to its knees, exhausted. Yet it had proved its courage and won a victory, for now it was destined to live until its next fight, in the ring.

In the next three hours many bulls were thrown, and some horsemen also rolled in the dust, but there was no serious accident. If a *picador* seemed in danger, the bull's attention was distracted, either by another rider or by some bystander who rushed forward waving his cloak with all the courage, if not the skill, of a professional. Two or three times, a bull charged the living wall of spectators who opened their ranks to let him pass, pursued by horse and rider, and at such close quarters as this I began to understand something of what a bull means to the men who fight him, how they perfect the *sang-froid* they display in every arena in Spain.

From a child, a Spaniard regards a bull as his born enemy, to be teased or provoked at every opportunity. I saw two little boys run up to a bull just thrown by the Count of Aguila. One seized the animal's tail and the other skipped over it as though it were a rope. Every young man who adopts the profession of bullfighting, in no matter what capacity, has spent years in studying his adversary, and what he will do on the stage he has practiced twenty times in the wings, so to speak. Ferdinand VII, who adored bullfighting, actually founded a *conservatoire* of tauromachy, here in Seville.

Toward 3 o'clock we drove back to Seville, followed by the whole population, and the rest of the day we spent in farewell visits and preparations for departure. Saint-Prix decided to come with us to Cadiz. The night before, he had a misword or two with his balcony, and hoped that a short absence might soften it a little.

To honor our final visit, a *grand ballet national* was given at the theater, and the producer's enterprise was well rewarded, for the place was packed. I went backstage to say good-by to Anita, Pietra, and Carmen, reminding myself not to kiss their hands, but the ladies regarded me as an old friend by now, and frankly offered me their cheeks. Carmen asked, in a whisper, whether I could help her to find work in a French theater. Unfortunately, she has had only six months' experience and is not yet fully trained, so I asked how long it would take her to equal Anita or Pietra.

"A year," she replied frankly, "if I could afford a good teacher."

I spoke a couple of words to Buisson, and Carmen will have her year's training. That evening I scarcely saw the performance, for I was visiting the boxes, saying *adieu* to the host of acquaintances I have made during my stay in Seville, whom on the morrow I would leave forever.

That morrow came, as morrows do, and our very good

friend, M. Buisson, was at our hotel at seven in the morning to accompany us to the quay. The captain of *El Rapido* was a friend of his, and he was allowed to come on board, where we stood exchanging those vague promises all travelers make: "I shall return to Seville one day," "I shall be coming to France." Soon the third bell rang, the gangplank was drawn in, the boat began to slip between the orange groves, and with tears in our eyes we watched Buisson waving to us until we could distinguish him no more.

Now *El Rapido* began to justify her name as she moved swiftly downstream, giving us a delightful change from the jolts of the stagecoach, and the weather was perfect, the brilliant sunshine tempered by the first cool winds of the coming winter. As we turned for one last look at Seville, the houses, steeples, trees, all seemed to have disappeared into the earth as, in the theater, scenery may disappear through a trapdoor. The cathedral loomed larger by contrast, until it, too, sank below the sky-line, and there remained only the rose-colored *Giralda*, with her figure of Faith like a shining golden bee. Then an elbow in the river drew across a green curtain, and Seville was gone.

39

❧ ❧ ❧

You may have quite a wrong impression of the Guadalquivir, Madame, for Arab poets, who had never seen so much water, praised it to the skies, and French writers, never having seen it at all, believed the Arabs. True, Spanish writers could have revealed the less picturesque truth, but since it is the only river in their country large enough to take a boat, why should they decry it? Besides, though its banks are flat and uninteresting, they are crowded with wild fowl, ducks, bustard, gulls almost as large as eagles.

I fired a shot or two, and passengers crowded around me, among them someone I thought I recognized, and I was right. There, decked in a *basquine*, her long lace veil hanging from her high comb to her waist, was a girl known as Julia, whom we had recently met at a house that was not precisely respectable. At the time she seemed greatly attracted to Boulanger, and we had teased him unmercifully, but now the situation threatened to be embarrassing, for she was well known. Discretion was not her strong point, and she gave us a charming smile. It would have been caddish to snub her or deny the acquaintance, and soon she was chatting away vivaciously, explaining that she was going to visit her mother in Cadiz, and had chosen today for the trip in the hope of seeing us again.

At lunchtime we went below, examined the menu and gave our order, but we had hardly put fork to our first cutlet when down the companionway came Julia. We could hardly object, for she had paid her passage and had as much right in the dining room as we had. She chose a seat near Boulanger and ordered one of those thimble-sized cups of chocolate, but before long she contrived to join our party and share our meal. It was humiliating, but what could we do? After coffee, however, she tactfully disappeared, and we firmly resolved that, even if we dined late, we would not dine on board.

By now the river was broader, its waters yellow under the hard blue of the sky, its banks flatter, with here and there a stork or heron standing motionless on one leg, and sea birds whirling in their thousands, their wings whistling shrilly in the wind. At San-Lucar the Guadalquivir merges with the sea, its waves begin to roll, its color changes to a greenish blue. Maquet and Giraud both grew pale in anticipation, and the remaining two hours of the voyage proved too much for both of them.

Toward 5 o'clock we cast anchor in the port of Cadiz, dazzling white between the blue of sky and sea, and crowded with sailing ships of every rig, size, and nationality. Eagerly we sought among their masts for the funnel of a steamship, and to our excitement there were two, which raised our hopes. We learned that they were French warships, the *Véloce* and the *Achéron,* newly arrived from Tangier. After a long, stormy interview with the customs officers, who viewed our arsenal with the utmost suspicion, we made our way to the *Fonda de la Europa,* recommended to us as the best hotel in Cadiz, and found it a veritable palace compared to the inns we had visited elsewhere in Spain.

Scarcely were we installed when a waiter inquired whether I would receive M. Vial, second lieutenant of the *Véloce.* I certainly would! He was a frank, pleasant man of forty, and he brought word in the name of Captain Béraud, that, by order of the Governor General of Algeria, the corvette *le Véloce* was released from her normal duties and placed at my service. He also brought a charming letter from Commandant Ferey, brother-in-law of M. de Salvandy and son-in-law of Maréchal Bugeaud, inviting me in the name of the Governor General of Algeria to come to Algiers, where, he said, I was eagerly awaited. M. de Salvandy had positively promised me a French warship for the crossing—in fact, I made it a condition of my acceptance—but I confess I never thought the government would agree, or carry it out with such good grace!*

We invited Lieutenant Vial to dine with us, and we were on the point of enjoying the best efforts of the French chef when, to our dismay, Julia entered the dining room. How could we be more stern with her at dinner than we had been at lunch? We looked apprehensively at M. Vial, but he was not the man to be afraid of a pretty girl, even though her manner was more free than conventional, so Julia joined our table and now regards herself as one of our party. We had difficulty in getting rid of her last night, and she came back this morning, but I did not see her myself for I had gone to call on the French con-

* This matter roused such fierce controversy in the Chamber of Deputies after Dumas returned to France that he actually challenged his bitterest critics to a duel.

223

sul, M. Huet, a charming man, and the rest of my time was occupied in writing feverishly to Paroldo in Cordova and Buisson in Seville, hoping to have news of Alexandre before we sail.

40

❦ ❦ ❦

Alas, Madame! I have something shocking and most humiliating to tell you. We have been turned out of the *Fonda de la Europa* for unseemly behavior! Poor Julia, of course, was the reason for this affront.

I will not specify which Ulysses among us this modern siren was pursuing, but her story of visiting her mother was quite false, and merely an excuse for traveling to Cadiz in our company. As you know, she dined with us last night, and also appeared at lunchtime today. Now Spain, Madame, observes strict conventions, and hotelkeepers are more rigidly puritanical than the rest of the population. Ours was scandalized by Julia's visits, and when she came back at dinnertime tonight he refused to admit her. The poor girl went away in tears, but very sensibly sent us a note telling us of the landlord's officious interference. Actually, he had done us a service, but there are some services one is not disposed to accept, so we summoned him and gave him a long lecture on showing proper respect to ladies. We rather expected him to stammer apologies and excuses, but no! He took full responsibility for his action, which he maintained was essential for preserving the reputation of his establishment. Haughtily I demanded his bill. Equally haughtily he presented it.

It was lucky for us, Madame, that he was so touchy about his hotel's good name! The total, for a mere twenty-four hours, was two hundred fifty francs! We howled in dismay, for our resources are at a low ebb. Fortunately Maquet, our economist, managed to secure a reduction of fifty francs, and we walked out, each carrying his own luggage, his spare clothes slung over his arm. Outside we met Julia, who was most anxious to help carry something and so attach herself to our company, but we made it plain that we thought we had already done enough to sustain the international reputation of French gallantry and at length she departed, sighing deeply and leaving us her address.

Not knowing the town, we wandered on with some uncertainty and happened to pause near an inn called *Les Quatre Nations*, whereupon a crowd of waiters, kitchen boys, and chambermaids rushed out at us like seagulls swooping on a shoal of sardines, each flying off again with something in its talons, while the proprietor welcomed us with an assurance that in his hotel we could receive anyone we wished. Our escapades were apparently the talk of all Cadiz! However, this place was almost as comfortable as the *Europa*, and much more obliging, so here we stayed, all our possessions, to my relief, being safely restored by the servants who had snatched them from us in the street.

Having told you of our tribulations, let me tell you what I have seen of the town. Cadiz is a true daughter of the sun, and lies bathed in dazzling light, her only colors the blue of sea and sky, the white of her houses, and the emerald green of their shutters. The streets are as narrow, and as badly paved, as any in Spain, but since Cadiz is virtually an island, able to extend only upward, the houses are very tall, and seem to be standing on tiptoe to gain a view of the harbor, the water, or even Tangier. For the rest, there is a cathedral in rather poor taste, but no other buildings of importance. Our French consul, M. Huet, has kindly taken me visiting, and a charming lady is giving a ball in my honor tomorrow evening. Captain Béraud, of *le Véloce*, a reserved, punctilious man, paid me a ceremonial call to ascertain when I wished to sail, and we agreed on the

23rd, two days from now, by which time Alexandre may have arrived. The officers and men of *le Véloce* will thus spend four days at Cadiz, an exhilarating change from Oran or Tangier. We have already won their hearts!

This morning I had a letter from Alexandre, or, rather, a drawing, dated November 18th. It shows a pretty little hand opening a door which Alexandre and Paroldo are about to enter, while following them, swathed to his eyes in his cloak, is a fierce-looking Spaniard with a dog at his heels. Not a word of explanation, but the meaning is clear enough. Alexandre is becoming involved in an *affaire* that might have serious consequences. I am uneasy, and glad to remember that he has his knife with him. Until we sail, I shall add a line or two as best I can in the intervals of sightseeing and packing, so that my letter, posted at the last moment, will bring you all the news I have.

This morning, M. Huet took us to see the famous harbor and jetty, then on toward the *Isla de Léon*, with the *Trocadero* on our left, and on our right the great plain where the Guadalete flows. It was on this plain, beside this river, centuries ago, that Roderique fought the bitter, eight-day battle which ended in his defeat and the capture of Spain by the Moors. Among other interesting sights we saw the wonderful cellars of Puerto Santa-Maria, famous for its sherry and much frequented by English tourists. Finally we explored, by steamer, the magnificent Bay of Cadiz, more than four times as large as the city itself.

Returning to our hotel at about 4 o'clock, I received another sketch from Alexandre. It bore the same date as the first but had obviously been drawn later, for it showed an interior, with the same pretty little hand that had opened the street door now admitting Alexandre to a cosy room furnished principally with a comfortable-looking bed. There was no word to say whether he might still rejoin us before we sail in the morning, but I did not lose all hope since a stagecoach was due in Cadiz from Cordova at midnight.

Fortunately, the ball given in my honor last night was held in a house which the coach would pass, and when I heard it roll by under the windows I slipped out and ran to the terminus. Everyone had already gone except the postillion, who was bedding down his mules, and all he could tell me was that the coach had brought two passengers only, an officer and a young lady. The thought struck me that perhaps Alexandre had kidnaped the girl and adopted the uniform as a disguise! Anxiously I rushed to the *Europa,* the address I had given him, but no one had arrived there. On I ran to *Les Quatre Nations.* No new guests there either, but I roused Desbarolles and Giraud. (Why were they not at the ball? That, Madame, is a secret between them and their wardrobe!)

Together we set off to find the coachman's lodging, a long and difficult quest, and it was almost an hour later that an old woman with a candle led us up to the garret where the coachman was sleeping. He woke terrified to see three cloaked men at his bedside, and it was some time before he would speak at all. I demanded to see his passenger list, and there, under the names of a soldier and a lady I saw Alexandre's signature. The coachman agreed that he had boarded the vehicle at Cordova, but said that he had stopped the coach a mile outside the town and had walked off across the fields, telling the driver not to wait. This seemed incredible! Had they murdered Alexandre and thrown his body into some ravine? I demanded more information, I threatened, and when I told the coachman my name he exclaimed that he had a letter for me which would be delivered in the morning. I insisted on seeing it at once, and found it was a third drawing from Alexandre. The scene was the same as in the second sketch, but now Alexandre was hiding under the bed with only his head visible, his nose close to that of the dog we had seen in the first picture. It was barking fiercely, and Alexandre, finger on lip, was trying to quiet it. As we gazed, the coachman gazed too, and ejaculated: "Yes! That's just how it was!"

Now, indeed, we were determined to hear all he knew of the affair! When he had made me swear solemnly that I was indeed Alexandre's father, and so had a right to know, he told us the whole story.

While in Cordova, Alexandre had fallen in love with a beautiful girl on a balcony, the jealously guarded daughter of a rich family, and when we left the town he inquired at a nearby tailor's for lodgings. He was directed to the home of this coachman, who found him an attractive, open-handed young man and championed his cause. On the occasion shown in the third sketch, the dog had indeed roused the household, and it was entirely due to his large knife that Alexandre had escaped unharmed. He swore he would elope with the lady; her family swore he should not, redoubled their guard, and set every *alguazil* in the town on Alexandre's track. That was why he had openly left Cordova in the coach, and then doubled back in secret.

"Then where is he now?"

"He's hiding at my house, unless he has already eloped. The lady is madly in love and will go with him anywhere. There's just one little formality she insists on, though. Marriage!"

"Marriage, eh?"

"Oh, that's easy to arrange in Spain. Any priest will perform the ceremony at a moment's notice!"

"And is it binding?"

"In Spain it is."

"I see! Well, how is he planning to elope?"

"With the help of some *contrabandistas* from Malaga, friends of mine. It's all arranged for this very night. The family believes he is in Cadiz by now, and will sleep soundly. The lady will slip quietly out of the house, your son and the *contrabandistas* will be waiting close by, and off they will go to Malaga. Everything will be all right, and they will join you when they can!"

"So you think he is safe enough, and I need not worry?"

"Not in the least, Monsieur. He's young, clever, resolute, and he has a good knife. God is on his side."

I looked at Desbarolles and Giraud. "What do you think?" I asked.

"He's a lucky man," said Desbarolles, dreamily. "I've been hoping for such an adventure ever since I came to Spain, but . . ."

"Wretch!" exclaimed Giraud. "You already have a wife and child!"

"Why, so I have!" said Desbarolles in a surprised tone, as though the circumstance had escaped his memory.

"I think," pursued Giraud, answering my question, "that it was Providence made him buy that knife in Châtellerault!"

Ten minutes later I was back in the ballroom, reassured in one way, more worried than ever in another, and when, hours later, I dropped off to sleep, my dreams were of Alexandre pursued by jealous Spaniards and an enormous dog.

On board *le Véloce*

At 7 o'clock I was awakened from an uneasy doze by the sailors arriving to collect our luggage, and in a hand's turn everyone was ready. No one had slept much, for they were all too busy talking of Alexandre's adventure. M. de Saint-Prix was particularly bewildered and depressed. For six weeks he had courted his balcony without even getting as far as the door, yet in twenty-four hours Alexandre managed to reach the spot where the dog found him!

Heaven knows where he has gone since! If you receive news of him, Madame, I implore you to let me know. Now, steam is up, the ship is just about to cast off, and I just have time to seal this for Saint-Prix to post in Cadiz. Once more, *adieu*, Madame. When I write to you again it will be from Africa.

Dumas published his adventures in Algeria under the title *En Véloce*, soon to be published in America for the first time by Chilton Company—Book Division, under the title *Adventures in Algeria*

Index

❧ ❧ ❧

233

234

235